HOW TO INVEST
IN REAL ESTATE
USING FREE MONEY

Other Books by Laurie Blum

Free Money for Humanities Students. HarperCollins Publishers.

Free Money for Science Students. HarperCollins Publishers.

Free Money for Professional Studies. HarperCollins Publishers.

Free Money for Humanities & Social Sciences. Paragon House.

Free Money for Mathematics & Natural Sciences. Paragon House.

Free Money for Small Businesses & Entrepreneurs. John Wiley & Sons.

Free Money for Small Businesses & Entrepreneurs,
        2nd Edition, John Wiley & Sons.

Free Money for Undergraduate Study. Facts on File.

Free Money for Graduate Study. Henry Holt.

Buying Real Estate with Free Money. John Wiley & Sons.

Free Money for Foreign Study. Facts on File.

Free Money For People in the Arts. Macmillan.

HOW TO INVEST IN REAL ESTATE USING FREE MONEY

Laurie Blum

John Wiley & Sons

New York • Chichester • Brisbane • Toronto • Singapore

This publication is designed to provide accurate and authoritative
information in regard to the subject matter covered. It is sold with
the understanding that the publisher is not engaged in rendering
legal, accounting, or other professional service. If legal advice or
other expert assistance is required, the services of a competent professional person should be sought. FROM A DECLARATION OF
PRINCIPLES JOINTLY ADOPTED BY A COMMITTEE OF THE AMERI-
CAN BAR ASSOCIATION AND A COMMITTEE OF PUBLISHERS.

Library of Congress Cataloging in Publication Data

Blum, Laurie.
   How to invest in real estate using free money / by Laurie Blum.
      p.   cm.
   Includes bibliographical references.
   ISBN 0-471-52488-3. — ISBN 0-471-52489-1 (pbk.)
   1. Real estate investment. I. Title.
HD1382.5.B58 1990
332.63'24—dc20   90-35675
                                                          CIP

Printed in the United States of America
91 92 10 9 8 7 6 5 4 3 2 1

"Buy land because they're not making it anymore."

Mark Twain

Contents

Introduction

This book is an outgrowth of my very successful book, *Free Money for Small Businesses and Entrepreneurs* (John Wiley & Sons, 1988). Although affordable housing—the American dream of owning one's own home—is becoming less and less a reality for too many Americans, the nonprofit community has billions of dollars available for the purchase of real estate.

The disbursement of monies varies. Various foundations and agencies will give money directly to individuals. Others require a nonprofit sponsor. Philanthropy is facing new challenges; to become more involved in the private sector and to address and help solve critical social issues such as the availability of affordable housing. Housing is a hot topic right now in philanthropy. With the recent changes in the tax law, the information in this book is a gold mine of untapped wealth.

Remember, however, that funding sources are not without restrictions. Do you just walk up, hold out your hand, and expect someone to put money in it? Of course not. It takes time, effort, and thought on your part. You are going to have to fill out applications. You may meet with frustration or rejection somewhere down the road. The odds, however, are in your favor that you will qualify for some sort of funding.

The hardest part has always been finding the sources of money. That is why I wrote this book. Much of the information in this book has never been made available to the general public.

I wanted to make this book as easy to use as possible. Since I find it tedious to use an index, I have organized the book to eliminate the need for one. The listings are divided into three sections: direct grants to individuals, (chapter 3), fiscal sponsorship funding (chapter 6), and federal monies (chapter 7). Within these chapters the listings are arranged by geographic location (where you live or where the property you intend to purchase or develop is). I have also included a chapter on charitable tax investments; this is a useful primer for tax benefits involving real estate that are still intact. Check all sections of the book to see which grants apply to you.

Each listing contains all the information you'll need, including the total amount of money awarded, the number of awards given, the range of monies given, and the average size of the award. Please note that the use of the word "minority" in this book refers to people who are either black, Hispanic, American Indian, or female.

By the time this book is published, some of the information contained here will have changed. No reference book can be as up-to-date as the reader (or author) would like. Names, addresses, dollar amounts, telephone numbers, and other data are always in flux; however, most of the information will not have changed.

Good Luck.

1

Tax Savings Using Free Money

The nonprofit sector, in spite of the changes in the tax code, still offers individuals many tax benefits. Individuals can make gifts of property to nonprofit organizations and still claim tax deductions. This can be done during one's lifetime or at the time of death. A person can give his or her home to a nonprofit organization and still live there until death. The donor gives the property but keeps the right to live there. This is called a gift of real estate with retained life estate. A gift of a personal residence or a portion of that residence can be made quite simply. All you need is a properly drawn deed. The donor can make a substantial gift in this way and claim immediate income estate and gift tax deductions that will be based on variables such as age and property values. Special advantages of a gift of real estate with retained life estate include the following:

1. A new roof or other capital improvements to the property will count as tax deductible. Since the nonprofit organization "owns" the property, permanent improvements are considered to benefit the nonprofit organization. The donor may claim the costs of such improvements as charitable gifts.
2. If the resident decides that he or she no longer wants to live in the donated house, the donor can give up that right and claim yet another tax deduction, again calculated on the basis of age and property value. Please note, however, that legally the donor/resident is still responsible for paying real estate and other taxes on the property.

There are other vehicles for tax savings. These include gift annuities, charitable remainder trusts, and pooled income funds. Check with your attorney or accountant for further details. Remember, you don't have to have a large estate to take advantage of these tax savings. Historically, forms of this giving have been associated only with the very rich, but today individuals from all walks of life may choose some of these methods.

3

2

How To Apply

Go through each section of the book and mark off all the foundations that could potentially give you money (don't be dissuaded from applying if the money given is a low-interest loan or if the award is donated technical services). Pay close attention to the restrictions and eliminate the least likely foundations. You should apply for a number of grants and awards; the same material you put together for one application can be used for most, if not all, of the other applications. Although none of the foundations in this book require an application fee, the effort you will have to put in will probably limit you to no more than eight applications (if you are ambitious and want to apply to more than eight foundations, go right ahead). Write or call the most likely foundations to get a copy of their guidelines. In cases where the contact's name is not listed, begin your letter: To Whom It May Concern. If you call, just request the guidelines; do not cross-examine the person who answers the phone.

Proposals should always be typed neatly and double spaced. Be sure to make a copy of the proposal. I have learned the hard way of the great inconvenience of having the foundation or governmental agency not be able to find my proposal and my having to reconstruct it because I didn't keep a copy. You may be asked for your tax return and other financial records. (Don't worry, you won't be penalized for having money in the bank.) You may be asked to include personal references. Be sure to get strong references. (Be sure to contact the people you are planning to use as references; it may be fatal to your request for your reference to be contacted by a foundation and have no idea what it is regarding.)

THE PROPOSAL

A grant proposal will include a concise narrative description of the project you are attempting to fund and/or the piece of real estate you are attempting to purchase. Remember, it is essential that you sell your

4

project to the potential grantor in the very first paragraph. The following outline should give you a good idea of how to put together the necessary components of a good proposal.

1. **Title page:** Name of applicant, address, and if there is a fiscal sponsor, name of fiscal sponor.
2. **First paragraph:** Clear and precise statement of purpose. Your statement of purpose should answer the following three questions:
   a. What do you hope to accomplish; purchase a piece of property, make a capital improvement on existing property, and/or develop multifamily dwelling units?
   b. How do you plan to accomplish your goals; are there other investors, lenders, zoning requirements, and so on?
   c. What need does the purchase or development of your property serve; individual, commercial, low-to middle-income housing?
3. **Body of Narrative:** Try to keep this to one or two typed, double-spaced pages. Brevity is the key! The body of the narrative should include a very specific indication of the proposed goals of the project and how the objectives will be met.
4. **Attachments:**
   a. Use of grant or loan (equity capital, capital improvement, feasibility study)
   b. Income revenue projections
   c. Your résumé or, if it is a multifamily or commercial building project, résumés of all principal participants as well as the architect's or planning and design consultant's feasibility study
   d. A list of other funding sources (yourself, other investors)
5. **Attachments for projects working with a fiscal sponsor:**
   a. A copy of the nonprofit organization's 501-C-3 IRS letter that documents tax-exempt status
   b. A board of directors list
   c. A list of past and present funding support to the organization (government, corporate, and foundation)
   d. Budgets (last year, current year, and projected year)
   e. One or two good press articles on the organization if available

3

Money for Individuals Listed by State

ALABAMA

Emhart Corporation
426 Colt Highway
Farmington, Connecticut 06032
(203) 678-3204

Areas of interest: Arts and humanities (museums/galleries, zoos, operas, arts centers, historic preservation/restoration), civic and public affairs (business/free enterprise, urban and community affairs), education, health, and social services.

Restrictions: Grants for general support, capital, endowment, and matching funds; grants to individuals.

Focus of giving: Giving primarily in areas where company has major facilities and a large number of employees: AL, CA (Anaheim, Los Angeles, Torrance), CT (Berlin, Farmington, Hartford, Shelton, Windsor), IL (Broadview), IN (Indianapolis), KY (Campbellsville), MA (Beverly, Fall River, Middleton, New Bedford, South Hadley, Whitman), MI (Mount Clemens), MO, NE (Lincoln), NH, NY (Elmira, Maspeth), OH (Cleveland), PA (Huntington Valley, Reading, Temple), TN, VT (Springfield).

$ Given: $738,865 for 200 grants: high $45,000; low $100; average $2,694.

Contact: John F. Budd, Jr., Chairman, Contributions and Grants Committee

    Initial approach: brief letter or proposal

    Deadlines: submit proposal before October

    Final notification: by December

ALASKA

Unocal Foundation
P. O. Box 7600
Los Angeles, California 90051
(213) 977-6171

Areas of interest: Arts and culture (museums/galleries, arts centers), civic and public affairs (business/free enterprise, economic development, and urban and community affairs), education, health, and social services.

Restrictions: Grants for capital, general support, and special projects; grants to individuals.

Focus of giving: Nationally, with preference given to areas where Unocal maintains corporate facilities: AK (Kenai), CA (Brea, Los Angeles, Mountain Pass, San Francisco, Santa Maria), CO, IL (Chicago, Palatine), LA, NC (Charlotte), OR (Rivergate), TX (Beaumont).

$ Given: $4,571,472 for 397 grants: high $491,860; low $250; average $500–$5,000.

Contact: R. P. Van Zandt, Vice-President and Trustee

    Initial approach: telephone

    Deadlines: requests in by September 15

ARKANSAS

Bemis Company Foundation
800 Northstar Center
Minneapolis, Minnesota 55402
(612) 340-6198

Areas of interest: Urban and community affairs, arts centers, cinema, performing arts (general), business/free enterprise, economic development, education, health, and social services.

Restrictions: Grants for general support, special projects, and matching funds; grants to individuals.

Focus of giving: Areas where company maintains facilities, with emphasis on Minneapolis, MN, AR (Crossett), CA (Los Angeles, Union City, Wilmington), CT (Plainfield, Stratford), FL (Panama City), IL (Murphysboro, Peoria, Schaumburg), IN (Indianapolis, Terre

Haute), KS (Wichita), KY (Florence, Henderson, Louisville), MA (East Pepperell), MI (Grand Rapids, Zeeland), MN (Mankato, Minneapolis, Minnetonka), MO (Louisiana, Saint Louis, Springfield), MS (Verona), NC (Statesville), NE (Omaha), NH (Hudson, Nashua, North Walpole), NJ (Flemington), NY (Buffalo), OH (Stow), TN (Memphis), TX (Jacksonville), WA (Seattle, Vancouver), WI (Green Bay, New London, Oshkosh, Sheboygan).

$ Given: $700,000 for 826 grants; average $832.

Contact: Edward T. Dougherty, Executive Director

> **Initial approach:** brief letter or proposal
>
> **Deadlines:** applications accepted throughout the year

Murphy Foundation
200 Jefferson Avenue
El Dorado, Arkansas 71730
(501) 862-6411

Areas of interest: Grants for capital, general support, individual, special projects, civic affairs (with emphasis on historic preservation/restoration, and museums/galleries).

Restrictions: grants to individuals.

Focus of giving: Major priority is for general purposes in Arkansas and Louisiana.

$ Given: $512,713 for 49 grants: high $106,969; low $175; average $1,000–$15,000.

Assets: $9,778,000

Contact: Lucy A. Ring

> **Application information:** application form required

Wal-Mart Foundation
702 Southwest Eighth Street
Bentonville, Arkansas 72716
(501) 273-4000

Areas of interest: Civic and public affairs (business/free enterprise, economic development, urban and community affairs), education, health, and social services (homes).

Restrictions: Grants for general support and to individuals.

Focus of giving: In communities where stores are located (950 stores in 20 states).

$ Given: $1,301,739 for 860 grants: high $102,018; low $17; average $500–$5,000.

Assets: $3,211,292

Contact: James Von Gremp, Director

    Initial approach: letter or proposal

    Deadlines: requests accepted throughout the year

Winthrop Rockefeller Foundation
308 East Eighth Street
Little Rock, Arkansas 72202
(501) 376-6854

Areas of interest: Program-related investments in community/economic development, including agricultural development.

Restrictions: With the exception of the Community Incentive Program, the foundation does not support construction.

Focus of giving: Arkansas.

Name of program: Community Incentive Program; offers support for construction and is restricted to eastern Arkansas residents who represent minority concerns.

$ Given: $1,927,623 for 46 grants: high $68,800; low $1,950.

Assets: $25,339,548

Publications: Annual report with application guidelines.

Contact: Thomas C. McRae, President

    Initial approach: through letter, telephone, or in person, must take place 8 weeks prior to quarterly meetings

    Copies of proposal: 1

    Board meeting dates: quarterly, the first weekend of March, June, September, and December

    Final notification: 2 weeks after board meeting

CALIFORNIA

Bemis Company Foundation
800 Northstar Center
Minneapolis, Minnesota 55402
(612) 340-6198

Areas of interest: Urban and community affairs, arts centers, cinema, performing arts (general), business/free enterprise, economic development, education, health, and social services.

Restrictions: Grants for general support, special projects, and matching funds; grants to individuals.

Focus of giving: Areas where company maintains facilities, with emphasis on Minneapolis, MN. AR (Crossett), CA (Los Angeles, Union City, Wilmington), CT (Plainfield, Stratford), FL (Panama City), IL (Murphysboro, Peoria, Schaumburg), IN (Indianapolis, Terre Haute), KS (Wichita), KY (Florence, Henderson, Louisville), MA (East Pepperell), MI (Grand Rapids, Zeeland), MN (Mankato, Minneapolis, Minnetonka), MO (Louisiana, Saint Louis, Springfield), MS (Verona), NC (Statesville), NE (Omaha), NH (Hudson, Nashua, North Walpole), NJ (Flemington), NY (Buffalo), OH (Stow), TN (Memphis), TX (Jacksonville), WA (Seattle, Vancouver), WI (Green Bay, New London, Oshkosh, Sheboygan).

$ Given: $700,000 for 826 grants; average $832.

Contact: Edward T. Dougherty, Executive Director
  Initial approach: brief letter or proposal
  Deadlines: applications accepted throughout the year

Emhart Corporation
426 Colt Highway
Farmington, Connecticut 06032
(203) 678-3204

Areas of interest: Arts and humanities (museums/galleries, zoos, operas, arts centers, historic preservation/restoration), civic and public affairs (business/free enterprise, urban and community affairs), education, health, and social services.

Restrictions: Grants for general support, capital, endowment, and matching funds; grants to individuals.

Focus of giving: Giving primarily in areas where company has major facilities and a large number of employees: AL, CA (Anaheim, Los Angeles, Torrance), CT (Berlin, Farmington, Hartford, Shelton, Windsor), IL (Broadview), IN (Indianapolis), KY (Campbellsville), MA (Beverly, Fall River, Middleton, New Bedford, South Hadley, Whitman), MI (Mount Clemens), MO, NE (Lincoln), NH, NY (Elmira, Maspeth), OH (Cleveland), PA (Huntington Valley, Reading, Temple), TN, VT (Springfield).

$ Given: $738,865 for 200 grants: high $45,000; low $100; average $2,694.

Contact: John F. Budd, Jr., Chairman, Contributions and Grants Committee

    Initial approach: brief letter or proposal

    Deadlines: submit proposal before October

    Final notification: by December

Unocal Foundation
P. O. Box 7600
Los Angeles, California 90051
(213) 977-6171

Areas of interest: Arts and culture (museums/galleries, arts centers), civic and public affairs (business/free enterprise, economic development, urban and community affairs), education, health, and social services.

Restrictions: Grants for capital, general support, and special projects; grants to individuals.

Focus of giving: Nationally, with preference given to areas where Unocal maintains corporate facilities: AK (Kenai), CA (Brea, Los Angeles, Mountain Pass, San Francisco, Santa Maria), CO, IL (Chicago, Palatine), LA, NC (Charlotte), OR (Rivergate), TX (Beaumont).

$ Given: $4,571,472 for 397 grants: high $491,860; low $250; average $500–$5,000.

Contact: R. P. Van Zandt, Vice-President and Trustee

    Initial approach: telephone

    Deadlines: requests in by September 15

Wells Fargo Foundation
420 Montgomery Street, MAC 0101-111
San Francisco, California 94163
(415) 396-3568

Areas of interest: Arts and culture (aquariums, museums/galleries, historic preservation/restoration), civic and public affairs (economic development, urban and community affairs), education, and social services.

Restrictions: Grants for capital, general support, matching funds, and special projects; grants to individuals.

Focus of giving: California communities where bank has offices.

$ Given: $4,431,506 for 598 grants: average $1,000–$10,000.

Contact: Mr. Ronald E. Eadie, President
  Initial approach: letter
  Deadlines: none
  Board meeting dates: quarterly

COLORADO

The Piton Foundation
511 16th Street, Suite 700
Denver, Colorado 80202
(303) 825-6246

Areas of interest: To encourage personal effort toward self-realization, to promote the development of strong cooperative relationships between the public and private sectors with emphasis on local involvement, and to improve conditions and opportunities for persons inadequately served by the institutions of society. Support for individual volunteer agencies to encourage improved management and service effectiveness; some giving also for civic, conservation, and health programs.

Restrictions: Grants awarded for operating budgets, seed money, emergency funds, consulting services, technical assistance, and program-related investments.

Focus of giving: Giving primarily in Colorado, with emphasis on the Denver metropolitan area, especially for community economic development and low-income, affordable housing. No grants for building or endowment funds.

$ Given: $5,660,983 for grants: high $350,000. Also $79,992 for 54 grants to individuals.

Contact: Phyllis Buehele, Grants Administrator Trust Officer

    Initial approach: letter

    Copies of proposal: 1

    Deadlines: none

    Board meeting dates: as required

    Final notification: approximately 4 months

Unocal Foundation
P. O. Box 7600
Los Angeles, California 90051
(213) 977-6171

Areas of interest: Arts and culture (museums/galleries, arts centers), civic and public affairs (business/free enterprise, economic development, urban and community affairs), education, health, and social services.

Restrictions: Grants for capital, general support, and special projects; grants to individuals.

Focus of giving: Nationally, with preference given to areas where Unocal maintains corporate facilities: AK (Kenai), CA (Brea, Los Angeles, Mountain Pass, San Francisco, Santa Maria), CO, IL (Chicago, Palatine), LA, NC (Charlotte), OR (Rivergate), TX (Beaumont).

$ Given: $4,571,472 for 397 grants: high $491,860; low $250; average $500–$5,000.

Contact: R. P. Van Zandt, Vice-President and Trustee

    Initial approach: telephone

    Deadlines: requests in by September 15

CONNECTICUT

Bemis Company Foundation
800 Northstar Center
Minneapolis, Minnesota 55402
(612) 340-6198

Areas of interest: Urban and community affairs, arts centers, cinema, performing arts (general), business/free enterprise, economic development, education, health, and social services.

Restrictions: Grants for general support, special projects, and matching funds; grants to individuals.

Focus of giving: Areas where company maintains facilities, with emphasis on Minneapolis, MN, AR (Crossett), CA (Los Angeles, Union City, Wilmington), CT (Plainfield, Stratford), FL (Panama City), IL (Murphysboro, Peoria, Schaumburg), IN (Indianapolis, Terre Haute), KS (Wichita), KY (Florence, Henderson, Louisville), MA (East Pepperell), MI (Grand Rapids, Zeeland), MN (Mankato, Minneapolis, Minnetonka), MO (Louisiana, Saint Louis, Springfield), MS (Verona), NC (Statesville), NE (Omaha), NH (Hudson, Nashua, North Walpole), NJ (Flemington), NY (Buffalo), OH (Stow), TN (Memphis), TX (Jacksonville), WA (Seattle, Vancouver), WI (Green Bay, New London, Oshkosh, Sheboygan).

$ Given: $700,000 for 826 grants; average $832.

Contact: Edward T. Dougherty, Executive Director

    Initial approach: brief letter or proposal

    Deadlines: applications accepted throughout the year

Emhart Corporation
426 Colt Highway
Farmington, Connecticut 06032
(203) 678-3204

Areas of interest: Arts and humanities (museums/galleries, zoos, operas, arts centers, historic preservation/restoration), civic and public affairs (business/free enterprise, urban and community affairs), education, health, and social services.

Restrictions: Grants for general support, capital, endowment, matching funds; grants to individuals.

Focus of giving: Giving primarily in areas where company has major facilities and a large number of employees: AL, CA (Anaheim, Los Angeles, Torrance), CT (Berlin, Farmington, Hartford, Shelton, Windsor), IL (Broadview), IN (Indianapolis), KY (Campbellsville), MA (Beverly, Fall River, Middleton, New Bedford, South Hadley, Whitman), MI (Mount Clemens), MO, NE (Lincoln), NH, NY (Elmira, Maspeth), OH (Cleveland), PA (Huntington Valley, Reading, Temple), TN, VT (Springfield).

$ Given: $738,865 for 200 grants: high $45,000; low $100; average $2,694.

Contact: John F. Budd, Jr., Chairman, Contributions and Grants Committee
  Initial approach: brief letter or proposal
  Deadlines: submit proposal before October
  Final notification: by December

ITT Rayonier Foundation
1177 Summer Street
Stamford, Connecticut 06904
(203) 348-7000

Areas of interest: Arts and humanities (aquariums, performing arts, museums/galleries), civic and public affairs (business/free enterprise, economic development, urban and community affairs), education, health, and social services (homes).

Restrictions: Grants for capital, general support, matching funds, and special projects; grants to individuals.

Focus of giving: Giving primarily near operating locations in Connecticut (Stamford), Florida, Georgia, and Washington.

$ Given: $259,985 for 129 grants: high $18,500; low $25; average $1,000—$5,000.

Assets: $2,635,096

Contact: Jerome D. Gregoire, Vice-President
  Initial approach: letter
  Deadlines: November 30
  Board meeting dates: February
  Final notification: 1 month

FLORIDA

Bemis Company Foundation
800 Northstar Center
Minneapolis, Minnesota 55402
(612) 340-6198

Areas of interest: Urban and community affairs, arts centers, cinema, performing arts (general), business/free enterprise, economic development, education, health, and social services.

Restrictions: Grants for general support, special projects, and matching funds; grants to individuals.

Focus of giving: Areas where company maintains facilities, with emphasis on Minneapolis, MN, AR (Crossett), CA (Los Angeles, Union City, Wilmington), CT (Plainfield, Stratford), FL (Panama City), IL (Murphysboro, Peoria, Schaumburg), IN (Indianapolis, Terre Haute), KS (Wichita), KY (Florence, Henderson, Louisville), MA (East Pepperell), MI (Grand Rapids, Zeeland), MN (Mankato, Minneapolis, Minnetonka), MO (Louisiana, Saint Louis, Springfield), MS (Verona), NC (Statesville), NE (Omaha), NH (Hudson, Nashua, North Walpole), NJ (Flemington), NY (Buffalo), OH (Stow), TN (Memphis), TX (Jacksonville), WA (Seattle, Vancouver), WI (Green Bay, New London, Oshkosh, Sheboygan).

$ Given: $700,000 for 826 grants; average $832.

Contact: Edward T. Dougherty, Executive Director

    Initial approach: brief letter or proposal

    Deadlines: applications accepted throughout the year

Gore Family Memorial Foundation
c/o Sun Bank
P. O. Box 14728
Fort Lauderdale, Florida 33302

Restrictions: Grants for housing and transportation costs, equipment for the handicapped, and medical expenses.

Focus of giving: Relief assistance to needy residents of Broward County, Florida, and surrounding areas.

$ Given: $627,434 for grants. Also $359,850 for 348 grants to individuals.

Assets: $14,623,583

Publications: Informational brochure.

    Initial approach: letter

    Deadlines: applications accepted throughout the year

ITT Rayonier Foundation
1177 Summer Street
Stamford, Connecticut 06904
(203) 348-7000

Areas of interest: Arts and humanities (aquariums, performing arts, museums/galleries), civic and public affairs (business/free enterprise, economic development, urban and community affairs), education, health, and social services (homes).

Restrictions: Grants for capital, general support, matching funds, and special projects; grants to individuals.

Focus of giving: Giving primarily near operating locations in Connecticut (Stamford), Florida, Georgia, and Washington.

$ Given: $259,985 for 129 grants: high $18,500; low $25; average $1,000–$5,000.

Assets: $2,635,096

Contact: Jerome D. Gregoire, Vice-President

    Initial approach: letter

    Deadlines: November 30

    Board meeting dates: February

    Final notification: 1 month

GEORGIA

ITT Rayonier Foundation
1177 Summer Street
Stamford, Connecticut 06904
(203) 348-7000

Areas of interest: Arts and humanities (aquariums, performing arts, museums/galleries), civic and public affairs (business/free enterprise, economic development, urban and community affairs), education, health, and social services (homes).

Restrictions: Grants for capital, general support, matching funds, and special projects; grants to individuals.

Focus of giving: Giving primarily near operating locations in Connecticut (Stamford), Florida, Georgia, and Washington.

$ Given: $259,985 for 129 grants: high $18,500; low $25; average $1,000–$5,000.

Assets: $2,635,096.

Contact: Jerome D. Gregoire, Vice-President
> **Initial approach:** letter
> **Deadlines:** November 30
> **Board meeting dates:** February
> **Final notification:** 1 month

HAWAII

The Hawaiian Foundation
111 South King Street
P. O. Box 3170
Honolulu, Hawaii 96802
(808) 525-8548

Restrictions: Grants for operating budgets, seed money, continuing support, equipment, special projects, and matching funds.

Focus of giving: Giving primarily in Hawaii.

$ Given: $357,395 for 61 grants and $28,686 for 75 grants to individuals.

Publications: Annual report, program policy statement, application guidelines, and informational brochure.

Contact: Mark J. O'Donnell, Trust Officer
> **Application information:** application forms required for grants to individuals
> **Initial approach:** telephone or proposal
> **Copies of proposal:** 9
> **Deadlines:** first day of month preceding board meeting
> **Board meeting dates:** January, April, July, and October

ILLINOIS

Abbot Laboratories
Abbot Park 6C
North Chicago, Illinois 60064
(312) 937-7075

Areas of interest: Education, health, and social services.

Restrictions: Capital grants for building funds, equipment, capital projects, matching funds, and land acquisition.

Focus of giving: Communities in which company has significant operations or employee populations.

$ Given: $13,000,000

Assets: $1,488,514

Contact: Charles S. Brown, President

    Initial approach: letter

    Deadlines: applications accepted throughout the year

    Board meeting dates: April and December

Bemis Company Foundation
800 Northstar Center
Minneapolis, Minnesota 55402
(612) 340-6198

Areas of interest: Urban and community affairs, arts centers, cinema, performing arts (general), business/free enterprise, economic development, education, health, and social services.

Restrictions: Grants for general support, special projects, and matching funds; grants to individuals.

Focus of giving: Areas where company maintains facilities, with emphasis on Minneapolis, MN, AR (Crossett), CA (Los Angeles, Union City, Wilmington), CT (Plainfield, Stratford), FL (Panama City), IL (Murphysboro, Peoria, Schaumburg), IN (Indianapolis, Terre Haute), KS (Wichita), KY (Florence, Henderson, Louisville), MA (East Pepperell), MI (Grand Rapids, Zeeland), MN (Mankato, Minneapolis, Minnetonka), MO (Louisiana, Saint Louis, Springfield), MS (Verona), NC (Statesville), NE (Omaha), NH (Hudson, Nashua, North Walpole), NJ (Flemington), NY (Buffalo), OH (Stow), TN (Memphis), TX (Jacksonville), WA (Seattle, Vancouver), WI (Green Bay, New London, Oshkosh, Sheboygan).

$ Given: $700,000 for 826 grants; average $832.

Contact: Edward T. Dougherty, Executive Director
  Initial approach: brief letter or proposal
  Deadlines: applications accepted throughout the year

Emhart Corporation
426 Colt Highway
Farmington, Connecticut 06032
(203) 678-3204

Areas of interest: Arts and humanities (museums/galleries, zoos, operas, arts centers, historic preservation/restoration), civic and public affairs (business/free enterprise, urban and community affairs), education, health, and social services.

Restrictions: Grants for general support, capital, endowment, and matching funds; grants to individuals.

Focus of giving: Giving primarily in areas where company has major facilities and a large number of employees: AL, CA (Anaheim, Los Angeles, Torrance), CT (Berlin, Farmington, Hartford, Shelton, Windsor), IL (Broadview), IN (Indianapolis), KY (Campbellsville), MA (Beverly, Fall River, Middleton, New Bedford, South Hadley, Whitman), MI (Mount Clemens), MO, NE (Lincoln), NH, NY (Elmira, Maspeth), OH (Cleveland), PA (Huntington Valley, Reading, Temple), TN, VT (Springfield).

$ Given: $738,865 for 200 grants: high $45,000; low $100; average $2,694.

Contact: John F. Budd, Jr., Chairman, Contributions and Grants Committee
  Initial approach: brief letter or proposal
  Deadlines: submit proposal before October
  Final notification: by December

Graham Foundation for Advanced Studies in the Fine Arts
4 West Burton Place
Chicago, Illinois 60610
(312) 787-4071

Areas of interest: Grants for historic preservation/restoration, and museums/galleries.

Focus of giving: Special interest in architecture. General support for cultural institutions and individuals; international distribution.

$ Given: $388,072 for 60 grants: high $12,000; low $470; average $2,500–$7,500.

Assets: $15,574,630

Contact: Carter H. Manny, Jr., Director
    Initial approach: letter

Inland Steel-Ryerson Foundation, Inc.
30 West Monroe Street
Chicago, Illinois 60603
(312) 899-3420

Areas of interest: Arts and culture (museums/galleries, arts centers, historic preservation/restoration), civic and public affairs (economic development, urban and community affairs), education, health, and social services (homes).

Restrictions: Grants for capital, general support, and special projects; grants to individuals.

Focus of giving: Giving primarily in northwestern Indiana and Chicago, Illinois (West Side and South suburbs).

$ Given: $1,697,817 for 306 grants: high $341,000; low $100; average $1,000–$10,000.

Contact: Earl Thompson, Secretary
    Initial approach: one- or two-page proposal
    Deadlines: submit proposal preferably during the first 9 months of the year
    Board meeting dates: April, August, and December

Sargent & Lundy Corporate Giving Program
55 East Monroe Street
Chicago, Illinois 60603
(312) 269-2000

Areas of interest: Education and private colleges, engineering, fine arts institutes, economic development, and environmental issues; also in-kind giving.

Restrictions: Grants for annual campaigns, building funds, capital campaigns, grants to individuals.

Contact: W. A. Chittenden, Senior Partner

Unocal Foundation
P. O. Box 7600
Los Angeles, California 90051
(213) 977-6171

Areas of interest: Arts and culture (museums/galleries, arts centers), civic and public affairs (business/free enterprise, economic development, urban and community affairs), education, health, and social services.

Restrictions: Grants for capital, general support, and special projects; grants to individuals.

Focus of giving: Nationally, with preference given to areas where Uno-cal maintains corporate facilities: AK (Kenai), CA (Brea, Los Angeles, Mountain Pass, San Francisco, Santa Maria), CO, IL (Chicago, Palatine), LA, NC (Charlotte), OR (Rivergate), TX (Beaumont).

$ Given: $4,571,472 for 397 grants: high $491,860; low $250; average $500–$5,000.

Contact: R. P. Van Zandt, Vice-President and Trustee
   Initial approach: telephone
   Deadlines: requests in by September 15

INDIANA

Bemis Company Foundation
800 Northstar Center
Minneapolis, Minnesota 55402
(612) 340-6198

Areas of interest: Urban and community affairs, arts centers, cinema, performing arts (general), business/free enterprise, economic develop-ment, education, health, and social services.

Restrictions: Grants for general support, special projects, and matching funds, grants to individuals.

Focus of giving: Areas where company maintains facilities, with emphasis on Minneapolis, MN, AR (Crossett), CA (Los Angeles, Union City, Wilmington), CT (Plainfield, Stratford), FL (Panama City), IL (Murphysboro, Peoria, Schaumburg), IN (Indianapolis, Terre Haute), KS (Wichita), KY (Florence, Henderson, Louisville), MA (East Pepperell), MI (Grand Rapids, Zeeland), MN (Mankato, Minneapolis, Minnetonka), MO (Louisiana, Saint Louis, Springfield), MS (Verona), NC (Statesville), NE (Omaha), NH (Hudson, Nashua, North Walpole), NJ (Flemington), NY (Buffalo), OH (Stow), TN (Memphis), TX (Jacksonville), WA (Seattle, Vancouver), WI (Green Bay, New London, Oshkosh, Sheboygan).

$ Given: $700,000 for 826 grants; average $832.

Contact: Edward T. Dougherty, Executive Director

    Initial approach: brief letter or proposal

    Deadlines: applications accepted throughout the year

Emhart Corporation
426 Colt Highway
Farmington, Connecticut 06032
(203) 678-3204

Areas of interest: Arts and humanities (museums/galleries, zoos, operas, arts centers, historic preservation/restoration), civic and public affairs (business/free enterprise, urban and community affairs), education, health, and social services.

Restrictions: Grants for general support, capital, endowment, and matching funds; grants to individuals.

Focus of giving: Giving primarily in areas where company has major facilities and a large number of employees: AL, CA (Anaheim, Los Angeles, Torrance), CT (Berlin, Farmington, Hartford, Shelton, Windsor), IL (Broadview), IN (Indianapolis), KY (Campbellsville), MA (Beverly, Fall River, Middleton, New Bedford, South Hadley, Whitman), MI (Mount Clemens), MO, NE (Lincoln), NH, NY (Elmira, Maspeth), OH (Cleveland), PA (Huntington Valley, Reading, Temple), TN, VT (Springfield).

$ Given: $738,865 for 200 grants: high $45,000; low $100; average $2,694.

Contact: John F. Budd, Jr., Chairman, Contributions and Grants Committee

> **Initial approach:** brief letter or proposal
>
> **Deadlines:** submit proposal before October
>
> **Final notification:** by December

Olive B. Cole Foundation, Inc.
Cole Capital Corporation
3242 Mallard Cove Lane
Fort Wayne, Indiana 46804
(219) 436-2182

Restrictions: Grants given for seed money, building funds, equipment, land acquisition, matching funds, program-related investments, general purposes, and continuing support.

Focus of giving: Giving limited to LaGrange, Steuben, and Noble counties.

$ Given: $337,462 for 28 grants: high $70,000; low $1,000; average $12,052. Also $118,018 for grants to individuals.

Contact: John E. Hogan, Jr., Executive Vice-President

> **Application information:** application form required
>
> **Initial approach:** letter
>
> **Copies of proposal:** 7
>
> **Deadlines:** none
>
> **Board meeting dates:** February, May, August, and November
>
> **Final notification:** 4 months

Inland Steel-Ryerson Foundation, Inc.
30 West Monroe Street
Chicago, Illinois 60603
(312) 899-3420

Areas of interest: Arts and culture (museums/galleries, arts centers, historic preservation/restoration), civic and public affairs (economic development, urban and community affairs), education, health, and social services (homes).

Restrictions: Grants for capital, general support, and special projects; grants to individuals.

Focus of giving: Giving primarily in northwestern Indiana and Chicago, Illinois (West Side and South suburbs).

$ Given: $1,697,817 for 306 grants: high $341,000; low $100; average $1,000–$10,000.

Contact: Earl Thompson, Secretary

> **Initial approach:** one- or two-page proposal
>
> **Deadlines:** submit proposal preferably during the first 9 months of the year
>
> **Board meeting dates:** April, August, and December

Northern Indiana Public Service Company Giving Program
5265 Hohman Avenue
Hammond, Indiana 46320
(219) 853-5200

Areas of interest: Supports energy assistance funds, education, health, hospital building funds, mental health, cultural programs, social welfare, arts and sciences, civic and community affairs, including youth programs.

Restrictions: Grants for building funds, capital campaigns, general purposes, matching funds, renovation projects, special projects; grants to individuals.

Focus of giving: Giving primarily in operating areas.

$ Given: $567,000 for grants: high $10,000; low $5,000.

Publications: Corporate report.

Contact: Jack W. Stine, Vice-President

> **Initial approach:** proposal
>
> **Copies of proposal:** 1
>
> **Deadlines:** none

IOWA

Maytag Company Foundation, Inc.
One Dependability Square
Newton, Iowa 50208
(515) 792-7000

Areas of interest: Arts and culture (museums/galleries, historic preservation/restoration), civic and public affairs (business/free enterprise), education, and social services.

Restrictions: Grants for general support, and matching funds; grants to individuals.

Focus of giving: Giving primarily in Newton and Central Iowa.

$ Given: $429,327 for 91 grants: high $49,000; low $66; average $500–$2,500.

Assets: $1,022,366

Contact: Betty J. Dickinson, Executive Director
   Initial approach: letter
   Deadlines: submit proposal before board meeting in late March

Pella Rolscreen Foundation
102 Main Street
Pella, Iowa 50219
(515) 628-1000

Areas of interest: Arts and culture (business/free enterprise, museums/galleries, arts centers, historic preservation/restoration), civic and public affairs (economic development, women's affairs, urban and community affairs), education, health, and social services (homes).

Restrictions: Grants for capital, general support, matching funds, and special projects; grants to individuals.

Focus of giving: Emphasis on Marion and Mahaska counties in Iowa.

$ Given: $919,015 for 115 grants: high $223,750; low $50; average $500–$10,000.

Assets: $6,118,677

Contact: William J. Anderson, Administrator
   Initial approach: full proposal
   Copies of proposal: 1
   Deadlines: applications accepted throughout the year
   Board meeting dates: monthly

KANSAS

Bemis Company Foundation
800 Northstar Center
Minneapolis, Minnesota 55402
(612) 340-6198

Areas of interest: Urban and community affairs, arts centers, cinema, performing arts (general), business/free enterprise, economic development, education, health, and social services.

Restrictions: Grants for general support, special projects, and matching funds; grants to individuals.

Focus of giving: Areas where company maintains facilities, with emphasis on Minneapolis, MN, AR (Crossett), CA (Los Angeles, Union City, Wilmington), CT (Plainfield, Stratford), FL (Panama City), IL (Murphysboro, Peoria, Schaumburg), IN (Indianapolis, Terre Haute), KS (Wichita), KY (Florence, Henderson, Louisville), MA (East Pepperell), MI (Grand Rapids, Zeeland), MN (Mankato, Minneapolis, Minnetonka), MO (Louisiana, Saint Louis, Springfield), MS (Verona), NC (Statesville), NE (Omaha), NH (Hudson, Nashua, North Walpole), NJ (Flemington), NY (Buffalo), OH (Stow), TN (Memphis), TX (Jacksonville), WA (Seattle, Vancouver), WI (Green Bay, New London, Oshkosh, Sheboygan).

$ Given: $700,000 for 826 grants; average $832.

Contact: Edward T. Dougherty, Executive Director

    Initial approach: brief letter or proposal

    Deadlines: applications accepted throughout the year

KENTUCKY

Bemis Company Foundation
800 Northstar Center
Minneapolis, Minnesota 55402
(612) 340-6198

Areas of interest: Urban and community affairs, arts centers, cinema, performing arts (general), business/free enterprise, economic development, education, health, and social services.

Restrictions: Grants for general support, special projects, and matching funds; grants to individuals.

Focus of giving: Areas where company maintains facilities, with emphasis on Minneapolis, MN, AR (Crossett), CA (Los Angeles, Union City, Wilmington), CT (Plainfield, Stratford), FL (Panama City), IL (Murphysboro, Peoria, Schaumburg), IN (Indianapolis, Terre Haute), KS (Wichita), KY (Florence, Henderson, Louisville), MA (East Pepperell), MI (Grand Rapids, Zeeland), MN (Mankato, Minneapolis, Minnetonka), MO (Louisiana, Saint Louis, Springfield), MS (Verona), NC (Statesville), NE (Omaha), NH (Hudson, Nashua, North Walpole), NJ (Flemington), NY (Buffalo), OH (Stow), TN (Memphis), TX (Jacksonville), WA (Seattle, Vancouver), WI (Green Bay, New London, Oshkosh, Sheboygan).

$ Given: $700,000 for 826 grants; average $832.

Contact: Edward T. Dougherty, Executive Director

   Initial approach: brief letter or proposal

   Deadlines: applications accepted throughout the year

Emhart Corporation
426 Colt Highway
Farmington, Connecticut 06032
(203) 678-3204

Areas of interest: Arts and humanities (museums/galleries, zoos, operas, arts centers, historic preservation/restoration), civic and public affairs (business/free enterprise, urban and community affairs), education, health, and social services.

Restrictions: Grants for general support, capital, endowment, and matching funds; grants to individuals.

Focus of giving: Giving primarily in areas where company has major facilities and a large number of employees: AL, CA (Anaheim, Los Angeles, Torrance), CT (Berlin, Farmington, Hartford, Shelton, Windsor), IL (Broadview), IN (Indianapolis), KY (Campbellsville), MA (Beverly, Fall River, Middleton, New Bedford, South Hadley, Whitman), MI (Mount Clemens), MO, NE (Lincoln), NH, NY (Elmira, Maspeth), OH (Cleveland), PA (Huntington Valley, Reading, Temple), TN, VT (Springfield).

$ Given: $738,865 for 200 grants: high $45,000; low $100; average $2,694.

Contact: John F. Budd, Jr., Chairman, Contributions and Grants Committee

Initial approach: brief letter or proposal

Deadlines: submit proposal before October

Final notification: by December

LOUISIANA

Murphy Foundation
200 Jefferson Avenue
El Dorado, Arkansas 71730
(501) 862-6411

Areas of interest: Civic affairs, historic preservation/restoration, museums/galleries.

Restrictions: Grants for capital, general support, and special projects; grants to individuals.

Focus of giving: Major priority is for general purposes in Arkansas and Louisiana.

$ Given: $512,713 for 49 grants: high $106,969; low $175; average $1,000–$15,000.

Assets: $9,778,000

Contact: Lucy A. Ring

   Application information: application form required

Unocal Foundation
P. O. Box 7600
Los Angeles, California 90051
(213) 977-6171

Areas of interest: Arts and culture (museums/galleries, arts centers), civic and public affairs (business/free enterprise, economic development, urban and community affairs), education, health, and social services.

Restrictions: Grants for capital, general support, and special projects; grants to individuals.

Focus of giving: Nationally, with preference given to areas where Unocal maintains corporate facilities: AK (Kenai), CA (Brea, Los Angeles, Mountain Pass, San Francisco, Santa Maria), CO, IL (Chicago, Palatine), LA, NC (Charlotte), OR (Rivergate), TX (Beaumont).

$ **Given:** $4,571,472 for 397 grants: high $491,860; low $250; average $500–$5,000.

Contact: R. P. Van Zandt, Vice-President and Trustee

  Initial approach: telephone

  Deadlines: requests in by September 15

MARYLAND

Abell Foundation
1116 Fidelity Building
210 North Charles Street
Baltimore, Maryland 21201
(301) 547-1300

Areas of interest: Arts and humanities, civic and public affairs, education, and social services.

Restrictions: Grants for building funds, land acquisitions, and renovations.

Focus of giving: Maryland; primarily metropolitan Baltimore.

$ **Given:** $1,376,626.

Assets: $112,957,546

Contact: Anne LaFarge Culman, Vice-President

  Initial approach: letter or brief proposal

  Copies of proposal: 1

  Deadlines: February 1, May 1, August 1, and November 1

MASSACHUSETTS

Bemis Company Foundation
800 Northstar Center
Minneapolis, Minnesota 55402
(612) 340-6198

Areas of interest: Urban and community affairs, arts centers, cinema, performing arts (general), business/free enterprise, economic development, education, health, and social services.

Restrictions: Grants for general support, special projects, and matching funds; grants to individuals.

Focus of giving: Areas where company maintains facilities, with emphasis on Minneapolis, MN, AR (Crossett), CA (Los Angeles, Union City, Wilmington), CT (Plainfield, Stratford), FL (Panama City), IL (Murphysboro, Peoria, Schaumburg), IN (Indianapolis, Terre Haute), KS (Wichita), KY (Florence, Henderson, Louisville), MA (East Pepperell), MI (Grand Rapids, Zeeland), MN (Mankato, Minneapolis, Minnetonka), MO (Louisiana, Saint Louis, Springfield), MS (Verona), NC (Statesville), NE (Omaha), NH (Hudson, Nashua, North Walpole), NJ (Flemington), NY (Buffalo), OH (Stow), TN (Memphis), TX (Jacksonville), WA (Seattle, Vancouver), WI (Green Bay, New London, Oshkosh, Sheboygan).

$ Given: $700,000 for 826 grants; average $832.

Contact: Edward T. Dougherty, Executive Director

   Initial approach: brief letter or proposal

   Deadlines: applications accepted throughout the year

Emhart Corporation
426 Colt Highway
Farmington, Connecticut 06032
(203) 678-3204

Areas of interest: Arts and humanities (museums/galleries, zoos, operas, arts centers, historic preservation/restoration), civic and public affairs (business/free enterprise, urban and community affairs), education, health, and social services.

Restrictions: Grants for general support, capital, endowment, and matching funds; grants to individuals.

Focus of giving: Giving primarily in areas where company has major facilities and a large number of employees: AL, CA (Anaheim, Los Angeles, Torrance), CT (Berlin, Farmington, Hartford, Shelton, Windsor), IL (Broadview), IN (Indianapolis), KY (Campbellsville), MA (Beverly, Fall River, Middleton, New Bedford, South Hadley, Whitman), MI (Mount Clemens), MO, NE (Lincoln), NH, NY (Elmira, Maspeth), OH (Cleveland), PA (Huntington Valley, Reading, Temple), TN, VT (Springfield).

$ Given: $738,865 for 200 grants: high $45,000; low $100; average $2,694.

Contact: John F. Budd, Jr., Chairman, Contributions and Grants Committee

   Initial approach: brief letter or proposal

   Deadlines: submit proposal before October

   Final notification: by December

MICHIGAN

Bemis Company Foundation
800 Northstar Center
Minneapolis, Minnesota 55402
(612) 340-6198

Areas of interest: Urban and community affairs, arts centers, cinema, performing arts (general), business/free enterprise, economic development, education, health, and social services.

Restrictions: Grants for general support, special projects, and matching funds; grants to individuals.

Focus of giving: Areas where company maintains facilities, with emphasis on Minneapolis, MN. AR (Crossett), CA (Los Angeles, Union City, Wilmington), CT (Plainfield, Stratford), FL (Panama City), IL (Murphysboro, Peoria, Schaumburg), IN (Indianapolis, Terre Haute), KS (Wichita), KY (Florence, Henderson, Louisville), MA (East Pepperell), MI (Grand Rapids, Zeeland), MN (Mankato, Minneapolis, Minnetonka), MO (Louisiana, Saint Louis, Springfield), MS (Verona), NC (Statesville), NE (Omaha), NH (Hudson, Nashua, North Walpole), NJ (Flemington), NY (Buffalo), OH (Stow), TN (Memphis), TX (Jacksonville), WA (Seattle, Vancouver), WI (Green Bay, New London, Oshkosh, Sheboygan).

$ Given: $700,000 for 826 grants; average $832.

Contact: Edward T. Dougherty, Executive Director

   Initial approach: brief letter or proposal

   Deadlines: applications accepted throughout the year

The Richard and Helen DeVos Foundation
7154 Windy Hill Road, SE
Grand Rapids, Michigan 49506
(616) 676-6225

Areas of interest: Civic affairs (economic development; urban and community affairs, business/free enterprise, community centers).

Restrictions: Grants for capital, general support, and special projects; grants to individuals.

Focus of giving: National distribution with priority given to religious programs and associations in Grand Rapids area.

$ Given: $783,078 for 65 grants: high $102,000; low $24; average $1,000–$25,000.

Assets: $6,883,417

Contact: Richard M. DeVos, President

   Initial approach: letter

Emhart Corporation
426 Colt Highway
Farmington, Connecticut 06032
(203) 678-3204

Areas of interest: Arts and humanities (museums/galleries, zoos, operas, arts centers, historic preservation/restoration), civic and public affairs (business/free enterprise, urban and community affairs), education, health, and social services.

Restrictions: Grants for general support, capital, endowment, and matching funds; grants to individuals.

Focus of giving: Giving primarily in areas where company has major facilities and a large number of employees: AL, CA (Anaheim, Los Angeles, Torrance), CT (Berlin, Farmington, Hartford, Shelton, Windsor), IL (Broadview), IN (Indianapolis), KY (Campbellsville), MA (Beverly, Fall River, Middleton, New Bedford, South Hadley, Whitman), MI (Mount Clemens), MO, NE (Lincoln), NH, NY (Elmira, Maspeth), OH (Cleveland), PA (Huntington Valley, Reading, Temple), TN, VT (Springfield).

$ Given: $738,865 for 200 grants: high $45,000; low $100; average $2,694.

Contact: John F. Budd, Jr., Chairman, Contributions and Grants Committee

   Initial approach: brief letter or proposal

   Deadlines: submit proposal before October

   Final notification: by December

Grand Rapids Foundation*
209-C Waters Building
161 Ottawa, NW
Grand Rapids, Michigan 49503
(616) 454-1751

Restrictions: Grants for seed money, building funds, emergency funds, equipment, matching funds, and land acquisition.

Focus of giving: Giving limited to Kent County, Michigan.

$ Given: $1,122,617 for 55 grants: high $123,300; low $83; average $500–$100,000. Also $51,904 for grants to individuals and $80,500 for 37 loans.

Publications: Annual report, program policy statement and application guidelines, informational brochure, and newsletter.

Contact: Diana Sieger, Executive Director

   Application information: application form required

   Initial approach: letter or telephone

   Copies of proposal: 10

   Deadlines: 4 weeks preceding board meeting

   Board meeting dates: bimonthly, beginning in August

   Final notification: 1 month

Hudson-Webber Foundation
333 West Fort Street
Detroit, Michigan 48226
(313) 963-8991

Areas of interest: Concentrates efforts and resources in support of physical revitalization of downtown Detroit, reduction of crime in Detroit, and economic development of southeastern Michigan, with emphasis on the creation of additional employment opportunities.

Focus of giving: Giving primarily in the Wayne, Oakland, and Macomb tricounty area of southeastern Michigan, particularly in Detroit.

* Community foundation established in 1922 in Michigan by resolution and declaration of trust.

$ Given: $2,176,592 for 62 grants: high $213,000; low $2,400; average $10,000–30,000. Also $188,871 for 236 grants to individuals and $43,946 for 11 employee matching gifts.

Contact: Gilbert Hudson, President

   Deadlines: April 15, August 15, and December 15

Muskegon County Community Foundation, Inc.*
Frauenthal Center, Suite 304
407 West Western Avenue
Muskegon, Michigan 49440
(616) 722-4538

Restrictions: Grants for seed money, building funds, equipment, special projects, matching funds, and land acquisition.

Focus of giving: Giving limited to Muskegon County, Michigan.

$ Given: $373,094 for 46 grants: high $58,600; low $200; average $1,000–$5,000. Also $163,259 for 192 grants to individuals and additional amounts as loans.

Publications: Annual report and application guidelines.

Contact: Patricia B. Johnson, Executive Director

   Application information: application form required

   Initial approach: letter or telephone

   Copies of proposal: 12

   Deadlines: January, April, July, or October

   Board meeting dates: February, May, August, and November

   Final notification: 2 to 3 weeks

MINNESOTA

Bemis Company Foundation
800 Northstar Center
Minneapolis, Minnesota 55402
(612) 340-6198

---

* Community foundation incorporated in 1961 in Michigan.

Areas of interest: Urban and community affairs, arts centers, cinema, performing arts (general), business/free enterprise, economic development, education, health, and social services.

Restrictions: Grants for general support, special projects, and matching funds; grants to individuals.

Focus of giving: Areas where company maintains facilities, with emphasis on Minneapolis, MN, AR (Crossett), CA (Los Angeles, Union City, Wilmington), CT (Plainfield, Stratford), FL (Panama City), IL (Murphysboro, Peoria, Schaumburg), IN (Indianapolis, Terre Haute), KS (Wichita), KY (Florence, Henderson, Louisville), MA (East Pepperell), MI (Grand Rapids, Zeeland), MN (Mankato, Minneapolis, Minnetonka), MO (Louisiana, Saint Louis, Springfield), MS (Verona), NC (Statesville), NE (Omaha), NH (Hudson, Nashua, North Walpole), NJ (Flemington), NY (Buffalo), OH (Stow), TN (Memphis), TX (Jacksonville), WA (Seattle, Vancouver), WI (Green Bay, New London, Oshkosh, Sheboygan).

$ Given: $700,000 for 826 grants; average $832.

Contact: Edward T. Dougherty, Executive Director

   Initial approach: brief letter or proposal

   Deadlines: applications accepted throughout the year

Charles K. Blandin Foundation[*]
100 Pokegama Avenue North
Grand Rapids, Minnesota 55744
(218) 326-0523

Areas of interest: Civic affairs (economic development, urban and community affairs, historic preservation/restoration).

Restrictions: Grants for general support, seed money, individual projects; grants to individuals.

Focus of giving: Giving primarily in the lake and forest regions of Itasca County, Minnesota.

$ Given: $4,992,106 for 92 grants: high $1,000,000; low $500; average $5,000–$50,000. Also $215,071 for 378 grants to individuals.

Assets: $18,526,203

[*] Incorporated in 1941 in Minnesota.

Publications: Annual report, program policy statement, and application guidelines.

Contact: Paul M. Olson, Executive Director

   Initial approach: letter

   Copies of proposal: 1

   Deadlines: submit proposal preferably 2 months prior to board meetings: March 1, June 1, September 1, and December 1

   Board meeting dates: first week of February, May, August, and November

   Final notification: 2 weeks after board meeting

MISSISSIPPI

Bemis Company Foundation
800 Northstar Center
Minneapolis, Minnesota 55402
(612) 340-6198

Areas of interest: Urban and community affairs, arts centers, cinema, performing arts (general), business/free enterprise, economic development, education, health, and social services.

Restrictions: Grants for general support, special projects, and matching funds; grants to individuals.

Focus of giving: Areas where company maintains facilities, with emphasis on Minneapolis, MN, AR (Crossett), CA (Los Angeles, Union City, Wilmington), CT (Plainfield, Stratford), FL (Panama City), IL (Murphysboro, Peoria, Schaumburg), IN (Indianapolis, Terre Haute), KS (Wichita), KY (Florence, Henderson, Louisville), MA (East Pepperell), MI (Grand Rapids, Zeeland), MN (Mankato, Minneapolis, Minnetonka), MO (Louisiana, Saint Louis, Springfield), MS (Verona), NC (Statesville), NE (Omaha), NH (Hudson, Nashua, North Walpole), NJ (Flemington), NY (Buffalo), OH (Stow), TN (Memphis), TX (Jacksonville), WA (Seattle, Vancouver), WI (Green Bay, New London, Oshkosh, Sheboygan).

$ Given: $700,000 for 826 grants; average $832.

Contact: Edward T. Dougherty, Executive Director

   Initial approach: brief letter or proposal

   Deadlines: applications accepted throughout the year

MISSOURI

Bemis Company Foundation
800 Northstar Center
Minneapolis, Minnesota 55402
(612) 340-6198

Areas of interest: Urban and community affairs, arts centers, cinema, performing arts (general), business/free enterprise, economic development, education, health, and social services.

Restrictions: Grants for general support, special projects, and matching funds; grants to individuals.

Focus of giving: Areas where company maintains facilities, with emphasis on Minneapolis, MN, AR (Crossett), CA (Los Angeles, Union City, Wilmington), CT (Plainfield, Stratford), FL (Panama City), IL (Murphysboro, Peoria, Schaumburg), IN (Indianapolis, Terre Haute), KS (Wichita), KY (Florence, Henderson, Louisville), MA (East Pepperell), MI (Grand Rapids, Zeeland), MN (Mankato, Minneapolis, Minnetonka), MO (Louisiana, Saint Louis, Springfield), MS (Verona), NC (Statesville), NE (Omaha), NH (Hudson, Nashua, North Walpole), NJ (Flemington), NY (Buffalo), OH (Stow), TN (Memphis), TX (Jacksonville), WA (Seattle, Vancouver), WI (Green Bay, New London, Oshkosh, Sheboygan).

$ Given: $700,000 for 826 grants; average $832.

Contact: Edward T. Dougherty, Executive Director

    Initial approach: brief letter or proposal

    Deadlines: applications accepted throughout the year

Butler Manufacturing Company Foundation*
BMA Tower, P. O. Box 917
Penn Valley Park
Kansas City, Missouri 64141

Areas of interest: Minorities and the handicapped, preservation of urban neighborhoods, and development and improvement of agriculture and industry.

Restrictions: Support for seed money, building funds, emergency funds, equipment, matching funds, general purposes, and special projects.

---

* Incorporated in 1922 in Missouri.

$ Given: $281,472 for 102 grants. $74,166 for 38 grants to individuals, and $4,550 for five loans.

Assets: $2,431,279

Publications: Annual report, program policy statement and application guidelines, and informational brochure.

Contact: Barbara Fay

    Initial approach: letter or telephone

    Copies of proposal: 1

    Deadlines: submit proposal preferably in month prior to board meetings

    Board meeting dates: March, June, September, and December

    Final notification: 6 months

Emhart Corporation
426 Colt Highway
Farmington, Connecticut 06032
(203) 678-3204

Areas of interest: Arts and humanities (museums/galleries, zoos, operas,
arts centers, historic preservation/restoration), civic and public affairs (business/free enterprise, urban and community affairs), education, health, and social services.

Restrictions: Grants for general support, capital, endowment, and matching funds; grants to individuals.

Focus of giving: Giving primarily in areas where company has major facilities and a large number of employees: AL, CA (Anaheim, Los Angeles, Torrance), CT (Berlin, Farmington, Hartford, Shelton, Windsor), IL (Broadview), IN (Indianapolis), KY (Campbellsville), MA (Beverly, Fall River, Middleton, New Bedford, South Hadley, Whitman), MI (Mount Clemens), MO, NE (Lincoln), NH, NY (Elmira, Maspeth), OH (Cleveland), PA (Huntington Valley, Reading, Temple), TN, VT (Springfield).

$ Given: $738,865 for 200 grants: high $45,000; low $100; average $2,694.

Contact: John F. Budd, Jr., Chairman, Contributions and Grants Committee

Initial approach: brief letter or proposal

Deadlines: submit proposal before October

Final notification: by December

The H&R Block Foundation
4410 Main Street
Kansas City, Missouri 64111
(816) 932-8424

Restrictions: Support for general purposes, building funds, emergency funds, equipment, matching funds, land acquisition, program-related investments, operating budgets, seed money, and deficit financing.

Focus of giving: Giving limited to the 50-mile area around Kansas City.

$ Given: $233,955 for 131 grants: high $26,000; low $50; average $500–25,000. Also $60,000 for 30 grants to individuals and $5,100 for 22 employee matching gifts.

Assets: $3,739,311

Publications: Informational brochure, program policy statement, and application guidelines.

Donor: H&R Block, Inc.

Contact: Terrance R. Wood, President

   Initial approach: full proposal

   Copies of proposal: 1

   Deadlines: 45 days prior to meetings

   Board meeting dates: March, June, September, and December

   Final notification: 2 weeks after board meeting

Hall Family Foundations
Charitable & Crown Investment—323
P. O. Box 419580
Kansas City, Missouri 64141-6580
(816) 274-5615

Areas of interest: Broad purposes, within four main areas of interest: (1) youth, especially education and programs that promote social welfare, health, and character building of young people; (2) economic development; (3) the performing and visual arts; and (4) the elderly.

Focus of giving: Giving limited to the Kansas City, Missouri, area.

$ Given: $3,768,407 for 52 grants: high $1,966,921; low $1,000; average $35,000. Also $130,600 for 89 loans and $155,550 for 110 grants to individuals.

Assets: $117,877,180

Contact: Sarah V. Hutchison, Margaret H. Pence, or Wendy Hockaday, Program Officers

    Initial approach: letter

    Copies of proposal: 1

    Deadlines: 4 weeks before board meetings

    Board meeting dates: March, June, September, and December

    Final notification: 4 to 6 weeks

Pulitzer Publishing Company Foundation
900 North Tucker Boulevard
St. Louis, Missouri 63101
(314) 622-7357

Areas of interest: Arts and culture (museums/galleries, historic preservation/restoration), civic and public affairs (business/free enterprise), education, health, and social services.

Restrictions: Grants for capital, endowment, general support, and special projects; grants to individuals.

Focus of giving: Giving primarily in St. Louis metropolitan area.

$ Given: $551,487 for 105 grants: high $100,000; low $100; average $1,000–$10,000.

Contact: Ronald H. Ridgeway, Treasurer and Director

    Initial approach: letter or proposal

    Deadlines: none

NEBRASKA

Bemis Company Foundation
800 Northstar Center
Minneapolis, Minnesota 55402
(612) 340-6198

Areas of interest: Urban and community affairs, arts centers, cinema, performing arts (general), business/free enterprise, economic development, education, health, and social services.

Restrictions: Grants for general support, special projects, and matching funds; grants to individuals.

Focus of giving: Areas where company maintains facilities, with emphasis on Minneapolis, MN, AR (Crossett), CA (Los Angeles, Union City, Wilmington), CT (Plainfield, Stratford), FL (Panama City), IL (Murphysboro, Peoria, Schaumburg), IN (Indianapolis, Terre Haute), KS (Wichita), KY (Florence, Henderson, Louisville), MA (East Pepperell), MI (Grand Rapids, Zeeland), MN (Mankato, Minneapolis, Minnetonka), MO (Louisiana, Saint Louis, Springfield), MS (Verona), NC (Statesville), NE (Omaha), NH (Hudson, Nashua, North Walpole), NJ (Flemington), NY (Buffalo), OH (Stow), TN (Memphis), TX (Jacksonville), WA (Seattle, Vancouver), WI (Green Bay, New London, Oshkosh, Sheboygan).

$ Given: $700,000 for 826 grants; average $832.

Contact: Edward T. Dougherty, Executive Director

    Initial approach: brief letter or proposal

    Deadlines: applications accepted throughout the year

Emhart Corporation
426 Colt Highway
Farmington, Connecticut 06032
(203) 678-3204

Areas of interest: Arts and humanities (museums/galleries, zoos, operas, arts centers, historic preservation/restoration), civic and public affairs (business/free enterprise, urban and community affairs), education, health, and social services.

Restrictions: Grants for general support, capital, endowment, and matching funds; grants to individuals.

Focus of giving: Giving primarily in areas where company has major facilities and a large number of employees: AL, CA (Anaheim, Los Angeles, Torrance), CT (Berlin, Farmington, Hartford, Shelton, Windsor), IL (Broadview), IN (Indianapolis), KY (Campbellsville), MA (Beverly, Fall River, Middleton, New Bedford, South Hadley, Whitman), MI (Mount Clemens), MO, NE (Lincoln), NH, NY (Elmira, Maspeth), OH (Cleveland), PA (Huntington Valley, Reading, Temple), TN, VT (Springfield).

$ Given: $738,865 for 200 grants: high $45,000; low $100; average $2,694.

Contact: John F. Budd, Jr., Chairman, Contributions and Grants Committee

    Initial approach: brief letter or proposal

    Deadlines: submit proposal before October

    Final notification: by December

NEW HAMPSHIRE

Bemis Company Foundation
800 Northstar Center
Minneapolis, Minnesota 55402
(612) 340-6198

Areas of interest: Urban and community affairs, arts centers, cinema, performing arts (general), business/free enterprise, economic development, education, health, and social services.

Restrictions: Grants for general support, special projects, and matching funds; grants to individuals.

Focus of giving: Areas where company maintains facilities, with emphasis on Minneapolis, MN, AR (Crossett), CA (Los Angeles, Union City, Wilmington), CT (Plainfield, Stratford), FL (Panama City), IL (Murphysboro, Peoria, Schaumburg), IN (Indianapolis, Terre Haute), KS (Wichita), KY (Florence, Henderson, Louisville), MA (East Pepperell), MI (Grand Rapids, Zeeland), MN (Mankato, Minneapolis, Minnetonka), MO (Louisiana, Saint Louis, Springfield), MS (Verona), NC (Statesville), NE (Omaha), NH (Hudson, Nashua, North Walpole), NJ (Flemington), NY (Buffalo), OH (Stow), TN (Memphis), TX (Jacksonville), WA (Seattle, Vancouver), WI (Green Bay, New London, Oshkosh, Sheboygan).

$ Given: $700,000 for 826 grants; average $832.

Contact: Edward T. Dougherty, Executive Director

    Initial approach: brief letter or proposal

    Deadlines: applications accepted throughout the year

Emhart Corporation
426 Colt Highway
Farmington, Connecticut 06032
(203) 678-3204

Areas of interest: Arts and humanities (museums/galleries, zoos, operas, arts centers, historic preservation/restoration), civic and public affairs (business/free enterprise, urban and community affairs), education, health, and social services.

Restrictions: Grants for general support, capital, endowment, and matching funds; grants to individuals.

Focus of giving: Giving primarily in areas where company has major facilities and a large number of employees: AL, CA (Anaheim, Los Angeles, Torrance), CT (Berlin, Farmington, Hartford, Shelton, Windsor), IL (Broadview), IN (Indianapolis), KY (Campbellsville), MA (Beverly, Fall River, Middleton, New Bedford, South Hadley, Whitman), MI (Mount Clemens), MO, NE (Lincoln), NH, NY (Elmira, Maspeth), OH (Cleveland), PA (Huntington Valley, Reading, Temple), TN, VT (Springfield).

$ Given: $738,865 for 200 grants: high $45,000; low $100; average $2,694.

Contact: John F. Budd, Jr., Chairman, Contributions and Grants Committee

    Initial approach: brief letter or proposal

    Deadlines: submit proposal before October

    Final notification: by December

The New Hampshire Charitable Fund*
One South Street
P. O. Box 1335
Concord, New Hampshire 03302-1335
(603) 255-6641

Restrictions: Grants for seed money, loans, general purposes, and special projects; grants to individuals.

Focus of giving: Giving limited to New Hampshire.

$ Given: $1,239,056 for 354 grants: high $207,966; low $78. Also $349,636 for 175 loans and $349,636 for 205 grants to individuals.

Publications: Annual report, program policy statement and application guidelines, and newsletter.

Contact: Deborah Cowan, Associate Director

---

* Community foundation incorporated in 1962 in New Hampshire.

Initial approach: telephone

Deadlines: February 1, May 1, August 1, and November 1

Board meeting dates: March, June, September, and December

Final notification: 4 to 6 weeks

NEW JERSEY

Bemis Company Foundation
800 Northstar Center
Minneapolis, Minnesota 55402
(612) 340-6198

Areas of interest: Urban and community affairs, arts centers, cinema, performing arts (general), business/free enterprise, economic development, education, health, and social services.

Restrictions: Grants for general support, special projects, and matching funds; grants to individuals.

Focus of giving: Areas where company maintains facilities, with emphasis on Minneapolis, MN, AR (Crossett), CA (Los Angeles, Union City, Wilmington), CT (Plainfield, Stratford), FL (Panama City), IL (Murphysboro, Peoria, Schaumburg), IN (Indianapolis, Terre Haute), KS (Wichita), KY (Florence, Henderson, Louisville), MA (East Pepperell), MI (Grand Rapids, Zeeland), MN (Mankato, Minneapolis, Minnetonka), MO (Louisiana, Saint Louis, Springfield), MS (Verona), NC (Statesville), NE (Omaha), NH (Hudson, Nashua, North Walpole), NJ (Flemington), NY (Buffalo), OH (Stow), TN (Memphis), TX (Jacksonville), WA (Seattle, Vancouver), WI (Green Bay, New London, Oshkosh, Sheboygan).

$ Given: $700,000 for 826 grants; average $832.

Contact: Edward T. Dougherty, Executive Director

Initial approach: brief letter or proposal

Deadlines: applications accepted throughout the year

NEW MEXICO

Carlsbad Foundation, Inc.*
116 South Canyon
Carlsbad, New Mexico 88220
(505) 887-1131

---

* Incorporated in 1977 in New Mexico.

Restrictions: Support given in the form of loans, operating budgets, building funds, emergency funds, equipment, special projects, matching funds, program-related investments, and seed money.

Focus of giving: Giving limited to South Eddy County, New Mexico.

$ Given: $249,513, including $62,853 for grants, $92,781 for grants to individuals, and $400,000 for one loan.

Assets: $2,464,031

Publications: Annual report, program policy statement, and application guidelines.

Contact: John Mills, Executive Director

NEW YORK

Bemis Company Foundation
800 Northstar Center
Minneapolis, Minnesota 55402
(612) 340-6198

Areas of interest: Urban and community affairs, arts centers, cinema, performing arts (general), business/free enterprise, economic development, education, health, and social services.

Restrictions: Grants for general support, special projects, and matching funds; grants to individuals.

Focus of giving: Areas where company maintains facilities, with emphasis on Minneapolis, MN, AR (Crossett), CA (Los Angeles, Union City, Wilmington), CT (Plainfield, Stratford), FL (Panama City), IL (Murphysboro, Peoria, Schaumburg), IN (Indianapolis, Terre Haute), KS (Wichita), KY (Florence, Henderson, Louisville), MA (East Pepperell), MI (Grand Rapids, Zeeland), MN (Mankato, Minneapolis, Minnetonka), MO (Louisiana, Saint Louis, Springfield), MS (Verona), NC (Statesville), NE (Omaha), NH (Hudson, Nashua, North Walpole), NJ (Flemington), NY (Buffalo), OH (Stow), TN (Memphis), TX (Jacksonville), WA (Seattle, Vancouver), WI (Green Bay, New London, Oshkosh, Sheboygan).

$ Given: $700,000 for 826 grants; average $832.

Contact: Edward T. Dougherty, Executive Director
    Initial approach: brief letter or proposal
    Deadlines: applications accepted throughout the year

The Buffalo Foundation
237 Main Street
Buffalo, New York 14203
(716) 852-2857

Restrictions: Grants for operating budgets, seed money, building funds, emergency funds, equipment, special projects, matching funds, and land acquisition.

Focus of giving: Programs and agencies must benefit and enhance the quality of life of residents of Erie County, New York.

$ Given: $1,289,111 for 123 grants: high $109,050; low $78. Also $245,263 for grants to individuals.

Contact: W. L. Van Schoonhoven, Director

    Initial approach: letter or proposal

    Copies of proposal: 1

    Deadlines: applications must be received by the last day of March, June, September, or December

    Board meeting dates: the Governing Committee meets on the first Wednesday of February, May, August, and November

    Final notification: 1st meeting after submission

Burlington Industries Foundation
P. O. Box 21207
Greensboro, North Carolina 27420
(919) 379-2515

Areas of interest: Urban and community affairs, arts centers, museums, libraries, business/free enterprise, economic development, education, health, and social services.

Restrictions: Grants for capital, general support, matching funds, and special projects; grants to individuals.

Focus of giving: Primarily in North and South Carolina, Virginia, and near corporate operating locations: NC (Burlington, Greensboro, Madison), NY (New Rochelle, New York), PA (King of Prussia, Norristown), and other states.

$ Given: $2,000,000 for 552 grants: high $60,000; low $10; average $2,640.

Contact: Park R. Davidson, Executive Director

   Initial approach: brief letter or proposal

   Deadlines: applications accepted throughout the year

The Clark Foundation
30 Wall Street
New York, New York 10005
(212) 269-1833

Restrictions: Grants for general purposes, urban and community affairs, and housing.

Focus of giving: Giving limited to northern New York and New York City.

$ Given: $5,166,843 for 783 grants: high $200,950; low $700; average $5,000–$25,000.

Assets: $160,554,423

Contact: Edward W. Stack, Secretary

   Initial approach: letter

   Copies of proposal: 1

   Board meeting dates: October and May (and other times during the year)

Emhart Corporation
426 Colt Highway
Farmington, Connecticut 06032
(203) 678-3204

Areas of interest: Arts and humanities (museums/galleries, zoos, operas, art centers, historic preservation/restoration), civic and public affairs (business/free enterprise, urban and community affairs), education, health, and social services.

Restrictions: Grants for general support, capital, endowment, and matching funds; grants to individuals.

Focus of giving: Giving primarily in areas where company has major facilities and a large number of employees: AL, CA (Anaheim, Los Angeles, Torrance), CT (Berlin, Farmington, Hartford, Shelton, Windsor),

IL (Broadview), IN (Indianapolis), KY (Campbellsville), MA (Beverly, Fall River, Middleton, New Bedford, South Hadley, Whitman), MI (Mount Clemens), MO, NE (Lincoln), NH, NY (Elmira, Maspeth), OH (Cleveland), PA (Huntington Valley, Reading, Temple), TN, VT (Springfield).

$ Given: $738,865 for 200 grants: high $45,000; low $100; average $2,694.

Contact: John F. Budd, Jr., Chairman, Contributions and Grants Committee

> **Initial approach:** brief letter or proposal
>
> **Deadlines:** submit proposal before October
>
> **Final notification:** by December

The Glens Falls Foundation
55 Colvin Avenue
Albany, New York 12206
(518) 793-6302

Areas of interest: Broad purposes, including the promotion of the mental, moral, and physical improvement of the people of Glens Falls and environs.

Restrictions: Grants for seed money, building funds, emergency funds, equipment, special projects, and matching funds; grants to individuals.

Focus of giving: Giving limited to Warren, Washington, and Saratoga counties, New York; no loans.

$ Given: $73,369 for 29 grants: high $10,000; low $35. Also $7,500 for 27 grants to individuals.

Contact: Robert Gibeault, Administrator

> **Initial approach:** letter, telephone, or full proposal
>
> **Copies of proposal:** 8
>
> **Deadlines:** submit proposal preferably in December, March, June, or September; deadline 1st day of months in which board meets
>
> **Board meeting dates:** second Wednesday in January, April, July, and October
>
> **Final notification:** two days after quarterly meetings

Margaret B. Monohan and Alberta W. Laighton Memorial Fund
P. O. Box 314
Pawling, New York 12564
(914) 855-1505

Restrictions: Grants for community funds and general charitable giving.

Focus of giving: Giving limited to Pawling, New York.

$ Given: $1,000 for 3 grants. Also $7,958 for 8 grants to individuals.

Assets: $196,743
  Initial approach: letter
  Deadlines: none

NORTH CAROLINA

ABC Foundation
1201 Maple
Greensboro, North Carolina 27405
(919) 379-6717

Areas of interest: Arts and humanities, civic and public affairs, education, and health.

Restrictions: Grants for building funds; foundation will fund part of a capital project.

Focus of giving: Primarily in communities where Cone Mills Corporation maintains production facilities.

$ Given: $397,786.

Assets: $4,343,589

Contact: William O. Leonard, Vice-President
  Initial approach: letter and brief proposal
  Copies of proposal: 1
  Deadlines: applications accepted throughout the year
  Board meeting dates: board meets annually and as necessary

Bemis Company Foundation
800 Northstar Center
Minneapolis, Minnesota 55402
(612) 340-6198

Areas of interest: Urban and community affairs, arts centers, cinema, performing arts (general), business/free enterprise, economic development, education, health, and social services.

Restrictions: Grants for general support, special projects, and matching funds; grants to individuals.

Focus of giving: Areas where company maintains facilities, with emphasis on Minneapolis, MN, AR (Crossett), CA (Los Angeles, Union City, Wilmington), CT (Plainfield, Stratford), FL (Panama City), IL (Murphysboro, Peoria, Schaumburg), IN (Indianapolis, Terre Haute), KS (Wichita), KY (Florence, Henderson, Louisville), MA (East Pepperell), MI (Grand Rapids, Zeeland), MN (Mankato, Minneapolis, Minnetonka), MO (Louisiana, Saint Louis, Springfield), MS (Verona), NC (Statesville), NE (Omaha), NH (Hudson, Nashua, North Walpole), NJ (Flemington), NY (Buffalo), OH (Stow), TN (Memphis), TX (Jacksonville), WA (Seattle, Vancouver), WI (Green Bay, New London, Oshkosh, Sheboygan).

$ Given: $700,000 for 826 grants; average $832.

Contact: Edward T. Dougherty, Executive Director

    Initial approach: brief letter or proposal

    Deadlines: applications accepted throughout the year

Burlington Industries Foundation
P. O. Box 21207
Greensboro, North Carolina 27420
(919) 379-2515

Areas of interest: Urban and community affairs, arts centers, museums, libraries, business/free enterprise, economic development, education, health, and social services.

Restrictions: Grants for capital, general support, matching funds, and special projects; grants to individuals.

Focus of giving: Primarily in North and South Carolina, Virginia, and near corporate operating locations: NC (Burlington, Greensboro, Madison), NY (New Rochelle, New York), PA (King of Prussia, Norristown), and other states.

$ Given: $2,000,000 for 552 grants: high $60,000; low $10; average $2,640.

Contact: Park R. Davidson, Executive Director
  Initial approach: brief letter or proposal
  Deadlines: applications accepted throughout the year

Foundation for the Carolinas
301 South Brevard Street
Charlotte, North Carolina
(704) 376-9541

Restrictions: Grants for operating budgets, seed money, building funds, emergency funds, equipment, special projects, matching funds, and land acquisition.

Focus of giving: Giving primarily in North Carolina and South Carolina.

$ Given: $2,385,853 for 1,225 grants: high $209,800; low $100; average $500–$10,000. Also $12,398 for grants to individuals.

Publications: Annual report, application guidelines, informational brochure, and newsletter.

Contact: William Spencer, President
  Application information: application form required
  Initial approach: letter
  Copies of proposal: 11
  Deadlines: none
  Board meeting dates: quarterly, with annual meeting in March; distribution committee meets monthly
  Final notification: 1 to 2 months

Unocal Foundation
P. O. Box 7600
Los Angeles, California 90051
(213) 977-6171

Areas of interest: Arts and culture (museums/galleries, arts centers), civic and public affairs (business/free enterprise, economic development, urban and community affairs), education, health, and social services.

Restrictions: Grants for capital, general support, and special projects; grants to individuals.

Focus of giving: Nationally, with preference given to areas where Unocal maintains corporate facilities: AK (Kenai), CA (Brea, Los Angeles, Mountain Pass, San Francisco, Santa Maria), CO, IL (Chicago, Palatine), LA, NC (Charlotte), OR (Rivergate), TX (Beaumont).

$ Given: $4,571,472 for 397 grants: high $491,860; low $250; average $500–$5,000.

Contact: R. P. Van Zandt, Vice-President and Trustee

    Initial approach: telephone

    Deadlines: requests in by September 15

The Wachovia Foundation Inc.
c/o Wachovia Bank & Trust Co., N.A.
P. O. Box 3099
Winston-Salem, North Carolina 27150

Areas of interest: Higher education and community projects, including community funds.

Restrictions: Grants for building funds, capital campaigns, endowments funds, special projects, renovation projects, annual campaigns; grants to individuals.

Focus of giving: Giving primarily in North Carolina.

$ Given: $913,144 for 142 grants: high $50,000; low $275.

Assets: $5,096,247

Contact: John F. McNair III, President

    Initial approach: contact local bank office

    Copies of proposal: 1

    Board meeting dates: monthly

OHIO

Bemis Company Foundation
800 Northstar Center
Minneapolis, Minnesota 55402
(612) 340-6198

Areas of interest: Urban and community affairs, arts centers, cinema, performing arts (general), business/free enterprise, economic development, education, health, and social services.

Restrictions: Grants for general support, special projects, and matching funds; grants to individuals.

Focus of giving: Areas where company maintains facilities, with emphasis on Minneapolis, MN, AR (Crossett), CA (Los Angeles, Union City, Wilmington), CT (Plainfield, Stratford), FL (Panama City), IL (Murphysboro, Peoria, Schaumburg), IN (Indianapolis, Terre Haute), KS (Wichita), KY (Florence, Henderson, Louisville), MA (East Pepperell), MI (Grand Rapids, Zeeland), MN (Mankato, Minneapolis, Minnetonka), MO (Louisiana, Saint Louis, Springfield), MS (Verona), NC (Statesville), NE (Omaha), NH (Hudson, Nashua, North Walpole), NJ (Flemington), NY (Buffalo), OH (Stow), TN (Memphis), TX (Jacksonville), WA (Seattle, Vancouver), WI (Green Bay, New London, Oshkosh, Sheboygan).

$ Given: $700,000 for 826 grants; average $832.

Contact: Edward T. Dougherty, Executive Director

   Initial approach: brief letter or proposal

   Deadlines: applications accepted throughout the year

Emhart Corporation
426 Colt Highway
Farmington, Connecticut 06032
(203) 678-3204

Areas of interest: Arts and humanities (museums/galleries, zoos, operas, arts centers, historic preservation/restoration), civic and public affairs (business/free enterprise, urban and community affairs), education, health, and social services.

Restrictions: Grants for general support, capital, endowment, and matching funds; grants to individuals.

Focus of giving: Giving primarily in areas where company has major facilities and a large number of employees: AL, CA (Anaheim, Los Angeles, Torrance), CT (Berlin, Farmington, Hartford, Shelton, Windsor), IL (Broadview), IN (Indianapolis), KY (Campbellsville), MA (Beverly, Fall River, Middleton, New Bedford, South Hadley, Whitman), MI (Mount Clemens), MO, NE (Lincoln), NH, NY (Elmira, Maspeth), OH (Cleveland), PA (Huntington Valley, Reading, Temple), TN, VT (Springfield).

$ **Given:** $738,865 for 200 grants: high $45,000; low $100; average $2,694.

Contact: John F. Budd, Jr., Chairman, Contributions and Grants Committee

    Initial approach: brief letter or proposal

    Deadlines: submit proposal before October

    Final notification: by December

Marathon Oil Foundation, Inc.
539 South Main Street
Findlay, Ohio 45840
(419) 422-2121 Ext. 3708

Restrictions: Support for seed money and building funds.

Focus of giving: Giving limited to areas of company operations.

$ **Given:** $1,789,407 for 368 grants: high $2,000,000; low $300. Also $197,778 for 50 grants to individuals.

Assets: $2,568,574

Contact: Carol Mittermaien, Assistant Secretary

    Initial approach: full proposal

    Copies of proposal: 1

    Deadlines: none

    Board meeting dates: as required

    Final notification: 6 to 8 weeks

National Machinery Foundation, Inc.
Greenfield Street
P. O. Box 747
Tiffin, Ohio 44883
(419) 447-5211

Areas of interest: Arts and humanities (museums/galleries, arts centers, historic preservation/restoration), civic and public affairs (economics, business/free enterprise, urban and community affairs), education, health, and social services (homes).

Restrictions: Grants for capital, general support, endowment, and special projects; grants to individuals.

Focus of giving: Giving primarily in county where company operates.

$ Given: $366,782 for 126 grants: high $35,000; low $50; average $500–$5,500.

Assets: $7,265,000

Contact: D. B. Bero, Secretary-Treasurer

    Application information: application form required

    Initial approach: brief letter or proposal

    Deadlines: applications accepted throughout the year

OKLAHOMA

Fort Howard Paper Foundation
P. O. Box 11325
Green Bay, Wisconsin 54307
(414) 435-8821

Areas of interest: Arts and humanities (museums/galleries, libraries, music, historic preservation/restoration), civic and public affairs (professional associations, urban and community affairs), education, health, and social services.

Restrictions: Grants for capital, general support, and special projects; grants to individuals.

Focus of giving: Giving primarily in Green Bay, Wisconsin; Muskogee, Oklahoma; and limited areas surrounding these communities.

$ Given: $622,396 for 31 grants: high $135,000; low $29; average $2,000–$12,000.

Assets: $11,303,956

Contact: Bruce W. Nagel, Assistant Secretary

    Initial approach: brief letter or proposal

    Deadlines: applications accepted throughout the year

OREGON

Unocal Foundation
P. O. Box 7600
Los Angeles, California 90051
(213) 977-6171

Areas of interest: Arts and culture (museums/galleries, arts centers), civic and public affairs (business/free enterprise, economic development, urban and community affairs), education, health, and social services.

Restrictions: Grants for capital, general support, and special projects; grants to individuals.

Focus of giving: Nationally, with preference given to areas where Unocal maintains corporate facilities: AK (Kenai), CA (Brea, Los Angeles, Mountain Pass, San Francisco, Santa Maria), CO, IL (Chicago, Palatine), LA, NC (Charlotte), OR (Rivergate), TX (Beaumont).

$ Given: $4,571,472 for 397 grants: high $491,860; low $250; average $500–$5,000.

Contact: R. P. Van Zandt, Vice-President and Trustee

  Initial approach: telephone

  Deadlines: requests in by September 15

PENNSYLVANIA

Burlington Industries Foundation
P. O. Box 21207
Greensboro, North Carolina 27420
(919) 379-2515

Areas of interest: Urban and community affairs, arts centers, museums, libraries, business/free enterprise, economic development, education, health, and social services.

Restrictions: Grants for capital, general support, matching funds, and special projects; grants to individuals.

Focus of giving: Primarily in North and South Carolina, Virginia, and near corporate operating locations: NC (Burlington, Greensboro, Madison), NY (New Rochelle, New York), PA (King of Prussia, Norristown), and other states.

$ Given: $2,000,000 for 552 grants: high $60,000; low $10; average $2,640.

Contact: Park R. Davidson, Executive Director

   Initial approach: brief letter or proposal

   Deadlines: applications accepted throughout the year

Emhart Corporation
426 Colt Highway
Farmington, Connecticut 06032
(203) 678-3204

Areas of interest: Arts and humanities (museums/galleries, zoos, operas, arts centers, historic preservation/restoration), civic and public affairs (business/free enterprise, urban and community affairs), education, health, and social services.

Restrictions: Grants for general support, capital, endowment, and matching funds; grants to individuals.

Focus of giving: Giving primarily in areas where company has major facilities and a large number of employees: AL, CA (Anaheim, Los Angeles, Torrance), CT (Berlin, Farmington, Hartford, Shelton, Windsor), IL (Broadview), IN (Indianapolis), KY (Campbellsville), MA (Beverly, Fall River, Middleton, New Bedford, South Hadley, Whitman), MI (Mount Clemens), MO, NE (Lincoln), NH, NY (Elmira, Maspeth), OH (Cleveland), PA (Huntington Valley, Reading, Temple), TN, VT (Springfield).

$ Given: $738,865 for 200 grants: high $45,000; low $100; average $2,694.

Contact: John F. Budd, Jr., Chairman, Contributions and Grants Committee

   Initial approach: brief letter or proposal

   Deadlines: submit proposal before October

   Final notification: by December

SOUTH CAROLINA

Burlington Industries Foundation
P. O. Box 21207
Greensboro, North Carolina 27420
(919) 379-2515

Areas of interest: Urban and community affairs, arts centers, museums, libraries, business/free enterprise, economic development, education, health, and social services.

Restrictions: Grants for capital, general support, matching funds, and special projects; grants to individuals.

Focus of giving: Primarily in North and South Carolina, Virginia, and near corporate operating locations: NC (Burlington, Greensboro, Madison), NY (New Rochelle, New York), PA (King of Prussia, Norristown), and other states.

$ Given: $2,000,000 for 552 grants: high $60,000; low $10; average $2,640.

Contact: Park R. Davidson, Executive Director

 Initial approach: brief letter or proposal

 Deadlines: applications accepted throughout the year

Foundation for the Carolinas
301 South Brevard Street
Charlotte, North Carolina
(704) 376-9541

Restrictions: Grants for operating budgets, seed money, building funds, emergency funds, equipment, special projects, matching funds, and land acquisition.

Focus of giving: Giving primarily in North Carolina and South Carolina.

$ Given: $2,385,853 for 1,225 grants: high $209,800; low $100; average $500–$10,000. Also $12,398 for grants to individuals.

Publications: Annual report, application guidelines, informational brochure, and newsletter.

Contact: William Spencer, President

Application information: application form required

Initial approach: letter

Copies of proposal: 11

Deadlines: none

Board meeting dates: quarterly, with annual meeting in March; distribution committee meets monthly

Final notification: 1 to 2 months

TENNESSEE

Bemis Company Foundation
800 Northstar Center
Minneapolis, Minnesota 55402
(612) 340-6198

Areas of interest: Urban and community affairs, arts centers, cinema, performing arts (general), business/free enterprise, economic development, education, health, and social services.

Restrictions: Grants for general support, special projects, and matching funds; grants to individuals.

Focus of giving: Areas where company maintains facilities, with emphasis on Minneapolis, MN. AR (Crossett), CA (Los Angeles, Union City, Wilmington), CT (Plainfield, Stratford), FL (Panama City), IL (Murphysboro, Peoria, Schaumburg), IN (Indianapolis, Terre Haute), KS (Wichita), KY (Florence, Henderson, Louisville), MA (East Pepperell), MI (Grand Rapids, Zeeland), MN (Mankato, Minneapolis, Minnetonka), MO (Louisiana, Saint Louis, Springfield), MS (Verona), NC (Statesville), NE (Omaha), NH (Hudson, Nashua, North Walpole), NJ (Flemington), NY (Buffalo), OH (Stow), TN (Memphis), TX (Jacksonville), WA (Seattle, Vancouver), WI (Green Bay, New London, Oshkosh, Sheboygan).

$ Given: $700,000 for 826 grants; average $832.

Contact: Edward T. Dougherty, Executive Director

Initial approach: brief letter or proposal

Deadlines: applications accepted throughout the year

Emhart Corporation
426 Colt Highway
Farmington, Connecticut 06032
(203) 678-3204

Areas of interest: Arts and humanities (museums/galleries, zoos, operas, arts centers, historic preservation/restoration), civic and public affairs (business/free enterprise, urban and community affairs), education, health, and social services.

Restrictions: Grants for general support, capital, endowment, and matching funds; grants to individuals.

Focus of giving: Giving primarily in areas where company has major facilities and a large number of employees: AL, CA (Anaheim, Los Angeles, Torrance), CT (Berlin, Farmington, Hartford, Shelton, Windsor), IL (Broadview), IN (Indianapolis), KY (Campbellsville), MA (Beverly, Fall River, Middleton, New Bedford, South Hadley, Whitman), MI (Mount Clemens), MO, NE (Lincoln), NH, NY (Elmira, Maspeth), OH (Cleveland), PA (Huntington Valley, Reading, Temple), TN, VT (Springfield).

$ Given: $738,865 for 200 grants: high $45,000; low $100; average $2,694.

Contact: John F. Budd, Jr., Chairman, Contributions and Grants Committee

> **Initial approach:** brief letter or proposal
>
> **Deadlines:** submit proposal before October
>
> **Final notification** by December

Lyndhurst Foundation
701 Tallan Building
Chattanooga, Tennessee 37402
(615) 756-0767

Areas of interest: Emphasis on health.

Restrictions: Support for general purposes, seed money, special projects, and matching funds.

Focus of giving: Grants generally limited to Chattanooga.

$ Given: $2,827,077 for 50 grants: high $355,000; low $2,000; average $30,000–$150,000. Also $305,000 for 13 grants to individuals.

Assets: $91,695,737

Contact: Deaderick C. Montague, President

Application information: application form required for grants to individuals; awards made only at the initiative of the foundation

Initial approach: letter

Copies of proposal: 1

Deadlines: 4 weeks before board meetings

Board meeting dates: February, May, August, and November

Final notification: 3 months

TEXAS

Bemis Company Foundation
800 Northstar Center
Minneapolis, Minnesota 55402
(612) 340-6198

Areas of interest: Urban and community affairs, arts centers, cinema, performing arts (general), business/free enterprise, economic development, education, health, and social services.

Restrictions: Grants for general support, special projects, and matching funds; grants to individuals.

Focus of giving: Areas where company maintains facilities, with emphasis on Minneapolis, MN, AR (Crossett), CA (Los Angeles, Union City, Wilmington), CT (Plainfield, Stratford), FL (Panama City), IL (Murphysboro, Peoria, Schaumburg), IN (Indianapolis, Terre Haute), KS (Wichita), KY (Florence, Henderson, Louisville), MA (East Pepperell), MI (Grand Rapids, Zeeland), MN (Mankato, Minneapolis, Minnetonka), MO (Louisiana, Saint Louis, Springfield), MS (Verona), NC (Statesville), NE (Omaha), NH (Hudson, Nashua, North Walpole), NJ (Flemington), NY (Buffalo), OH (Stow), TN (Memphis), TX (Jacksonville), WA (Seattle, Vancouver), WI (Green Bay, New London, Oshkosh, Sheboygan).

$ Given: $700,000 for 826 grants; average $832.

Contact: Edward T. Dougherty, Executive Director

Initial approach: brief letter or proposal

Deadlines: applications accepted throughout the year

The Clayton Fund
c/o Anderson, Clayton and Company
P. O. Box 2538
Houston, Texas 77252
(713) 651-0641

Restrictions: Grants for general support, housing, community centers, and historic preservation/restoration; grants to individuals.

Focus of giving: Giving primarily to Texas, with limited support elsewhere.

$ Given: $1,223,936 for 47 grants: high $200,000; low $100; average $5,000–$20,000.

Assets: $16,254,955

Contact: S. M. McAshan, Jr., Trustee

Communities Foundation of Texas, Inc.
4605 Live Oak Street
Dallas, Texas 75204
(214) 826-5231

Areas of interest: Broad purposes: to promote the well-being of the inhabitants of Texas, primarily in the Dallas area.

Restrictions: Support for operating budgets, building funds, emergency funds, equipment, special projects, matching funds, land acquisition, program-related investments, and seed money.

Focus of giving: Giving primarily in Dallas, Texas, area.

$ Given: $11,310,838 for 925 grants: high $1,050,923; low $15; average $10,000–$25,000.

Assets: $89,520,522

Contact: Edward M. Fjorbak, Executive Vice-President

    Initial approach: letter

    Copies of proposal: 1

    Deadlines: 30 days before distribution committee meetings

    Board meeting dates: distribution committee for unrestricted funds meets in March, August, and November

    Final notification: 1 week after distribution committee meeting

The Moody Foundation
704 Moody National Bank Building
Galveston, Texas 77550
(409) 763-5333

Areas of interest: Local historic restoration projects, performing arts organizations, cultural programs, health, science, education, community and social services, and religion.

Restrictions: Support given for seed money, building funds, emergency funds, equipment, special projects, and matching funds.

Focus of giving: Giving limited to Texas.

$ Given: $9,452,399 for 142 grants: high $515,000; low $600. Also $350,495 for 518 grants to individuals.

Publications: Annual report and application guidelines.

Contact: Peter M. Moore, Grants Officer
    Initial approach: letter or telephone
    Copies of proposal: 1
    Deadlines: 4 weeks prior to board meetings
    Board meeting dates: quarterly
    Final notification: 2 weeks after board meeting

Unocal Foundation
P. O. Box 7600
Los Angeles, California 90051
(213) 977-6171

Areas of interest: Arts and culture (museums/galleries, arts centers), civic and public affairs (business/free enterprise, economic development, urban and community affairs), education, health, and social services.

Restrictions: Grants for capital, general support, and special projects; grants to individuals.

Focus of giving: Nationally, with preference given to areas where Unocal maintains corporate facilities: AK (Kenai), CA (Brea, Los Angeles, Mountain Pass, San Francisco, Santa Maria), CO, IL (Chicago, Palatine), LA, NC (Charlotte), OR (Rivergate), TX (Beaumont).

$ Given: $4,571,472 for 397 grants: high $491,860; low $250; average $500–$5,000.

Contact: R. P. Van Zandt, Vice-President and Trustee

    Initial approach: telephone

    Deadlines: requests in by September 15

VERMONT

Emhart Corporation
426 Colt Highway
Farmington, Connecticut 06032
(203) 678-3204

Areas of interest: Arts and humanities (museums/galleries, zoos, operas, arts centers, historic preservation/restoration), civic and public affairs (business/free enterprise, urban and community affairs), education, health, and social services.

Restrictions: Grants for general support, capital, endowment, and matching funds; grants to individuals.

Focus of giving: Giving primarily in areas where company has major facilities and a large number of employees: AL, CA (Anaheim, Los Angeles, Torrance), CT (Berlin, Farmington, Hartford, Shelton, Windsor), IL (Broadview), IN (Indianapolis), KY (Campbellsville), MA (Beverly, Fall River, Middleton, New Bedford, South Hadley, Whitman), MI (Mount Clemens), MO, NE (Lincoln), NH, NY (Elmira, Maspeth), OH (Cleveland), PA (Huntington Valley, Reading, Temple), TN, VT (Springfield).

$ Given: $738,865 for 200 grants: high $45,000; low $100; average $2,694.

Contact: John F. Budd, Jr., Chairman, Contributions and Grants Committee

    Initial approach: brief letter or proposal

    Deadlines: submit proposal before October

    Final notification: by December

The Windham Foundation, Inc.
P. O. Box 70
Grafton, Vermont 05146
(802) 843-2211

Restrictions: A private operating foundation in which 85 percent of adjusted net income is applied to operating programs of the foundation. The foundation's primary activity is the preservation of properties in rural areas of Vermont to maintain their charm and historic, native, or unusual features, with emphasis on restoration of houses in Grafton. The remaining 15 percent of the foundation's income is used for general charitable giving.

Focus of giving: Giving limited to Vermont, with emphasis on Windham County.

$ Given: $230,641 for 57 grants: high $30,000; low $100. Also $116,590 for 357 grants to individuals.

Contact: Stephan A. Morse, Executive Director

    Initial approach: letter

    Copies of proposal: 1

    Deadlines: none

    Board meeting dates: February, May, July, and October

    Final notification: following the board meeting

VIRGINIA

Burlington Industries Foundation
P. O. Box 21207
Greensboro, North Carolina 27420
(919) 379-2515

Areas of interest: Urban and community affairs, arts centers, museums, libraries, business/free enterprise, economic development, education, health, and social services.

Restrictions: Grants for capital, general support, matching funds, and special projects; grants to individuals.

Focus of giving: Primarily in North and South Carolina, Virginia, and near corporate operating locations: NC (Burlington, Greensboro, Madison), NY (New Rochelle, New York), PA (King of Prussia, Norristown), and other states.

$ Given: $2,000,000 for 552 grants: high $60,000; low $10; average $2,640.

Contact: Park R. Davidson, Executive Director

Initial approach: brief letter or proposal

Deadlines: applications accepted throughout the year

WASHINGTON

Bemis Company Foundation
800 Northstar Center
Minneapolis, Minnesota 55402
(612) 340-6198

Areas of interest: Urban and community affairs, arts centers, cinema, performing arts (general), business/free enterprise, economic development, education, health, and social services.

Restrictions: Grants for general support, special projects, and matching funds; grants to individuals.

Focus of giving: Areas where company maintains facilities, with emphasis on Minneapolis, MN, AR (Crossett), CA (Los Angeles, Union City, Wilmington), CT (Plainfield, Stratford), FL (Panama City), IL (Murphysboro, Peoria, Schaumburg), IN (Indianapolis, Terre Haute), KS (Wichita), KY (Florence, Henderson, Louisville), MA (East Pepperell), MI (Grand Rapids, Zeeland), MN (Mankato, Minneapolis, Minnetonka), MO (Louisiana, Saint Louis, Springfield), MS (Verona), NC (Statesville), NE (Omaha), NH (Hudson, Nashua, North Walpole), NJ (Flemington), NY (Buffalo), OH (Stow), TN (Memphis), TX (Jacksonville), WA (Seattle, Vancouver), WI (Green Bay, New London, Oshkosh, Sheboygan).

$ Given: $700,000 for 826 grants; average $832.

Contact: Edward T. Dougherty, Executive Director

Initial approach: brief letter or proposal

Deadlines: applications accepted throughout the year

Inland Northwest Community Foundation
400 Paulsen Center
Spokane, Washington 99201
(509) 624-2606

Restrictions: Grants for operating budgets, continuing support, seed money, building funds, special projects, matching funds, and land acquisition.

Focus of giving: Giving primarily limited to the inland Northwest.

$ Given: $169,024 for 157 grants: high $3,500; low $242; average $1,000. Also $18,550 for 53 grants to individuals.

Publications: Annual report, program policy statement and application guidelines, and 990-PF.

Contact: Jeanne L. Ager, Executive Director

  Application information: application form required

  Initial approach: letter

  Copies of proposal: 11

  Deadlines: varies depending on area of grant

  Board meeting dates: September through June

  Final notification: 3 months

ITT Rayonier Foundation
1177 Summer Street
Stamford, Connecticut 06904
(203) 348-7000

Areas of interest: Arts and humanities (aquariums, performing arts, museums/galleries), civic and public affairs (business/free enterprise, economic development, urban and community affairs), education, health, and social services (homes).

Restrictions: Grants for capital, general support, matching funds, and special projects; grants to individuals.

Focus of giving: Giving primarily near operating locations in Connecticut (Stamford), Florida, Georgia, and Washington.

$ Given: $259,985 for 129 grants: high $18,500; low $25; average $1,000–$5,000.

Assets: $2,635,096

Contact: Jerome D. Gregoire, Vice-President

  Initial approach: letter

  Deadlines: November 30

Board meeting dates: February
Final notification: 1 month

Puget Sound Power & Light Company
P. O. Box 97034
Bellevue, Washington 98009
(206) 462-3799

Areas of interest: Arts and culture (museums/galleries), civic and public affairs (economics, business/free enterprise, urban and community affairs), education, health, and social services.

Restrictions: Grants for capital and general support; grants to individuals.

Focus of giving: Primarily in Washington State.

$ Given: $500,000 for grants: average $1,000–$10,000.

Contact: Neil L. McReynolds, Senior Vice-President, Corporate Relations

Initial approach: letter or proposal

Deadlines: submit proposal preferably during late summer/early fall

---

WEST VIRGINIA

The Greater Kanawha Valley Foundation*
P. O. Box 3041
Charleston, West Virginia
(304) 346-3620

Restrictions: Grants for operating budgets, continuing support, seed money, building funds, emergency funds, equipment, special projects, matching funds, and land acquisition.

Focus of giving: Giving limited to the Greater Kanawha Valley, West Virginia, area.

$ Given: $406,559 for 91 grants: high $25,000; low $89; average $500–$5,000. Also $200,371 for 200 grants to individuals.

*Community foundation established in 1962 in West Virginia.

Publications: Annual report and application guidelines.

Contact: Stanley Loewenstein, Executive Director
   Initial approach: letter or telephone full proposal

WISCONSIN

Bemis Company Foundation
800 Northstar Center
Minneapolis, Minnesota 55402
(612) 340-6198

Areas of interest: Urban and community affairs, arts centers, cinema, performing arts (general), business/free enterprise, economic development, education, health, and social services.

Restrictions: Grants for general support, special projects, and matching funds; grants to individuals.

Focus of giving: Areas where company maintains facilities, with emphasis on Minneapolis, MN, AR (Crossett), CA (Los Angeles, Union City, Wilmington), CT (Plainfield, Stratford), FL (Panama City), IL (Murphysboro, Peoria, Schaumburg), IN (Indianapolis, Terre Haute), KS (Wichita), KY (Florence, Henderson, Louisville), MA (East Pepperell), MI (Grand Rapids, Zeeland), MN (Mankato, Minneapolis, Minnetonka), MO (Louisiana, Saint Louis, Springfield), MS (Verona), NC (Statesville), NE (Omaha), NH (Hudson, Nashua, North Walpole), NJ (Flemington), NY (Buffalo), OH (Stow), TN (Memphis), TX (Jacksonville), WA (Seattle, Vancouver), WI (Green Bay, New London, Oshkosh, Sheboygan).

$ Given: $700,000 for 826 grants; average $832.

Contact: Edward T. Dougherty, Executive Director
   Initial approach: brief letter or proposal
   Deadlines: applications accepted throughout the year

Fort Howard Paper Foundation
P. O. Box 11325
Green Bay, Wisconsin 54307
(414) 435-8821

Areas of interest: Arts and humanities (museums/galleries, libraries, music, historic preservation/restoration), civic and public affairs (professional associations, urban and community affairs), education, health, and social services.

Restrictions: Grants for capital, general support, and special projects; grants to individuals.

Focus of giving: Giving primarily in Green Bay, Wisconsin, Muskogee, Oklahoma, and limited areas surrounding these communities.

$ Given: $622,396 for 31 grants: high $135,000; low $29; average $2,000–$12,000.

Assets: $11,303,956

Contact: Bruce W. Nagel, Assistant Secretary

    Initial approach: brief letter or proposal

    Deadlines: applications accepted throughout the year

La Crosse Foundation
P. O. Box 489
La Crosse, Wisconsin 54602-0489
(608) 782-1148

Restrictions: Local giving for charitable purposes to benefit the citizens of La Crosse County, Wisconsin.

Focus of giving: Giving limited to La Crosse County, Wisconsin.

$ Given: $142,059 for 45 grants: high $30,000; low $100; average $2,300. Also $9,816 for 20 grants to individuals.

Contact: Carol B. Popelka, Program Director

    Deadlines: submit proposal preferably 1 month before committee meetings

4

Program-Related Investments

A program-related investment (PRI) is an investment a foundation makes in a nonprofit organization, a profit-making business, or an individual that furthers the charitable objectives of the foundation (housing for low-middle income residents, urban renewal). PRIs traditionally take the form of outright grants, equity investments, letters of credit, donated services, and direct loans (the loans are usually offered at extremely low interest rates, such as 4 percent, and often with extended time periods and flexible terms for repayment).

PRIs as they exist today date back only as far as 1968. There were, however, a few earlier examples. Benjamin Franklin created a charitable trust in the late eighteenth century to lend money to "young married artificers" at one percentage point below prevailing interest rates to help them establish themselves in business. The United Housing Foundation was responsible for the building of Co-Op City (New York City)—the largest single apartment development in the United States—a "city" of 50,000 to 60,000 people in 15,382 apartments piled onto 300 acres.

The nonprofit sector has entered the housing field. Working in partnership with state, local, and private developers, nonprofit organizations have gained considerable experience and expertise. These organizations may well hold the answers to resolving the nation's many-sided housing crisis. Economic development projects that are organized to better the community may aim at creating new jobs, building low-income housing, or revitalizing neighborhood businesses. These programs should also generate revenues, but income is secondary to the primary social objective. Many conventional lenders are unwilling to invest in socially beneficial projects because they perceive the financial return to be too low. Nonprofit housing projects should never ask conventional lenders to lose money; conventional lenders should be able to make some money, even if less than their normal spreads. If a foundation is willing to provide a portion of the needed financing through a PRI with a below-market rate of return (or no return at all), the recipient may be able to obtain the remainder of the financing from commercial investors or lenders. Remember, though, that the main function of the PRI is to fulfill a major charitable objective.

The Bay Area Residential Investment and Development Group (BRIDGE) is one of the few nonprofit housing developers operating on a regional scale and one of the leading nonprofit developers in the United States producing low- and moderate-income housing. Magnolia Plaza, a 124-unit complex in South San Francisco, is an excellent example of how BRIDGE operates. First, the property was bought from the school district. The city then bought the property back from BRIDGE, subsequently leasing it to them. That relieved the project of having to put a lot of money up front. Tax-exempt mortgage-revenue bonds issued by the City of San Francisco helped reduce the cost of financing Magnolia Plaza. The 15 to 20 percent developers profit "thrown back into the deal" by BRIDGE also lowered project costs (and ultimately rental and ownership payments). For the half of the projects apartments qualifying as affordable, BRIDGE's deal making brought monthly rents down to approximately $450. But since that was felt to be too high, BRIDGE provided tax credits to limited-partner investors, with proceeds of the sale used for equity capital. The tax credits dropped the rent another $80. The Magnolia Plaza project used an innovative financing device: An arcane loan agreement known as a tax-exempt "lower floater," which provided the project with funds at a discounted interest rate. Normally a project of this size (the Magnolia Plaza project and a companion project totalled $11 million) would require a lot of security to be posted. Wells Fargo Bank, confident of BRIDGE's ability, originated the lower floater and the construction loan for the very low rate of one-and-a-half points. All told, Magnolia Plaza is an excellent example of a partnership between the city, the private sector, and a program-related investment (BRIDGE had been a recipient of a PRI from the Ford Foundation).

Program-related investments can be made directly to profit-making businesses and individuals although some foundations will fund only nonprofit organizations. An individual or business can use an established nonprofit organization as a "flow-through," utilizing their tax-exempt status, and thereby eliminating the need to set up a separate nonprofit organization. If possible, it is a good idea to work through a nonprofit organization whose purposes and activities are compatible with your own (if you are building low-income housing in an inner-city neighborhood, for example, work with a foundation that makes grants for community development). Custom dictates that the nonprofit organization is usually given 3 to 7 percent of monies raised as a flow-through fee. For further information please see Chapter 5.

5

Flow-Through Funding/Fiscal Sponsorship

As explained in my book, *Free Money for Small Businesses and Entrepreneurs*, many foundations will not fund individuals or businesses directly, but instead will give money only to enterprises that are designated as charitable under section 501 (c) (3) of the Internal Revenue Code. However, an individual or business can work through a nonprofit organization, which will act as a sponsor or parent organization. There are many past examples of public/private partnerships; it is currently a very hot topic in philanthropy. The way it works is as follows: The monies given to an individual or business are paid directly to the non-profit organization, which in turn pays its private partner. Usually the nonprofit organization receives a fee of between three and seven percent of monies raised. There is no upfront fee paid to the sponsor or parent organization. The three to seven percent fee is customary; it is not an obligation.

How does one go about finding a nonprofit conduit? Check any local directory of nonprofit organizations (public libraries will usually have such directories). Check national organizational reference books, such as the *Encyclopedia of Associations*, for other potential candidates.

6

Fiscal Sponsors by State (Nonprofit Organizations)

ALABAMA

J. L. Bedsole Foundation
c/o AmSouth Bank, N.A.
P. O. Box 1628
Mobile, Alabama 36621

Areas of interest: Higher education and social services.

Restrictions: Grants for building funds and special projects.

Focus of giving: Giving primarily in Alabama.

$ Given: $488,250 for 21 grants: high $300,000; low $500.

Assets: $27,398,438

Contact: Mabel B. Ward
  Initial approach: letter
  Deadlines: none

The Blount Foundation, Inc.[*]
c/o Blount, Inc.
4520 Executive Park Drive
Montgomery, Alabama 36116
(205) 244-4000

Areas of interest: Culture and the arts, higher and secondary education, civic affairs, and health care.

---

* Incorporated in 1970 in Alabama.

Restrictions: Grants for building funds and general purposes.

Focus of giving: No grants to individuals. No loans; no in-kind grants.

$ Given: $576,565 for 164 grants: high $100,000; low $25.

Assets: $112,646

Publications: Informational brochure including application guidelines.

Contact: D. Joseph McInnes, President

   Initial approach: 2- or 3-page letter

   Copies of proposal: 1

   Deadlines: none

   Board meeting dates: as needed

   Final notification: 12 weeks after board meeting

Central Bank Foundation*
P. O. Box 10566
Birmingham, Alabama 35296

Areas of interest: Support for community funds, health, social service, education, civic affairs, and arts and cultural programs.

Restrictions: Grants for building funds and general purposes.

Focus of giving: Giving primarily in Alabama. No grants to individuals.

$ Given: $204,935 for 121 grants: high $25,000; low $25.

   Copies of proposal: 1

   Deadlines: none

Durr-Fillauer Medical Foundation**
P. O. Box 951
Montgomery, Alabama 36192

Areas of interest: Support primarily for education, culture, and community funds.

Restrictions: Grants for building funds.

---

* Established in 1981 in Alabama.
** Established in 1982 in Alabama.

$ Given: $134,218 for 51 grants: high $25,000; low $100.

Emhart Corporation
426 Colt Highway
Farmington, Connecticut 06032
(203) 678-3204

Areas of interest: Arts and humanities (museums/galleries, zoos, operas, arts centers, historic preservation/restoration), civic and public affairs (business/free enterprise, and urban and community affairs), education, health, and social services.

Restrictions: Grants for general support, capital, endowment, and matching funds; grants to individuals.

Focus of giving: Giving primarily in areas where company has major facilities and a large number of employees: AL, CA (Anaheim, Los Angeles, Torrance), CT (Berlin, Farmington, Hartford, Shelton, Windsor), IL (Broadview), IN (Indianapolis), KY (Campbellsville), MA (Beverly, Fall River, Middleton, New Bedford, South Hadley, Whitman), MI (Mount Clemens), MO, NE (Lincoln), NH, NY (Elmira, Maspeth), OH (Cleveland), PA (Huntington Valley, Reading, Temple), TN, VT (Springfield).

$ Given: $738,865 for 200 grants: high $45,000; low $100; average $2,694.

Contact: John F. Budd, Jr., Chairman, Contributions and Grants Committee

    Initial approach: brief letter or proposal

    Deadlines: submit proposal before October

    Final notification: by December

Robert R. Meyer Foundation*
c/o AmSouth Bank, N.A., Trust Department
P. O. Box 11426
Birmingham, Alabama 35202

Areas of interest: Health, welfare, educational, and cultural organizations and institutions.

* Trust established in 1942 in Alabama.

Restrictions: Grants for building funds and land acquisition.

Focus of giving: Giving limited to the Birmingham, Alabama, metropolitan area. No grants to individuals.

$ Given: $874,450 for 40 grants: high $100,000; low $3,000.

Assets: $19,055,754

Publications: Application guidelines.

Contact: C. Dowd Ritter, Executive Vice-President
  Initial approach: proposal
  Copies of proposal: 5
  Deadlines: April 15
  Board meeting dates: June and December
  Final notification: 4 weeks

Sonat Foundation, Inc.
1900 Fifth Avenue
P. O. Box 2563
Birmingham, Alabama 35203
(205) 325-7133

Restrictions: Grants for building funds and community development (performing arts, hospitals).

Contact: John C. Griffin, Secretary

Susan Mott Webb Charitable Trust
c/o AmSouth Bank, N.A., Trust Department
P. O. Box 11426
Birmingham, Alabama 35202
(205) 326-5396

Areas of interest: Health projects, social welfare, colleges and universities, libraries, science.

Restrictions: Grants for building funds.

Contact: Mrs. Virginia Ramsey, Vice-President

ALASKA

Fred Meyer Charitable Trust
1515 Southwest Fifth Avenue, Suite 500
Portland, Oregon 97201
(503) 228-5512

Restrictions: Support for seed money, building funds, equipment, special projects, and matching funds.

Focus of giving: Support primarily in Oregon, with occasional grants at the initiative of the trust for programs in Washington, Idaho, Montana, and Alaska.

$ Given: $6,365,583 for 94 grants: high $555,000; low $964; average $20,000–$75,000.

Assets: $171,639,900

Contact: Charles S. Rooks, Executive Director
   Application information: application form required
   Initial approach: letter or full proposal
   Copies of proposal: 1
   Deadlines: none
   Board meeting dates: monthly
   Final notification: 4 to 6 months for proposals that pass first screening; 2 to 3 months for those that do not

Unocal Foundation
P. O. Box 7600
Los Angeles, California 90051
(213) 977-6171

Areas of interest: Arts and culture (museums/galleries, arts centers), civic and public affairs (business/free enterprise, economic development, urban and community affairs), education, health, and social services.

Restrictions: Grants for capital, general support, and special projects; grants to individuals.

Focus of giving: Nationally, with preference given to areas where Unocal maintains corporate facilities: AK (Kenai), CA (Brea, Los Angeles, Mountain Pass, San Francisco, Santa Maria), CO, IL (Chicago, Palatine), LA, NC (Charlotte), OR (Rivergate), TX (Beaumont).

$ Given: $4,571,472 for 397 grants: high $491,860; low $250; average $500–$5,000.

Contact: R. P. Van Zandt, Vice President and Trustee
   Initial approach: telephone
   Deadlines: requests in by September 15

ARKANSAS

Bemis Company Foundation
800 Northstar Center
Minneapolis, Minnesota 55402
(612) 340-6198

Areas of interest: Urban and community affairs, arts centers, cinema, performing arts (general), business/free enterprise, economic development, education, health, and social services.

Restrictions: Grants for general support, special projects, and matching funds; grants to individuals.

Focus of giving: Areas where company maintains facilities, with emphasis on Minneapolis, MN. AR (Crossett), CA (Los Angeles, Union City, Wilmington), CT (Plainfield, Stratford), FL (Panama City), IL (Murphysboro, Peoria, Schaumburg), IN (Indianapolis, Terre Haute), KS (Wichita), KY (Florence, Henderson, Louisville), MA (East Pepperell), MI (Grand Rapids, Zeeland), MN (Mankato, Minneapolis, Minnetonka), MO (Louisiana, Saint Louis, Springfield), MS (Verona), NC (Statesville), NE (Omaha), NH (Hudson, Nashua, North Walpole), NJ (Flemington), NY (Buffalo), OH (Stow), TN (Memphis), TX (Jacksonville), WA (Seattle, Vancouver), WI (Green Bay, New London, Oshkosh, Sheboygan).

$ Given: $700,000 for 826 grants; average $832.

Contact: Edward T. Dougherty, Executive Director
   Initial approach: brief letter or proposal
   Deadlines: applications accepted throughout the year

Winthrop Rockefeller Foundation
308 East Eighth Street
Little Rock, Arkansas 72202
(501) 376-6854

Areas of interest: Program-related investments in community/economic development, including agricultural development.

Restrictions: With the exception of the Community Incentive Program, the foundation does not support construction.

Focus of giving: Arkansas.

Name of program: Community Incentive Program; offers support for construction and is restricted to eastern Arkansas residents who represent minority concerns.

$ Given: $1,927,623 for 46 grants: high $68,800; low $1,950; average: $1,000.

Assets: $25,339,548

Publications: Annual report with application guidelines.

Contact: Thomas C. McRae, President

> **Initial approach:** initial contact, through letter, telephone, or in person, must take place 8 weeks prior to quarterly meetings
>
> **Copies of proposal:** 1
>
> **Board meeting dates:** quarterly, the first weekend of March, June, September, and December
>
> **Final notification:** 2 weeks after board meeting

Murphy Foundation
200 Jefferson Avenue
El Dorado, Arkansas 71730
(501) 862-6411

Areas of Interest: Civic affairs (historic preservation/restoration, museums/galleries).

Restrictions: Grants for capital, general support, and special projects; grants to individuals.

Focus of giving: Major priority is for general purposes in Arkansas and Louisiana.

$ Given: $512,713 for 49 grants: high $106,969; low $175; average $1,000–$15,000.

Assets: $9,778,000

Contact: Lucy A. Ring

   Application information: application form required

CALIFORNIA

Ahmanson Foundation
9215 Wilshire Boulevard
Beverly Hills, California 90210
(213) 383-1381

Areas of interest: Higher education (including performing arts and museums), secondary education, social welfare, libraries, youth organizations, health projects, hospitals, and minorities.

Restrictions: Grants for building funds.

Contact: Kathleen A. Gilcrest, Vice-President

American Honda Foundation
P.O. Box 2205
Torrance, California 90509-2205
(213) 781-4090

Restrictions: Grants for special projects, building funds, operating budgets, seed money, and matching funds.

$ Given: $613,418 for 16 grants: high $71,854; low $2,500; average $25,000–$50,000.

Assets: $10,040,895

Publications: Grants list, newsletter, informational brochure, program policy statement, and application guidelines.

Contact: Kathryn A. Carey, Manager
   Application information: application form required
   Initial approach: letter or telephone
   Copies of proposal: 1
   Deadlines: November 1, February 1, May 1, and August 1
   Board meeting dates: January, April, July, and October
   Final notification: 2 months

AMFAC, INC.
Amfac Foundation
P. O. Box 7813
San Francisco, California 94120
(415) 772-3374

Areas of interest: Building funds, capital campaigns, miscellaneous, and general support.

Restrictions: No grants to individuals, current United Way recipients, or national organizations.

Focus of giving: National (most grants in company-operating areas), California (San Francisco), Hawaii (Honolulu), Oregon.

$ Given: Grants: high $160,000; low $25; average $100–$1,000.

Assets: $1,078,308,000 (corporate); $15,561 (foundation).

Contact: Norma Luther, Contributions Director
    Initial approach: letter
    Copies of proposal: 1
    Deadlines: applications accepted throughout the year

Atkinson Foundation
10 West Orange Avenue
South San Francisco, California 94080
(415) 876-1559

Areas of interest: Universities, museums, child welfare, libraries, youth organizations, recreation, hospitals, community development, and minorities.

Restrictions: Grants for building funds.

Contact: Donald K. Grant, Treasurer

BankAmerica Foundation, Dept. 3246
P. O. Box 37000
San Francisco, California 94137
(415) 953-3175

Areas of interest: All levels of education, health projects, community development, and arts and humanities.

Restrictions: Grants for building funds.

Focus of giving: Grants given in areas of company operations.

Contact: Edward F. Truschke, Executive Director

Bothin Foundation
873 Sutter Street, Suite B
San Francisco, California 94109
(415) 771-4300

Areas of interest: Community development, social welfare, health projects, culture, and youth.

Restrictions: Grants for building funds.

Contact: Lyman H. Casey, Executive Director

Bemis Company Foundation
800 Northstar Center
Minneapolis, Minnesota 55402
(612) 340-6198

Areas of interest: Urban and community affairs, arts centers, cinema, performing arts (general), business/free enterprise, economic development, education, health, and social services.

Restrictions: Grants for general support, special projects, and matching funds; grants to individuals.

Focus of giving: Areas where company maintains facilities, with emphasis on Minneapolis, MN. AR (Crossett), CA (Los Angeles, Union City, Wilmington), CT (Plainfield, Stratford), FL (Panama City), IL (Murphysboro, Peoria, Schaumburg), IN (Indianapolis, Terre Haute), KS (Wichita), KY (Florence, Henderson, Louisville), MA (East Pepperell), MI (Grand Rapids, Zeeland), MN (Mankato, Minneapolis, Minnetonka), MO (Louisiana, Saint Louis, Springfield), MS (Verona), NC (Statesville), NE (Omaha), NH (Hudson, Nashua, North Walpole), NJ (Flemington), NY (Buffalo), OH (Stow), TN (Memphis), TX (Jacksonville), WA (Seattle, Vancouver), WI (Green Bay, New London, Oshkosh, Sheboygan).

$ Given: $700,000 for 826 grants; average $832.

Contact: Edward T. Dougherty, Executive Director
    Initial approach: brief letter or proposal
    Deadlines: applications accepted throughout the year

California Community Foundation*
3580 Wilshire Boulevard, Suite 1660
Los Angeles, California 90010
(213) 413-4042

Restrictions: Grants for community development, special projects, and matching funds. Grants are not made to individuals.

Focus of giving: Giving limited to Los Angeles, Orange, Riverside, San Bernardino, and Ventura counties.

$ Given: $3,719,458 for 226 grants: high $64,540; low $100; average $5,000–$20,000.

Publications: Annual report, application guidelines, and informational brochure.

Contact: Jack Shakely, Executive Director
   Initial approach: full proposal
   Copies of proposal: 1
   Deadlines: none
   Board meeting dates: quarterly
   Final notification: 3 months after board meets

Clorox Company Foundation
1221 Broadway
Oakland, California 94612
(415) 271-7747

Areas of interest: Community development, social welfare, health projects, culture, youth, minorities, the disabled, and the elderly.

Restrictions: Grants for building funds.

Focus of giving: Grants given in areas of company operations.

The Columbia Foundation
1090 Sansome Street
San Francisco, California 94111
(415) 986-5179

* California Community Foundation established in 1915 in California by bank resolution.

Areas of interest: Community development/neighborhood revitalization.

Restrictions: Generally no support for building campaigns.

Focus of giving: For the most part, grants are made to organizations in the San Francisco Bay area.

$ Given: $1,188,490 for 60 grants: high $30,000; low $1,000; average $10,000.

Assets: $16,178,359

Publications: Annual report, program policy statement, and application guidelines.

Contact: Susan Clark Silk, Executive Director
   Initial approach: letter
   Deadlines: accepted throughout the year, at least three months prior to board meetings
   Board meeting dates: 3 times a year

Community Foundation for Monterey County
P. O. Box 1384
Monterey, California 93942
(408) 375-9712

Areas of interest: Arts and humanities and social welfare.

Restrictions: Grants for building funds.

Contact: Todd Lueders, Executive Director

James S. Copley Foundation
7776 Ivanhoe Avenue
P. O. Box 1530
La Jolla, California 92038
(619) 454-0411

Areas of interest: Community development, performing arts and museums, hospitals, and universities.

Restrictions: Grants for building funds.

Contact: Anita Baumgardner

The Corcoran Community Foundation
P. O. Box 655
Corcoran, California 93212
(209) 992-5551

Areas of interest: Broad purposes: to support organizations benefiting the inhabitants of Corcoran and its surrounding area.

Restrictions: Grants awarded for operating budgets, continuing support, seed money, emergency funds, building funds, equipment, land acquisition, matching funds, consulting services, technical assistance, program-related investments, loans, special projects, publications, conferences, and seminars.

$ Given: $104,000 for 26 grants: high $32,500; low $233. Also $12,000 for two loans.

Assets: $1,023,453

Contact: Mike Graville, Executive Director

    Initial approach: letter

    Copies of proposal: 1

    Deadlines: submit proposal preferably in the month preceding board meetings

    Board meeting dates: October, December, February, April, June, and August

    Final notification: after board meeting

Emhart Corporation
426 Colt Highway
Farmington, Connecticut 06032
(203) 678-3204

Areas of interest: Arts and humanities (museums/galleries, zoos, operas, arts centers, historic preservation/restoration), civic and public affairs (business/free enterprise, urban and community affairs), education, health, and social services.

Restrictions: Grants for general support, capital, endowment, and matching funds; grants to individuals.

Focus of giving: Giving primarily in areas where company has major facilities and a large number of employees: AL, CA (Anaheim, Los Angeles, Torrance), CT (Berlin, Farmington, Hartford, Shelton, Windsor), IL (Broadview), IN (Indianapolis), KY (Campbellsville), MA (Beverly, Fall River, Middleton, New Bedford, South Hadley, Whitman), MI (Mount Clemens), MO, NE (Lincoln), NH, NY (Elmira, Maspeth), OH (Cleveland), PA (Huntington Valley, Reading, Temple), TN, VT (Springfield).

$ Given: $738,865 for 200 grants: high $45,000; low $100; average $2,694.

Contact: John F. Budd, Jr., Chairman, Contributions and Grants Committee

  Initial approach: brief letter or proposal

  Deadlines: submit proposal before October

  Final notification: by December

Fluor Foundation
3333 Michelson Drive
Irvine, California 92730
(714) 975-6326

Areas of interest: Community development, special education, health projects, culture, social welfare, and colleges and universities.

Restrictions: Grants for building funds.

Focus of giving: Grants given in areas of company operations.

Contact: Cindy Linneberger

Samuel Goldwyn Foundation
10203 Santa Monica Boulevard
Los Angeles, California 90067
(213) 552-2255

Areas of interest: Medical research, colleges and universities, social welfare, libraries, youth organizations, and community development.

Restrictions: Grants for building funds.

Contact: Priscilla J. Mick, Executive Director

Walter and Elise Hass Fund
1155 Battery Street, 7th Floor
San Francisco, California 94111
(415) 398-4474

Areas of interest: Jewish organizations, performing arts, museums, colleges and universities, hospitals, and social welfare.

Restrictions: Grants for building funds.

Contact: Bruce R. Sievers, Executive Director

Hedco Foundation
1221 Broadway
Oakland, California 94612

Areas of interest: Medical centers, social welfare, youth, health projects, and education.

Restrictions: Grants for building funds.

Contact: Mary A. Goriup, Foundation Manager

Herbst Foundation
Two Embarcadero Center, Suite 2400
San Francisco, California 94111
(415) 627-8384

Areas of interest: Arts and humanities, recreation, health projects, and all levels of education.

Restrictions: Grants for building funds.

Contact: John T. Seigle, President

William Knox Holt Foundation
505 Sansome Street, Suite 1001
San Francisco, California 94111

Areas of interest: All levels of education, and science projects.

Restrictions: Grants for building funds.

Contact: Stephen W. Veitch, Secretary

James Irvine Foundation
One Market Plaza
Spear Street Tower, Suite 1715
San Francisco, California 94105
(415) 777-2244

Areas of interest: Arts and humanities, recreation, colleges and universities, social welfare, youth, health projects, hospitals, minorities, disabled, and the elderly.

Restrictions: Grants for building funds.

Contact: Luz A. Vega, Program Director

William G. Irwin Charity Foundation
1662 Russ Building
235 Montgomery Street
San Francisco, California 94104
(415) 362-6954

Areas of interest: Secondary education, colleges (including libraries), social welfare, hospitals, and arts and humanities.

Restrictions: Grants for building funds.

Contact: Fred R. Grant, Secretary

George Frederick Jewett Foundation
One Maritime Plaza
The Alcoa Building, Suite 1340
San Francisco, California 94111
(415) 421-1351

Areas of interest: Arts and humanities, medical research, health projects, and colleges.

Restrictions: Grants for building funds.

Contact: Sara C. Fernandez, Program Director

Jones Foundation
One Wilshire Building, Suite 1210
624 South Grand Avenue
Los Angeles, California 90017
(213) 689-9292

Areas of interest: Social welfare, colleges and universities, museums, health projects, and zoo renovation.

Restrictions: Grants for building funds.

Contact: Harvey L. Price, Executive Director

W. M. Keck Foundation
555 South Flower Street, Suite 3230
Los Angeles, California 90071
(213) 680-3830

Areas of interest: Higher education (including libraries, science), medical research, community development, youth, women, hospitals, and culture.

Restrictions: Grants for building funds.

Levi Strauss Foundation
Levi's Plaza
1155 Battery Street, P. O. Box 7215
San Francisco, California 94120-6906
(415) 544-6579

Areas of Interest: Community development, women, culture, health projects, and secondary and higher education.

Restrictions: Grants for building funds; no grants to individuals.

Focus of giving: Grants are made to community-based organizations; some grants are made to national or regional organizations for general support.

$ Given: $2,034,300 for 89 grants: high $100,000; low $500; average $15,000.

Assets: $13,554,841

Publications: Annual report, program policy statement, application guidelines, and list of communities where the company has facilities.

Contact: Suzanne Ward Seidel, Director of Community Affairs
>   **Initial approach:** letter
>   **Board meeting dates:** quarterly, in March, June, September, and December
>   **Final notification:** 60 to 90 days

Ralph B. Lloyd Foundation
9441 Olympic Boulevard
P. O. Box 3037
Los Angeles, California 90212
(213) 879-3080

Areas of interest: Colleges and universities, community development, and culture.

Restrictions: Grants for building funds.

David and Lucille Packard Foundation
330 Second Street
P. O. Box 1330
Los Altos, California 94022
(415) 948-7658

Areas of interest: Social welfare, education, arts and humanities, minorities, and child care centers.

Restrictions: Grants for building funds.

Contact: Colburn S. Wilbur, Executive Director

Ralph M. Parsons Foundation
1035 Wilshire Boulevard, Suite 1701
Los Angeles, California 90017
(213) 482-3185

Areas of interest: Social welfare, youth, hospitals, and colleges and universities.

Restrictions: Grants for building funds.

Contact: Christine Sisley, Executive Director

Peninsula Community Foundation
1204 Burlingame Avenue
P. O. Box 627
Burlingame, California 94011
(415) 342-2477

Areas of interest: Mental health, youth organizations, health projects, culture, and recreation.

Restrictions: Grants for building funds.

Contact: Bill Somerville, Executive Director

San Diego Community Foundation
525 B Street, Suite 410
San Diego, California 92101
(619) 239-8815

Areas of interest: Mental health, social welfare, youth, culture, education, and recreation.

Restrictions: Grants for building funds.

Contact: Helen Monroe, Executive Director

The San Francisco Foundation
685 Market Street, Suite 910
San Francisco, California 94105
(415) 543-0223

Restrictions: Grants awarded for operating budgets, seed money, building funds, equipment, land acquisition, program-related investments, special projects, loans, and technical assistance.

Focus of giving: Giving limited to the Bay Area, in the counties of Alameda, Contra Costa, Marin, San Francisco, and San Mateo.

$ Given: $37,753,057 for 683 grants: high $1,000,000; low $100; average $5,000–$75,000. Also $4,307,903 for five loans.

Assets: $461,040,287

Contact: Martin A. Paley, Director
    Application information: application form required
    Initial approach: letter
    Copies of proposal: 1
    Deadlines: none
    Board meeting dates: monthly except August; applications are reviewed 6 times each year
    Final notification: 3 to 4 months

Santa Barbara Community Foundation
15 East Carrillo Street
Santa Barbara, California 93101
(805) 963-1873

Areas of interest: Social welfare, youth organizations, mental health, women, and hospitals.

Restrictions: Grants for building funds.

Contact: Marti Erickson, Executive Director

Security Pacific Foundation
333 South Hope Street
Los Angeles, California 90071
(213) 345-6688

Areas of interest: Social welfare, museums, community development, performing arts, colleges, and youth organizations.

Restrictions: Grants for building funds.

Focus of giving: Grants given in areas of company operations.

Contact: Susan Swinburne, Executive Director

Harry and Grace Steele Foundation
441 Old Newport Boulevard, Room 301
Newport Beach, California 92663
(714) 631-0418

Areas of interest: Secondary and higher education, social welfare, performing arts, and museums.

Restrictions: Grants for building funds.

Contact: Richard Steele, Vice-President

Sidney Stern Memorial Trust
P. O. Box 893
Pacific Palisades, California 90272

Areas of interest: Arts and humanities, recreation, health projects, hospitals, social welfare, and colleges.

Restrictions: Grants for building funds.

Contact: Marvin Hoffenberg

Morris Stulsaft Foundation
100 Bush Street, Room 500
San Francisco, California 94104
(415) 986-7117

Areas of interest: Arts and humanities, recreation, social welfare, hospitals, science, minorities, and the disabled.

Restrictions: Grants for building funds.

Contact: Joan Nelson Dills, Administrator

Times Mirror Foundation
Times Mirror Square
Los Angeles, California 90012
(213) 237-3945

Areas of interest: Colleges (including performing arts centers), community development, culture, and hospitals.

Restrictions: Grants for building funds.

Contact: Cindy Beyl, Corporate Contributions

Unocal Foundation
P. O. Box 7600
Los Angeles, California 90051
(213) 977-6171

Areas of interest: Arts and culture (museums/galleries, arts centers), civic and public affairs (business/free enterprise, economic development, urban and community affairs), education, health, and social services.

Restrictions: Grants for capital, general support, and special projects; grants to individuals.

Focus of giving: Nationally, with preference given to areas where Unocal maintains corporate facilities: AK (Kenai), CA (Brea, Los Angeles, Mountain Pass, San Francisco, Santa Maria), CO, IL (Chicago, Palatine), LA, NC (Charlotte), OR (Rivergate), TX (Beaumont).

$ Given: $4,571,472 for 397 grants: high $491,860; low $250; average $500–$5,000.

Contact: R. P. Van Zandt, Vice-President and Trustee

     Initial approach: telephone

     Deadlines: requests in by September 15

Weingart Foundation
1200 Wilshire Boulevard, Suite 305
Los Angeles, California 90017

Areas of interest: Higher education (including libraries), social welfare, women, secondary education, medical centers, and youth.

Restrictions: Grants for building funds.

Contact: Charles W. Jacobson, Grant Administrator

Wells Fargo Foundation
420 Montgomery Street, MAC 0101-111
San Francisco, California 94163
(415) 396-3568

Areas of interest: Arts and culture (aquariums, museums/galleries, historic preservation/restoration), civic and public affairs (economic development, urban and community affairs), education, and social services.

Restrictions: Grants for capital, general support, matching funds, and special projects; grants to individuals.

Focus of giving: California communities where bank has offices.

$ Given: $4,431,506 for 598 grants: average $1,000–$10,000.

Contact: Mr. Ronald E. Eadie, President

     Initial approach: letter

     Deadlines: none

     Board meeting dates: quarterly

COLORADO

Boettcher Foundation
1670 Broadway, Suite 3301
Denver, Colorado 80202
(303) 571-5510

Areas of interest: Community development, all levels of education, social welfare, culture, the disabled, and recreation.

Restrictions: Grants for building funds.

Contact: John C. Mitchell II, President

Coors (Adolph) Foundation
350-C Clayton Street
Denver, Colorado 80206
(303) 388-1636

Restrictions: Grants given for building funds, general purposes, seed money, and program-related investments.

Focus of giving: Giving primarily in Colorado.

$ Given: $4,425,146, including $3,265,690 for grants.

Contact: Linda S. Tafoya, Executive Director
  Initial approach: letter
  Copies of proposal: 1
  Deadlines: 6 weeks prior to meetings
  Board meeting dates: February, May, August, and November
  Final notification: 3 months

El Pomar Foundation
Ten Lake Circle Drive
P. O. Box 158
Colorado Springs, Colorado 80901
(303) 633-7733

Areas of interest: Mental health, education, social welfare, arts and humanities, recreation, health projects, and youth.

Restrictions: Grants for building funds.

Frost Foundation, Ltd.
Cherry Creek Plaza II, Suite 810
Denver, Colorado 80222
(303) 388-1687

Areas of interest: All levels of education, performing arts, social welfare, health projects, and medical centers.

Restrictions: Grants for building funds.

Contact: Theodore R. Kauss, Executive Director

Gates Foundation
3200 Cherry Creek South Drive, Suite 630
Denver, Colorado 80209-3247
(303) 722-1881

Restrictions: Grants for continuing support, building funds, capital campaigns, endowment funds, matching funds, program-related investments, renovation projects, seed money, special projects, equipment, fellowships, general purposes, land acquisition, publications, and technical assistance.

Focus of giving: Giving limited to Colorado, especially the Denver area, except for foundation-initiated grants.

$ Given: $3,367,020 for 106 grants: high $850,000; average $5,000–$100,000.

Assets: $84,600,000

Publications: Annual report, informational brochure (including application guidelines), program policy statement, and grants list.

Contact: F. Charles Froelicher, Executive Director
   Initial approach: telephone
   Copies of proposal: 1
   Deadlines: February 1, April 15, August 1, and December 15
   Board meeting dates: April 1, June 15, October 1, and December 15
   Final notification: 2 weeks following meetings

Will E. Heginbotham Trust
P. O. Box 245
Holyoke, Colorado 80734

Areas of interest: Secondary schools, health projects, municipalities, and medical centers.

Restrictions: Grants for building funds.

Contact: Glen E. Stenson, Trustee

Hill Foundation
Terminal Annex, Box 5825
Denver, Colorado 80217
(303) 297-2400

Areas of interest: Colleges and universities, museums, social welfare, health projects, the elderly, and medical institutions.

Restrictions: Grants for building funds.

Contact: John R. Moran, Jr., Trustee

Mabel Y. Hughes Charitable Trust
c/o The First Interstate Bank of Denver
Terminal Annex, Box 5825
Denver, Colorado 80217
(303) 293-5324

Areas of interest: Community development, higher education, health, hospitals, and culture.

Restrictions: Grants for building funds.

Focus of giving: Grants given in areas of company operations.

Contact: Yvonne J. Baca, Vice-President

Helen K. and Arthur E. Johnson Foundation
1700 Broadway, Room 2302
Denver, Colorado 80202
(303) 861-4127

Areas of interest: Community development, education, health projects, social welfare, hospitals, and youth organizations.

Restrictions: Grants for building funds.

Contact: Robert L. Mitton, Executive Director

Lowe Foundation
Colorado Judicial Center
Two East 14th Avenue
Denver, Colorado 80203
(303) 837-3750

Restrictions: Grants for building funds, equipment, general purposes, operating budgets, program-related investments, and seed money.

Focus of giving: Giving primarily in Colorado.

$ Given: $115,000 for 21 grants: high $15,000; low $1,500; average $6,000.

Assets: $2,395,000

Publications: 990-PF, and application guidelines.

Contact: Luis D. Rovina, President

> **Initial approach:**   letter
>
> **Copies of proposal:**   5
>
> **Deadlines:**   submit proposal preferably in January; deadline February 28
>
> **Board meeting dates:**   March and November

Carl A. Norgren Foundation
2696 S. Colorado Boulevard, Suite 585
Denver, Colorado 80222
(303) 758-8393

Areas of interest: Community development, all levels of education, museums, performing arts, youth organizations, health, and the disabled.

Restrictions: Grants for building funds.

Contact: Leigh H. Norgren, President

The Piton Foundation
511 16th Street, Suite 700
Denver, Colorado 80202
(303) 825-6246

Areas of interest: To encourage personal effort toward self-realization, to promote the development of strong cooperative relationships between the public and private sectors with emphasis on local involvement, and to improve conditions and opportunities for persons inadequately served by the institutions of society. Support for individual volunteer agencies to encourage improved management and service effectiveness; some giving also for civic, conservation, and health programs.

Restrictions: Grants awarded for operating budgets, seed money, emergency funds, consulting services, technical assistance, and program-related investments.

Focus of giving: Giving primarily in Colorado, with emphasis on the Denver metropolitan area, especially for community economic development and low-income, affordable housing. No grants for building or endowment funds.

$ Given: $5,660,983 for grants: high $350,000. Also $79,992 for 54 grants to individuals.

Contact: Phyllis Buehele, Grants Administrator Trust Officer
    Initial approach: letter
    Copies of proposal: 1
    Deadlines: none
    Board meeting dates: as required
    Final notification: approximately 4 months

Ruth and Vernon Taylor Foundation
1670 Denver Club Building
Denver, Colorado 80202
(303) 893-5284

Areas of interest: Colleges and universities, hospitals, social welfare, and secondary education.

Restrictions: Grants for building funds.

Contact: Ms. Friday A. Green, Treasurer

Unocal Foundation
P. O. Box 7600
Los Angeles, California 90051
(213) 977-6171

Areas of interest: Arts and culture (museums/galleries, arts centers), civic and public affairs (business/free enterprise, economic development, urban and community affairs), education, health, and social services.

Restrictions: Grants for capital, general support, and special projects; grants to individuals.

Focus of giving: Nationally, with preference given to areas where Unocal maintains corporate facilities: AK (Kenai), CA (Brea, Los Angeles, Mountain Pass, San Francisco, Santa Maria), CO, IL (Chicago, Palatine), LA, NC (Charlotte), OR (Rivergate), TX (Beaumont).

$ Given: $4,571,472 for 397 grants: high $491,860; low $250; average $500–$5,000.

Contact: R. P. Van Zandt, Vice-President and Trustee
 Initial approach: telephone
 Deadlines: requests in by September 15

CONNECTICUT

Aetna Life & Casualty Foundation
151 Farmington Avenue
Hartford, Connecticut 06156
(203) 273-2465

Restrictions: Urban neighborhood revitalization, support of national and regional organizations that provide technical assistance to neighborhood-based organizations engaged in revitalization efforts. The Foundation also supports innovative efforts to reduce arson, a major destructive element in many low-income neighborhoods.

$ Given: Foundation dispersed $7,995,738 in 1984; corporate grants totaled $1,491,421.

Contact: Contributions Program

Amax Foundation, Inc.
Amax Center
Greenwich, Connecticut 06836
(203) 629-6901

Areas of interest: Social welfare, culture, the elderly and disabled, and recreation, and colleges (mining, science).

Restrictions: Grants for building funds.

Contact: Sonja B. Weill, President

Bemis Company Foundation
800 Northstar Center
Minneapolis, Minnesota 55402
(612) 340-6198

Areas of interest: Urban and community affairs, arts centers, cinema, performing arts (general), business/free enterprise, economic development, education, health, and social services.

Restrictions: Grants for general support, special projects, and matching funds; grants to individuals.

Focus of giving: Areas where company maintains facilities, with emphasis on Minneapolis, MN. AR (Crossett), CA (Los Angeles, Union City, Wilmington), CT (Plainfield, Stratford), FL (Panama City), IL (Murphysboro, Peoria, Schaumburg), IN (Indianapolis, Terre Haute), KS (Wichita), KY (Florence, Henderson, Louisville), MA (East Pepperell), MI (Grand Rapids, Zeeland), MN (Mankato, Minneapolis, Minnetonka), MO (Louisiana, Saint Louis, Springfield), MS (Verona), NC (Statesville), NE (Omaha), NH (Hudson, Nashua, North Walpole), NJ (Flemington), NY (Buffalo), OH (Stow), TN (Memphis), TX (Jacksonville), WA (Seattle, Vancouver), WI (Green Bay, New London, Oshkosh, Sheboygan).

$ Given: $700,000 for 826 grants; average $832.

Contact: Edward T. Dougherty, Executive Director
   Initial approach: brief letter or proposal
   Deadlines: applications accepted throughout the year

Bridgeport Area Foundation
446 University Avenue
Bridgeport, Connecticut 06604
(203) 334-7511

Areas of interest: Broad purposes for the local community.

Restrictions: Grants for building funds.

Contact: Richard O. Dietrich, President

Connecticut Mutual Life Foundation
140 Garden Street
Hartford, Connecticut 06154
(203) 727-6500

Areas of interest: Largely for education, low- and moderate-income housing, and social purposes.

Restrictions: Grants given for operating budgets, continuing support, seed money, building funds, matching funds, consulting services, technical assistance, program-related investments, special projects, conferences, and seminars.

Focus of giving: Giving primarily in Hartford, Connecticut, area.

$ Given: $769,691 for 102 grants: average $3,000–$6,000

Assets: $8,043,787

Contact: Astrida R. Olds, Assistant Vice-President
    Initial approach: letter, full proposal, or telephone
    Copies of proposal: 1
    Deadlines: none
    Board meeting dates: March and November
    Final notification: 3 months

Emhart Corporation
426 Colt Highway
Farmington, Connecticut 06032
(203) 678-3204

Areas of interest: Arts and humanities (museums/galleries, zoos, operas, arts centers, historic preservation/restoration), civic and public affairs (business/free enterprise, urban and community affairs), education, health, and social services.

Restrictions: Grants for general support, capital, endowment, and matching funds; grants to individuals.

Focus of giving: Giving primarily in areas where company has major facilities and a large number of employees: AL, CA (Anaheim, Los Angeles, Torrance), CT (Berlin, Farmington, Hartford, Shelton, Windsor), IL (Broadview), IN (Indianapolis), KY (Campbellsville), MA (Beverly, Fall River, Middleton, New Bedford, South Hadley, Whitman), MI (Mount Clemens), MO, NE (Lincoln), NH, NY (Elmira, Maspeth), OH (Cleveland), PA (Huntington Valley, Reading, Temple), TN, VT (Springfield).

$ Given: $738,865 for 200 grants: high $45,000; low $100; average $2,694.

Contact: John F. Budd, Jr., Chairman, Contributions and Grants Committee

    Initial approach: brief letter or proposal

    Deadlines: submit proposal before October

    Final notification: by December

ITT Rayonier Foundation
1177 Summer Street
Stamford, Connecticut 06904
(203) 348-7000

Areas of interest: Arts and humanities (aquariums, performing arts, museums/galleries), civic and public affairs (business/free enterprise, economic development, urban and community affairs), education, health, and social services (homes).

Restrictions: Grants for capital, general support, matching funds, and special projects; grants to individuals.

Focus of giving: Giving primarily near operating locations in Connecticut (Stamford), Florida, Georgia, and Washington.

$ Given: $259,985 for 129 grants: high $18,500; low $25; average $1,000–$5,000.

Assets: $2,635,096

Contact: Jerome D. Gregoire, Vice-President

    Initial approach: letter

    Deadlines: November 30

    Board meeting dates: February

    Final notification: one month

GTE Foundation
One Stamford Forum
Stamford, Connecticut 06904
(203) 965-2000

Areas of interest: Community development, all levels of education, mental health, hospitals, social welfare, arts and humanities, and minorities.

Restrictions: Grants for building funds.

Contact: Ann C. Robin, Secretary

Hartford Courant Foundation, Inc.
285 Broad Street
Hartford, Connecticut 06105
(203) 241-6472

Areas of interest: Community development, social welfare, culture, health projects, universities, and recreation.

Restrictions: Grants for building funds.

Contact: Martha S. Newman, Executive Director

Howard and Bush Foundation, Inc.
c/o Connecticut Bank & Trust
P. O. Box 3334
Hartford, Connecticut 06103

Areas of interest: Social welfare, youth, health projects, culture, and the disabled.

Restrictions: Grants for building funds.

New Haven Foundation
One State Street
New Haven, Connecticut 06510
(203) 777-2386

Areas of interest: Community development, education, health projects, arts and humanities, and recreation.

Restrictions: Grants for building funds.

Contact: Helmer Ekstrom, Director

Olin Corporation Charitable Trust
120 Long Ridge Road
Stamford, Connecticut 06904
(203) 356-3301

Areas of interest: Community development, universities, youth organizations, health projects, hospitals, and recreation.

Restrictions: Grants for building funds.

Focus of giving: Grants given in areas of company operations.

Contact: Carmella V. Piacentini, Administrator

Scovill Foundation, Inc.
1600 Summer Street
Stamford, Connecticut 06904
(203) 757-6061

Areas of interest: Youth organizations, hospitals, community development, and arts and humanities.

Restrictions: Grants for building funds.

Contact: Paul Beetz, Secretary

Alix Stanley Charitable Foundation, Inc.
235 Main Street
New Britain, Connecticut 06051
(203) 224-6473

Areas of interest: Hospitals, community development, and culture.

Restrictions: Grants for building funds.

Contact: David A. Hurley III, Secretary

Stanley Works Foundation
c/o Connecticut Bank and Trust Company
P. O. Box 3334
Hartford, Connecticut 06103

Areas of interest: Libraries, hospitals, community development, science, colleges, and arts and humanities.

Restrictions: Grants for building funds.

Contact: Ronald F. Gilrain, Vice-President, Public Affairs

DELAWARE

Crystal Trust
1088 DuPont Building
Wilmington, Delaware 19898
(302) 774-8421

Restrictions: Grants awarded for seed money, building funds, equipment, land acquisition, and program-related investments.

Focus of giving: Giving primarily in Delaware.

$ Given: $843,260 for 46 grants: high $100,000; low $2,000; average $10,000–$20,000.

Contact: Burt C. Pratt, Director

    Initial approach: letter

    Copies of proposal: 1

    Deadlines: October 1

    Board meeting dates: November

    Final notification: December 31

Laffrey-McHugh Foundation
1200 Market Building
P. O. Box 2207
Wilmington, Delaware 19899
(302) 658-9141

Areas of interest: Performing arts, social welfare, and community development.

Restrictions: Grants for building funds.

Marmot Foundation
c/o Wilmington Trust Company
1004 Wilmington Trust Center
Wilmington, Delaware 19801
(302) 654-2477

Areas of interest: Community development, culture, social welfare, colleges, and secondary education.

Restrictions: Grants for building funds.

Raskob Foundation for Catholic Activities, Inc.
P. O. Box 4019
Wilmington, Delaware 19807
(302) 655-4440

Restrictions: Grants for operating budgets, seed money, emergency funds, equipment, land acquisition, matching funds, conferences and seminars, program-related investments, renovation projects, and special projects.

$ Given: $2,879,026 for grants.

Publications: Biennial report and application guidelines.

Contact: Gerard S. Garey, President

    Application information: application form required

    Initial approach: letter

    Copies of proposal: 1

    Deadlines: applications accepted for spring meeting from December 15 to February 15; applications accepted for fall meeting from June 15 to August 15

    Board meeting dates: spring and fall

    Final notification: 6 months

Welfare Foundation, Inc.
1004 Wilmington Trust Center
Wilmington, Delaware 19801
(302) 654-2477

Areas of interest: Community development, performing arts, education, social welfare, youth organizations, and health projects.

Restrictions: Grants for building funds.

Contact: Endsley P. Fairman, Executive Secretary

DISTRICT OF COLUMBIA

America The Beautiful Fund
219 Shoreham Building
Washington, DC 20005
(202) 638-1649

Areas of interest: Architecture, history, museums and libraries, creative and performing arts, the elderly, children and youth, cultural relations, community gardens, and rural development.

Restrictions: Seed grants available to innovative community projects to enrich the quality of the natural, historic, and man-made environment. Local projects to protect, enhance, or restore a community with broad-scale participation by a significant number of people.

$ Given: $620,130 in grants; average $1,000.

Contact: P. B. Dowling, Executive Director

The Kiplinger Foundation, Inc.
1729 H Street, N.W.
Washington, D.C. 20006
(202) 887-6537

Areas of interest: Community development, performing arts, social welfare, and hospitals.

Restrictions: Grants for building funds.

Contact: Arnold B. Barach, Secretary

National Trust for Historic Preservation
1785 Massachusetts Avenue, N.W.
Washington, DC 20036
(202) 673-4054

Areas of interest: A private, nonprofit organization chartered by Congress to encourage public participation in the preservation of sites, buildings, and objects significant in American history and culture.

Name of program: National Preservation Loan Fund

Restrictions: To assist nonprofit or public member organizations in establishing or expanding preservation revolving funds, and in undertaking other real estate development projects that preserve historic buildings, sites, and districts. To encourage the preservation of endangered National Historic Landmarks, the fund includes an endangered properties component which offers specialized assistance for eligible projects.

$ Given: Low-interest loans and lines of credit and loan guarantees for terms of five to ten years.

National Trust For Historic Preservation
1785 Massachusetts Avenue, N.W.
Washington, DC 20036
(202) 673-4054

Name of program: Inner-City Ventures Fund

Restrictions: Preservation projects of nonprofit neighborhood organizations.

$ Given: Grants, low-interest loans and technical assistance.

Administration for Native Americans
Room 5300 N
U.S. Department of Health and Human Services
330 Independence Avenue, S.W.
Washington, D.C. 20201
(202) 245-7714

Name of program: Native American Programs—Financial Assistance Grants

Restrictions: To promote the economic and social self-sufficiency of American Indians, Native Hawaiians, and Alaskan Natives.

Eligibility: Nonprofit organizations, state and local governments.

$ Given: Grants ranging from $15,000 to $400,000.

Public Welfare Foundation, Inc.
2600 Virginia Avenue, N.W., Room 505
Washington, D.C. 20037
(202) 965-1800

Areas of interest: Community development in education, child welfare, youth agencies, and health services.

Restrictions: No grants are made directly to individuals.

$ Given: Range per award is $1,500–$100,000.

Contact: C. Glenn Ihrig, Executive Director
   Initial approach: phone or letter
   Deadlines: none

FLORIDA

Bemis Company Foundation
800 Northstar Center
Minneapolis, Minnesota 55402
(612) 340-6198

Areas of interest: Urban and community affairs, arts centers, cinema, performing arts (general), business/free enterprise, economic development, education, health, and social services.

Restrictions: Grants for general support, special projects, and matching funds; grants to individuals.

Focus of giving: Areas where company maintains facilities, with emphasis on Minneapolis, MN. AR (Crossett), CA (Los Angeles, Union City, Wilmington), CT (Plainfield, Stratford), FL (Panama City), IL (Murphysboro, Peoria, Schaumburg), IN (Indianapolis, Terre Haute), KS (Wichita), KY (Florence, Henderson, Louisville), MA (East Pepperell), MI (Grand Rapids, Zeeland), MN (Mankato, Minneapolis, Minnetonka), MO (Louisiana, Saint Louis, Springfield), MS (Verona), NC (Statesville), NE (Omaha), NH (Hudson, Nashua, North Walpole), NJ (Flemington), NY (Buffalo), OH (Stow), TN (Memphis), TX (Jacksonville), WA (Seattle, Vancouver), WI (Green Bay, New London, Oshkosh, Sheboygan).

$ Given: $700,000 for 826 grants; average $832.

Contact: Edward T. Dougherty, Executive Director
   Initial approach: brief letter or proposal
   Deadlines: applications accepted throughout the year

Edyth Bush Charitable Foundation
199 East Welbourne Avenue
Winter Park, Florida 32790
(305) 647-4322

Areas of interest: Colleges and universities, minorities, arts and humanities, and recreation.

Restrictions: Grants for building funds.

Contact: H. Clifford Lee, Executive Vice-President

Dade Foundation
200 S. Biscayne Boulevard, Suite 520
Miami, Florida 33131
(305) 371-2711

Areas of interest: Arts and humanities, youth, health projects, hospitals, and the disabled.

Restrictions: Grants for building funds.

Contact: Ruth Shack, Executive Director

Arthur Vining Davis Foundations
645 Riverside Avenue, Suite 520
Jacksonville, Florida 32204
(904) 359-0670

Areas of interest: Colleges (including art centers, auditoriums and libraries), medicine, and recreation.

Restrictions: Grants for building funds.

Contact: Max Morris, Executive Director

Jack Eckerd Corporation Foundation
P. O. Box 4689
Clearwater, Florida 33518
(813) 397-7461

Areas of interest: Arts and humanities, health projects, hospitals, community development, and colleges.

Restrictions: Grants for building funds.

Focus of giving: Grants given in areas of company operations.

Harris Foundation
1025 West NASA Boulevard
Melbourne, Florida 32919
(305) 727-9378

Areas of interest: Health projects, culture, community development, and colleges.

Restrictions: Grants for building funds.

Contact: O.W. Hudson, Secretary

ITT Rayonier Foundation
1177 Summer Street
Stamford, Connecticut 06904
(203) 348-7000

Areas of interest: Arts and humanities (aquariums, performing arts, museums/galleries), civic and public affairs (business/free enterprise, economic development, urban and community affairs), education, health, and social services (homes).

Restrictions: Grants for capital, general support, matching funds, and special projects; grants to individuals.

Focus of giving: Giving primarily near operating locations in Connecticut (Stamford), Florida, Georgia, and Washington.

$ Given: $259,985 for 129 grants: high $18,500; low $25; average $1,000–$5,000.

Assets: $2,635,096

Contact: Jerome D. Gregoire, Vice-President
    Initial approach: letter
    Deadlines: November 30
    Board meeting dates: February
    Final notification: 1 month

George W. Jenkins Foundation, Inc.
P. O. Box 407
Lakeland, Florida 33802
(813) 688-1188

Areas of interest: Community development, colleges and universities, disabled, hospitals, and health projects.

Restrictions: Grants for building funds.

Contact: Barbara O. Hart, Director

Dr. P. Phillips Foundation
60 West Robinson Street
Orlando, Florida 32802
(305) 422-6105

Areas of interest: Youth organizations and community development.

Restrictions: Grants for building funds.

John E. and Aliese Price Foundation, Inc.
P. O. Box 4607
North Ft. Myers, Florida 33918
(813) 656-0196

Areas of interest: The blind, health projects, and churches.

Restrictions: Grants for building funds.

The Wilder Foundation
P. O. Box 99
Key Biscayne, Florida 33149

Restrictions: Support for general purposes, building funds, endowment funds, research, scholarship funds, and matching funds.

Focus of giving: Giving primarily in Florida.

$ Given: $126,956 for 18 grants: high $55,000; low $80.

Assets: $962,796

Contact: Rita Wilder, President, or Gary Wilder, Vice-President
    Initial approach: proposal
    Copies of proposal: 1
    Deadlines: submit proposal before September
    Board meeting dates: monthly

GEORGIA

Metropolitan Atlanta Community Foundation, Inc.
The Hurt Building, Suite 449
Atlanta, Georgia 30303
(404) 688-5525

Restrictions: Grants for seed money, emergency funds, building funds, equipment, land acquisition, technical assistance, program-related investments, special projects, publications, capital campaigns, matching funds, and renovation projects.

$ Given: $10,223,081 for grants: high $1,000,000; low $50; average $3,000–$5,000.

Publications: Annual report, program policy statement, and application guidelines.

Contact: Alicia Philip, Executive Director

   Application information: application form required

   Initial approach: letter or telephone

   Copies of proposal: 1

   Deadlines: June 1, September 1, December 1, and March 1

   Board meeting dates: July, October, January, and April

   Final notification: 6 weeks

Atlanta Foundation
c/o First National Bank of Atlanta
P. O. Box 4148
Atlanta, Georgia 30302
(404) 332-6677

Areas of interest: Community development.

Restrictions: Grants for building funds.

Contact: Frank Rozelle, Secretary

Callaway Foundation, Inc.
209 Broome Street
LaGrange, Georgia 30240
(404) 884-7348

Areas of interest: Community development.

Restrictions: Grants for building funds.

Contact: J.T. Gresham, General Manager

The Coca-Cola Foundation
One Coca-Cola Plaza
Atlanta, Georgia 30313
(404) 676-3740

Restrictions: Grants for annual campaigns, scholarship funds, continuing support, operating budgets, program-related investments, and special projects.

$ Given: $3,666,464 for 149 grants: high $371,031; low $200. $500,000 for loans.

Assets: $8,772,658

Contact: Margaret J. Cox, Executive Director
    Initial approach: proposal
    Board meeting dates: February, May, July, and November
    Final notification: 90 to 120 days

Fund for Southern Communities
57 Forsyth Street, Suite 1603
P. O. Box 927
Atlanta, Georgia 30303
(404) 577-3178

Areas of interest: Housing and economic development. The Fund supports organizations working against discrimination based on race, sex, age, religion, economic status, sexual preference, ethnic background, or physical or mental disabilities.

Restrictions: Seed grants to new projects; general support and project grants to small organizations.

Focus of giving: Requests must be submitted from projects/programs operating in North Carolina, South Carolina, or Georgia.

$ Given: $144,700 for grants: high $3,000; low $750; average $1,570.

Publications: Annual report, program policy statement, and application guidelines.

Contact: Alan McGregor, Executive Director

    Application information: application form required

    Initial approach: telephone or letter

    Copies of proposal: 1

    Deadlines: the fund accepts applications once a year, usually in the fall

    Board meeting dates: once a year

    Final notification: 4 months

John H. and Wilhelmina D. Harland Charitable Foundation
2939 Miller Road
Decatur, Georgia 30035
(404) 981-9460

Areas of interest: Community development.

Restrictions: Grants for building funds.

Contact: John A. Conant, Secretary

ITT Rayonier Foundation
1177 Summer Street
Stamford, Connecticut 06904
(203) 348-7000

Areas of interest: Arts and humanities (aquariums, performing arts, museums/galleries), civic and public affairs (business/free enterprise, economic development, urban and community affairs), education, health, and social services (homes).

Restrictions: Grants for capital, general support, matching funds, and special projects; grants to individuals.

Focus of giving: Giving primarily near operating locations in Connecticut (Stamford), Florida, Georgia, and Washington.

$ Given: $259,985 for 129 grants: high $18,500; low $25; average $1,000–$5,000.

Assets: $2,635,096

Contact: Jerome D. Gregoire, Vice-President
  Initial approach: letter
  Deadlines: November 30.
  Board meeting dates: February
  Final notification: 1 month

Rich Foundation, Inc.
45 Broad Street
Atlanta, Georgia 30303
(404) 586-2488

Areas of interest: Community development.

Restrictions: Grants for building funds.

Contact: Anne Poland Berg, Grant Consultant

Trust Company of Georgia Foundation
P. O. Box 4418
Atlanta, Georgia 30302
(404) 588-8246

Areas of interest: Community development.

Restrictions: Grants for building funds.

Contact: Victor A. Gregory, Secretary

HAWAII

Alexander & Baldwin, Inc.
822 Bishop Street
P. O. Box 3440
Honolulu, Hawaii 96801
(808) 525-6611

Areas of interest: Community and urban affairs, property development and investments, culture (museums, performing arts), capital campaigns, general support, in-kind donations of land, and seed money.

Restrictions: Organizations must be tax-exempt under 501 (c) 3. No grants to individuals or religious organizations for religious purposes.

Focus of giving: Giving to CA (San Francisco), HI (Honolulu, Puunene, Kahului, Puhi, Eleele, Wailea, and the islands of Maui, Oahu, and Kauai).

$ Given: $2,517,000 for grants: high $250,000; low $50; average $1,000–$10,000.

Assets: $981,737,000

Contact: Scott Matsuura, Manager, Community Relations
  Application information: application form required
  Initial approach: letter
  Copies of proposal: 1
  Deadlines: applications accepted throughout the year

Samuel N. and Mary Castle Foundation
c/o Hawaiian Trust Company, Ltd.
111 South King
Honolulu, Hawaii 96802
(808) 525-6512

Areas of interest: Community development.

Restrictions: Grants for building funds.

Contact: Mark J. O'Donnell, Secretary

The Hawaiian Foundation
111 South King Street
P. O. Box 3170
Honolulu, Hawaii 96802
(808) 525-8548

Restrictions: Grants for operating budgets, seed money, continuing support, equipment, special projects, and matching funds.

Focus of giving: Giving primarily in Hawaii.

$ Given: $357,395 for 61 grants and $28,686 for 75 grants to individuals.

Publications: Annual report, program policy statement, application guidelines, and informational brochure.

Contact: Mark J. O'Donnell, Trust Officer

    Application information: application forms required for grants to individuals

    Initial approach: telephone or proposal

    Copies of proposal: 9

    Deadlines: first day of month preceding board meeting

    Board meeting dates: January, April, July, and October

G. N. Wilcox Trust
c/o Bishop Trust Company, Ltd.
140 South King Street
Honolulu, Hawaii 96813
(808) 523-2111

Areas of interest: Community development.

Restrictions: Grants for building funds.

IDAHO

Fred Meyer Charitable Trust
1515 Southwest Fifth Avenue, Suite 500
Portland, Oregon 97201
(503) 228-5512

Restrictions: Support for seed money, building funds, equipment, special projects, and matching funds.

Focus of giving: Support primarily in Oregon, with occasional grants at the initiative of the trust for programs in Washington, Idaho, Montana, and Alaska.

$ Given: $6,365,583 for 94 grants: high $555,000; low $964; average $20,000–$75,000.

Assets: $171,639,900

Contact: Charles S. Rooks, Executive Director

Application information: application form required

Initial approach: letter or full proposal

Copies of proposal: 1

Deadlines: none

Board meeting dates: monthly

Final notification: 4 to 6 months for proposals that pass first screening; 2 to 3 months for those that do not

Northwest Area Foundation
West 975 First National Bank Building
St. Paul, Minnesota 55101
(612) 224-9635

Restrictions: Grants generally for experimental and demonstration projects that promise significant impact on the community and the well-being of society but for which there is not now general support.

Focus of giving: Giving limited to an eight-state region that includes Idaho, Iowa, Minnesota, Montana, North Dakota, Oregon, South Dakota, and Washington.

$ Given: $6,967,105 for 196 grants: high $250,000; low $150; average $20,000–$60,000.

Contact: Terry Tinson, President

Initial approach: letter, telephone, or proposal

Copies of proposal: 2

Deadlines: varies

Board meeting dates: bimonthly, beginning in February

Final notification: 60 to 90 days

ILLINOIS

Abbot Laboratories
Abbot Park 6C
North Chicago, Illinois 60064
(312) 937-7075

Areas of interest: Education, health, and social services.

Restrictions: Capital grants for building funds, equipment, capital projects, matching funds, and land acquisition.

Focus of giving: Communities in which company has significant operations or employee populations.

$ Given: $13,000,000.

Assets: $1,488,514

Contact: Charles S. Brown, President
   Initial approach: letter
   Deadlines: applications accepted throughout the year
   Board meeting dates: April and December

American National Bank and Trust Company of Chicago Foundation
33 North LaSalle Street
Chicago, Illinois 60602
(312) 661-5000

Areas of interest: Community development.

Restrictions: Grants for building funds.

Contact: Linda Septow, Public Relations Coordinator

Amoco Foundation, Inc.
200 East Randolph Drive
Chicago, Illinois 60601
(312) 856-6306

Areas of interest: Community development.

Restrictions: Grants for building funds.

Contact: Bob L. Arganbright, Executive Director

Amsted Industries Foundation
Boulevard Towers South, 44th Floor
205 N. Michigan Avenue
Chicago, Illinois 60601
(312) 645-1700

Areas of interest: Community development.

Restrictions: Grants for building funds.

Aurora Foundation
111 W. Downer Place, Suite 312
Aurora, Illinois 60506
(708) 896-7800

Areas of interest: Community development.

Restrictions: Grants for building funds.

Contact: Sharon Stredde, Corporate Secretary

Bemis Company Foundation
800 Northstar Center
Minneapolis, Minnesota 55402
(612) 340-6198

Areas of interest: Urban and community affairs, arts centers, cinema, performing arts (general), business/free enterprise, economic development, education, health, and social services.

Restrictions: Grants for general support, special projects, and matching funds; grants for individuals.

Focus of giving: Areas where company maintains facilities, with emphasis on Minneapolis, MN. AR (Crossett), CA (Los Angeles, Union City, Wilmington), CT (Plainfield, Stratford), FL (Panama City), IL (Murphysboro, Peoria, Schaumburg), IN (Indianapolis, Terre Haute), KS (Wichita), KY (Florence, Henderson, Louisville), MA (East Pepperell), MI (Grand Rapids, Zeeland), MN (Mankato, Minneapolis, Minnetonka), MO (Louisiana, Saint Louis, Springfield), MS (Verona), NC (Statesville), NE (Omaha), NH (Hudson, Nashua, North Walpole), NJ (Flemington), NY (Buffalo), OH (Stow), TN (Memphis), TX (Jacksonville), WA (Seattle, Vancouver), WI (Green Bay, New London, Oshkosh, Sheboygan).

$ Given: $700,000 for 826 grants; average $832.

Contact: Edward T. Dougherty, Executive Director
  Initial approach: brief letter or proposal
  Deadlines: applications accepted throughout the year

Borg-Warner Foundation, Inc.
200 South Michigan Avenue
Chicago, Illinois 60604
(312) 322-8659

Areas of interest: Neighborhood revitalization, community development, and building funds.

Restrictions: Grants are limited to Chicago-area nonprofit organizations.

Contact: Ellen J. Benjamin, Director, Corporate Contributions
   Deadlines: none

Clark Foundation
2300 Sixth Street
Rockford, Illinois 61108
(815) 962-8861

Areas of interest: Community development.

Restrictions: Grants for building funds.

Contact: V. E. Zumhagen, Chairman

Arie and Ida Crown Memorial
300 W. Washington Street, Room 1200
Chicago, Illinois 60606
(312) 236-6300

Areas of interest: Community development.

Restrictions: Grants for building funds.

Contact: Susan Crown, President

Emhart Corporation
426 Colt Highway
Farmington, Connecticut 06032
(203) 678-3204

Areas of interest: Arts and humanities (museums/galleries, zoos, operas, arts centers, historic preservation/restoration), civic and public affairs (business/free enterprise, urban and community affairs), education, health, and social services.

Restrictions: Grants for general support, capital, endowment, and matching funds; grants for individuals.

Focus of giving: Giving primarily in areas where company has major facilities and a large number of employees: AL, CA (Anaheim, Los Angeles, Torrance), CT (Berlin, Farmington, Hartford, Shelton, Windsor), IL (Broadview), IN (Indianapolis), KY (Campbellsville), MA (Beverly, Fall River, Middleton, New Bedford, South Hadley, Whitman), MI (Mount Clemens), MO, NE (Lincoln), NH, NY (Elmira, Maspeth), OH (Cleveland), PA (Huntington Valley, Reading, Temple), TN, VT (Springfield).

$ Given: $738,865 for 200 grants: high $45,000; low $100; average $2,694.

Contact: John F. Budd, Jr., Chairman, Contributions and Grants Committee

    Initial approach: brief letter or proposal

    Deadlines: submit proposal before October

    Final notification: by December

The Field Foundation of Illinois, Inc.
135 South LaSalle Street
Chicago, Illinois 60603
(312) 263-3211

Areas of interest: Health, welfare, education, cultural activities and civic affairs, youth agencies, race relations, and the aged.

Restrictions: Support for building funds, emergency funds, equipment, special projects, and land acquisition.

Focus of giving: Giving primarily in Chicago, Illinois, area.

$ Given: $1,475,357 for 69 grants: high $60,000; low $1,000; average $10,000–$20,000.

Assets: $22,926,924

Contact: Lorraine Madsen, President

    Initial approach: full proposal

    Board meeting dates: quarterly

FMC Foundation
200 E. Randolph Drive
Chicago, Illinois 60601
(312) 861-6102

Areas of interest: Community development.

Restrictions: Grants for building funds.

Contact: Catherine Johnston, Executive Director

Gould Incorporated Foundation
Ten Gould Center
Rolling Meadows, Illinois 60008
(708) 640-4255

Areas of interest: Community development.

Restrictions: Grants for building funds.

Contact: Jan A. Britt, Director, Employee Relations

Graham Foundation for Advanced Studies in the Fine Arts
4 West Burton Place
Chicago, Illinois 60610
(312) 787-4071

Areas of interest: Grants for historic preservation/restoration and museums/galleries, special interest in architecture. General support for cultural institutions and individuals; international distribution.

$ Given: $388,072 for 60 grants: high $12,000; low $470; average $2,500–$7,500.

Assets: $15,574,630

Contact: Carter H. Manny, Jr., Director
   Initial approach: letter

Inland Steel-Ryerson Foundation, Inc.
30 West Monroe Street
Chicago, Illinois 60603
(312) 899-3420

Areas of interest: Arts and culture (museums/galleries, arts centers, historic preservation/restoration), civic and public affairs (economic development, urban and community affairs), education, health, and social services (homes).

Restrictions: Grants for capital, general support, and special projects; grants to individuals.

Focus of giving: Giving primarily in northwestern Indiana and Chicago, Illinois (West Side and South suburbs).

$ Given: $1,697,817 for 306 grants: high $341,000; low $100; average $1,000–$10,000.

Contact: Earl Thompson, Secretary

> **Initial approach:** one- or two-page proposal
>
> **Deadlines:** submit proposal preferably during the first 9 months of the year
>
> **Board meeting dates:** April, August, and December

John Deere Foundation
John Deere Road
Moline, Illinois 61265
(309) 752-4137

Areas of interest: Social welfare, secondary and higher education, minorities, the disabled, recreation, and projects relating to agriculture.

Restrictions: Grants for building funds and community development.

Focus of giving: Grants given in areas of company operations.

$ Given: $3,162,348 in grants.

Contact: John F. Coy, President

> **Initial approach:** one- or two-page letter outlining the purpose of the organization, the geographic area to be served, and how private funds will be used
>
> **Deadlines:** none

Illinois Arts Council
State of Illinois Center
100 West Randolph, Suite 10-500
Chicago, IL 60601
(312) 917-6755

Restrictions: Special Assistance Grants and Community Development Grants.

Illinois Tool Works Foundation
8501 W. Higgins Road
Chicago, Illinois 60631
(312) 692-3040

Areas of interest: Community development.

Restrictions: Grants for building funds.

Contact: Stephen B. Smith, Director

Motorola Foundation
1303 E. Algonquin Road
Schaumburg, Illinois 60195
(708) 576-6200

Areas of interest: Community development.

Restrictions: Grants for building funds.

Contact: Herta Betty Nikolai, Administrator

Quaker Oats Foundation
345 Merchandise Mart Plaza
Chicago, Illinois 60654
(312) 222-7033

Areas of interest: Community development.

Restrictions: Grants for building funds.

Contact: W. Thomas Phillips, Secretary

Square D Foundation
1415 S. Roselle Road
Palatine, Illinois 60067
(708) 397-2600

Areas of interest: Community development.

Restrictions: Grants for building funds.

Contact: Donald E. Wilson, Secretary-Treasurer

Sunstrand Corporation Foundation
4751 Harrison Avenue
Rockford, Illinois 61125
(815) 226-6000

Areas of interest: Community development.

Restrictions: Grants for building funds.

Contact: John A. Thayer, Secretary

Unocal Foundation
P. O. Box 7600
Los Angeles, California 90051
(213) 977-6171

Areas of interest: Arts and culture (museums/galleries, arts centers), civic and public affairs (business/free enterprise, economic development, urban and community affairs), education, health, and social services.

Restrictions: Grants for capital, general support, and special projects; grants to individuals.

Focus of giving: Nationally, with preference given to areas where Unocal maintains corporate facilities: AK (Kenai), CA (Brea, Los Angeles, Mountain Pass, San Francisco, Santa Maria), CO, IL (Chicago, Palatine), LA, NC (Charlotte), OR (Rivergate), TX (Beaumont).

$ Given: $4,571,472 for 397 grants: high $491,860; low $250; average $500–$5,000.

Contact: R. P. Van Zandt, Vice-President and Trustee
    Initial approach: telephone
    Deadlines: requests in by September 15

INDIANA

John W. Anderson
402 Wall Street
Valparaiso, Indiana 46383
(219) 462-4611

Areas of interest: Community development.

Restrictions: Grants for building funds.

Contact: Paul G. Wallace, Secretary

Bemis Company Foundation
800 Northstar Center
Minneapolis, Minnesota 55402
(612) 340-6198

Areas of interest: Urban and community affairs, arts centers, cinema, performing arts (general), business/free enterprise, economic development, education, health, and social services.

Restrictions: Grants for general support, special projects, and matching funds; grants to individuals.

Focus of giving: Areas where company maintains facilities, with emphasis on Minneapolis, MN. AR (Crossett), CA (Los Angeles, Union City, Wilmington), CT (Plainfield, Stratford), FL (Panama City), IL (Murphysboro, Peoria, Schaumburg), IN (Indianapolis, Terre Haute), KS (Wichita), KY (Florence, Henderson, Louisville), MA (East Pepperell), MI (Grand Rapids, Zeeland), MN (Mankato, Minneapolis, Minnetonka), MO (Louisiana, Saint Louis, Springfield), MS (Verona), NC (Statesville), NE (Omaha), NH (Hudson, Nashua, North Walpole), NJ (Flemington), NY (Buffalo), OH (Stow), TN (Memphis), TX (Jacksonville), WA (Seattle, Vancouver), WI (Green Bay, New London, Oshkosh, Sheboygan).

$ Given: $700,000 for 826 grants; average $832.

Contact: Edward T. Dougherty, Executive Director
   Initial approach: brief letter or proposal
   Deadlines: applications accepted throughout the year

Cummins Engine Foundation
Box 3005
Columbus, Indiana 47202
(812) 377-3114

Areas of interest: Community development.

Restrictions: Grants are given to tax-exempt organizations or institutions. No grants are made to individuals or for denominational religious organizations.

$ Given: Grants vary in amount, depending upon the needs and nature of the request.

Contact: David L. Dodson, Executive Director.

Emhart Corporation
426 Colt Highway
Farmington, Connecticut 06032
(203) 678-3204

Areas of interest: Arts and humanities (museums/galleries, zoos, operas, arts centers, historic preservation/restoration), civic and public affairs (business/free enterprise, urban and community affairs), education, health, and social services.

Restrictions: Grants for general support, capital, endowment, and matching funds; grants to individuals.

Focus of giving: Giving primarily in areas where company has major facilities and a large number of employees: AL, CA (Anaheim, Los Angeles, Torrance), CT (Berlin, Farmington, Hartford, Shelton, Windsor), IL (Broadview), IN (Indianapolis), KY (Campbellsville), MA (Beverly, Fall River, Middleton, New Bedford, South Hadley, Whitman), MI (Mount Clemens), MO, NE (Lincoln), NH, NY (Elmira, Maspeth), OH (Cleveland), PA (Huntington Valley, Reading, Temple), TN, VT (Springfield).

$ Given: $738,865 for 200 grants: high $45,000; low $100; average $2,694.

Contact: John F. Budd, Jr., Chairman, Contributions and Grants Committee

  Initial approach: brief letter or proposal

  Deadlines: submit proposal before October

  Final notification: by December

Foellinger Foundation, Inc.
5800 Fairfield Avenue, Suite 230
Ft. Wayne, Indiana 46807
(219) 456-4441

Areas of interest: Community development.

Restrictions: Grants for building funds.

Contact: Helene R. Foellinger, President

Heritage Fund of Bartholomew County, Inc.
P. O. Box 1547
Columbus, Indiana 47202
(812) 376-7772

Restrictions: Grants given for operating budgets, continuing support, seed money, emergency funds, deficit financing, building funds, equipment, land acquisition, matching funds, consulting services, technical assistance, program-related investments, special projects, conferences, and seminars.

Focus of giving: Giving primarily in Bartholomew County, Indiana.

$ Given: $9,938 for four grants.

Contact: Edward F. Sullivan, Executive Director

Inland Steel-Ryerson Foundation, Inc.
30 West Monroe Street
Chicago, Illinois 60603
(312) 899-3420

Areas of interest: Arts and culture (museums/galleries, arts centers, historic preservation/restoration), civic and public affairs (economic development, urban and community affairs), education, health, and social services (homes).

Restrictions: Grants for capital, general support, and special projects; grants to individuals.

Focus of giving: Giving primarily in northwestern Indiana and Chicago, Illinois (West Side and South suburbs).

$ Given: $1,697,817 for 306 grants: high $341,000; low $100; average $1,000–$10,000.

Contact: Earl Thompson, Secretary

    Initial approach: one- or two-page proposal

    Deadlines: submit proposal preferably during the first 9 months of the year

    Board meeting dates: April, August, and December

Indianapolis Foundation
615 N. Alabama Street, Room 119
Indianapolis, Indiana 46204
(317) 634-7497

Areas of interest: Community development.

Restrictions: Grants for building funds.

Contact: Kenneth I. Chapman, Executive Director

Lilly Endowment, Inc.
2801 North Meridian Street
P.O. Box 88068
Indianapolis, Indiana 46208
(317) 924-5471

Areas of interest: Community development.

Restrictions: Tax-exempt organizations and institutions with appropriate interests are eligible.

$ Given: Grants vary in amount, depending upon the needs and nature of the request. Range is $10,000–$25,000; average, $40,000.

Contact: Program Office
    Initial approach: letter
    Deadlines: none

Olive B. Cole Foundation, Inc.
Cole Capital Corporation
3242 Mallard Cove Lane
Fort Wayne, Indiana 46804
(219) 436-2182

Restrictions: Grants given for seed money, building funds, equipment, land acquisition, matching funds, program-related investments, general purposes, and continuing support.

Focus of giving: Giving limited to LaGrange, Steuben, and Noble counties.

$ Given: $337,462 for 28 grants: high $70,000; low $1,000; average $12,052. Also $118,018 for grants to individuals.

Contact: John E. Hogan, Jr., Executive Vice-President

Application information: application form required

Initial approach: letter

Copies of proposal: 7

Deadlines: none

Board meeting dates: February, May, August, and November

Final notification: 4 months

The Plumsock Fund
312 Fairbanks Building
9292 North Meridian Street
Indianapolis, Indiana 46260
(317) 846-8115

Areas of interest: Community development.

Restrictions: No established procedures for grants to individuals. Grants are limited to tax-exempt organizations.

$ Given: Varies.

Contact: John G. Rauch, Jr., Secretary

Trust Corporation, Inc. Foundation
c/o Trust Corporation Bank, Ohio
Three Seagate
Toledo, Ohio 43603
(419) 259-8217

Restrictions: Charitable purposes: primarily local giving, with emphasis on community funds. Grants given for continuing support, building funds, emergency funds, equipment, and land acquisition.

Focus of giving: Giving primarily in tristate area of Indiana, Michigan, and Ohio.

$ Given: $212,350 for 19 grants: high $148,000; low $100; average $1,000–$10,000.

Assets: $291,394

Contact: J. E. Lupe, Vice-President

Initial approach: letter

Deadlines: none

Board meeting dates: monthly

Final notification: 2 months

IOWA

Hall Foundation, Inc.
803 Merchants National Bank Building
Grand Rapids, Iowa 52401
(319) 362-9079

Areas of interest: Community development.

Restrictions: Grants for building funds.

Contact: John G. Lidvall, Executive Director

Maytag Company Foundation, Inc.
Newton, Iowa 50208
(515) 792-7000

Areas of interest: Arts and culture (museums/galleries, historic preservation/restoration), civic and public affairs (business/free enterprise), education, and social services.

Restrictions: Grants for general support and matching funds; grants to individuals.

Focus of giving: Giving primarily in Newton and central Iowa.

$ Given: $429,327 for 91 grants: high $49,000; low $66; average $500–$2,500.

Assets: $1,022,366

Contact: Betty J. Dickinson, Executive Director
    Initial approach: letter
    Deadlines: submit proposal before board meeting in late March

Northwest Area Foundation
West 975 First National Bank Building
St. Paul, Minnesota 55101
(612) 224-9635

Restrictions: Grants generally for experimental and demonstration projects that promise significant impact on the community and the well-being of society but for which there is not now general support.

Focus of giving: Giving limited to an eight-state region that includes Idaho, Iowa, Minnesota, Montana, North Dakota, Oregon, South Dakota, and Washington.

$ Given: $6,967,105 for 196 grants: high $250,000; low $150; average $20,000–$60,000.

Contact: Terry Tinson, President

  Initial approach: letter, telephone, or proposal

  Copies of proposal: 2

  Deadlines: varies

  Board meeting dates: bimonthly, beginning in February

  Final notification: 60 to 90 days

Pella Rolscreen Foundation
102 Main Street
Pella, Iowa 50219
(515) 628-1000

Areas of interest: Arts and culture (business/free enterprise, museums/galleries, arts centers, historic preservation/restoration), civic and public affairs (economic development, womens affairs, urban and community affairs), education, health, and social services (homes).

Restrictions: Grants for capital, general support, matching funds, and special projects; grants to individuals.

Focus of giving: Emphasis on Marion and Mahaska counties in Iowa.

$ Given: $919,015 for 115 grants: high $223,750; low $50; average $500–$10,000.

Assets: $6,118,677

Contact: William J. Anderson, Administrator

Initial approach: full proposal

Copies of proposal: 1

Deadlines: applications accepted throughout the year

Board meeting dates: monthly

KANSAS

Bemis Company Foundation
800 Northstar Center
Minneapolis, Minnesota 55402
(612) 340-6198

Areas of interest: Urban and community affairs, arts centers, cinema, performing arts (general), business/free enterprise, economic development, education, health, and social services.

Restrictions: Grants for general support, special projects, and matching funds; grants to individuals.

Focus of giving: Areas where company maintains facilities, with emphasis on Minneapolis, MN. AR (Crossett), CA (Los Angeles, Union City, Wilmington), CT (Plainfield, Stratford), FL (Panama City), IL (Murphysboro, Peoria, Schaumburg), IN (Indianapolis, Terre Haute), KS (Wichita), KY (Florence, Henderson, Louisville), MA (East Pepperell), MI (Grand Rapids, Zeeland), MN (Mankato, Minneapolis, Minnetonka), MO (Louisiana, Saint Louis, Springfield), MS (Verona), NC (Statesville), NE (Omaha), NH (Hudson, Nashua, North Walpole), NJ (Flemington), NY (Buffalo), OH (Stow), TN (Memphis), TX (Jacksonville), WA (Seattle, Vancouver), WI (Green Bay, New London, Oshkosh, Sheboygan).

$ Given: $700,000 for 826 grants; average $832.

Contact: Edward T. Dougherty, Executive Director

Initial approach: brief letter or proposal

Deadlines: applications accepted throughout the year

Cessna Foundation, Inc.
5800 E. Pawnee Road
P. O. Box 1521
Wichita, Kansas 67201
(316) 685-9111

Areas of interest: Community development.

Restrictions: Grants for building funds.

Focus of giving: Grants given in areas of company operations.

Contact: H. D. Humphrey, Secretary

The Powell Family Foundation
10990 Roe Avenue
P. O. Box 7270
Shawnee Mission, Kansas 66207
(913) 345-3000

Restrictions: Grants given for operating budgets, seed money, emergency funds, equipment, program-related investments, conferences and seminars, matching funds, and general purposes.

Focus of giving: Giving limited to Kansas City, Kansas, and the surrounding community.

$ Given: $1,191,538 for 119 grants: high $147,000; low $200.

Assets: $44,354,020

Contact: Marjorie P. Allen, President
    Initial approach: letter
    Copies of proposal: 2
    Deadlines: 30 days preceding board meetings
    Board meeting dates: usually in January, April, July, and October
    Final notification: 4 to 6 weeks

KENTUCKY

Bemis Company Foundation
800 Northstar Center
Minneapolis, Minnesota 55402
(612) 340-6198

Areas of interest: Urban and community affairs, arts centers, cinema, performing arts (general), business/free enterprise, economic development, education, health, and social services.

Restrictions: Grants for general support, special projects, and matching funds, grants to individuals.

Focus of giving: Areas where company maintains facilities, with emphasis on Minneapolis, MN. AR (Crossett), CA (Los Angeles, Union City, Wilmington), CT (Plainfield, Stratford), FL (Panama City), IL (Murphysboro, Peoria, Schaumburg), IN (Indianapolis, Terre Haute), KS (Wichita), KY (Florence, Henderson, Louisville), MA (East Pepperell), MI (Grand Rapids, Zeeland), MN (Mankato, Minneapolis, Minnetonka), MO (Louisiana, Saint Louis, Springfield), MS (Verona), NC (Statesville), NE (Omaha), NH (Hudson, Nashua, North Walpole), NJ (Flemington), NY (Buffalo), OH (Stow), TN (Memphis), TX (Jacksonville), WA (Seattle, Vancouver), WI (Green Bay, New London, Oshkosh, Sheboygan).

$ Given: $700,000 for 826 grants; average $832.

Contact: Edward T. Dougherty, Executive Director

    Initial approach: brief letter or proposal

    Deadlines: applications accepted throughout the year

Emhart Corporation
426 Colt Highway
Farmington, Connecticut 06032
(203) 678-3204

Areas of interest: Arts and humanities (museums/galleries, zoos, operas, arts centers, historic preservation/restoration), civic and public affairs (business/free enterprise, urban and community affairs), education, health, and social services.

Restrictions: Grants for general support, capital, endowment, and matching funds; grants to individuals.

Focus of giving: Giving primarily in areas where company has major facilities and a large number of employees: AL, CA (Anaheim, Los Angeles, Torrance), CT (Berlin, Farmington, Hartford, Shelton, Windsor), IL (Broadview), IN (Indianapolis), KY (Campbellsville), MA (Beverly, Fall River, Middleton, New Bedford, South Hadley, Whitman), MI (Mount Clemens), MO, NE (Lincoln), NH, NY (Elmira, Maspeth), OH (Cleveland), PA (Huntington Valley, Reading, Temple), TN, VT (Springfield).

$ Given: $738,865 for 200 grants: high $45,000; low $100; average $2,694.

Contact: John F. Budd, Jr., Chairman, Contributions and Grants Committee

> **Initial approach:** brief letter or proposal
>
> **Deadlines:** submit proposal before October
>
> **Final notification:** by December

LOUISIANA

Eugene and Joseph Jones Family Foundation
835 Union Street, Suite 333
New Orleans, Louisiana 70115
(504) 581-2424

Areas of interest: Community development.

Restrictions: Grants for building funds.

Contact: Joseph M. Jones, Jr., Vice-President

The Lupin Foundation
3715 Prytania Street, Suite 403
New Orleans, Louisiana 70115
(504) 897-6125

Restrictions: Grants for equipment, research, scholarship funds, special projects, matching funds, continuing support, general purposes, program-related investments, renovation projects, and seed money. No grants to individuals; no loans.

Focus of giving: Giving primarily in Louisiana.

$ Given: $1,222,469, including $774,650 for 52 grants: high $75,000; low $800; average $15,000.

Assets: $19,482,186

Publications: Application guidelines.

> **Application information:** application form required
>
> **Initial approach:** brief proposal
>
> **Copies of proposal:** 9
>
> **Deadlines:** none

Board meeting dates: monthly

Final notification: 4 to 6 weeks

Murphy Foundation
200 Jefferson Avenue
El Dorado, Arkansas 71730
(501) 862-6411

Areas of interest: Civic affairs (historic preservation/restoration; museums/galleries).

Focus of giving: Major priority is for general purposes in Arkansas and Louisiana.

Restrictions: Grants for capital, general support, special projects; grants to individuals.

$ Given: $512,713 for 49 grants: high $106,969; low $175; average $1,000–$15,000.

Assets: $9,778,000

Contact: Lucy A. Ring

   Application information: application form required

Unocal Foundation
P. O. Box 7600
Los Angeles, California 90051
(213) 977-6171

Areas of interest: Arts and culture (museums/galleries, arts centers), civic and public affairs (business/free enterprise, economic development, urban and community affairs), education, health, and social services.

Restrictions: Grants for capital, general support, and special projects; grants to individuals.

Focus of giving: Nationally, with preference given to areas where Unocal maintains corporate facilities: AK (Kenai), CA (Brea, Los Angeles, Mountain Pass, San Francisco, Santa Maria), CO, IL (Chicago, Palatine), LA, NC (Charlotte), OR (Rivergate), TX (Beaumont).

$ Given: $4,571,472 for 397 grants: high $491,860; low $250; average $500–$5,000.

Contact: R. P. Van Zandt, Vice-President and Trustee

Initial approach: telephone

Deadlines: requests in by September 15

MAINE

George P. Davenport Trust Fund
55 Front Street
Bath, Maine 04530
(207) 443-3431

Areas of interest: Community development.

Restrictions: Grants for building funds.

MARYLAND

Morris Goldseker Foundation of Maryland, Inc.
300 North Charles Street, Suite 350
Baltimore, Maryland 21201
(301) 837-5100

Areas of interest: To address long-term solutions to community problems, strengthen neighborhoods, and strengthen the private, nonprofit sector; community affairs and housing.

Restrictions: Groups must have tax-exempt status; no grants to individuals or for building campaigns.

$ Given: $961,671 for 34 grants: high $53,807; low $5,000; median: $20,000.

Assets: $26,005,727

Publications: Annual report

Contact: Timothy D. Armbruster, Executive Director

   Application information: application form required

   Initial approach: letter

   Copies of proposal: 1

   Deadlines: preliminary letters and grant proposals are welcomed throughout the year; specific deadlines for fully-developed proposals: December 1, April 1, and August 1

   Board meeting dates: March, June, and October

Marion I. and Henry J. Knott Foundation, Inc.
Two West University Parkway
Baltimore, Maryland 21218
(301) 235-7068

Areas of interest: Community development.

Restrictions: Grants for building funds.

Contact: Joan Notarangelo

Noxell Foundation, Inc.
11050 York Road
Baltimore, Maryland 21031
(301) 628-7300

Areas of interest: Community development.

Restrictions: Grants for building funds.

Contact: Robert W. Lindsay, Treasurer

USF & G Foundation, Inc.
100 Light Street
Baltimore, Maryland 21202
(301) 547-3000

Areas of interest: Community development.

Restrictions: Grants for building funds.

Focus of giving: Grants given in areas of company operations.

Contact: Jack Moseley, President

MASSACHUSETTS

Bank of Boston Corporation Charitable Foundation
c/o Bank of Boston
P. O. Box 1861
Boston, Massachusetts 02108
(617) 434-2171

Areas of interest: Community development.

Restrictions: Grants for building funds.

Focus of giving: Grants given in areas of company operations.

Contact: Judith Kidd, Corporate Contributions

Bemis Company Foundation
800 Northstar Center
Minneapolis, Minnesota 55402
(612) 340-6198

Areas of interest: Urban and community affairs, arts centers, cinema, performing arts (general), business/free enterprise, special projects, economic development, education, health, and social services.

Restrictions: Grants for general support and matching funds; grants to individuals.

Focus of giving: Areas where company maintains facilities, with emphasis on Minneapolis, MN. AR (Crossett), CA (Los Angeles, Union City, Wilmington), CT (Plainfield, Stratford), FL (Panama City), IL (Murphysboro, Peoria, Schaumburg), IN (Indianapolis, Terre Haute), KS (Wichita), KY (Florence, Henderson, Louisville), MA (East Pepperell), MI (Grand Rapids, Zeeland), MN (Mankato, Minneapolis, Minnetonka), MO (Louisiana, Saint Louis, Springfield), MS (Verona), NC (Statesville), NE (Omaha), NH (Hudson, Nashua, North Walpole), NJ (Flemington), NY (Buffalo), OH (Stow), TN (Memphis), TX (Jacksonville), WA (Seattle, Vancouver), WI (Green Bay, New London, Oshkosh, Sheboygan).

$ Given: $700,000 for 826 grants; average $832.

Contact: Edward T. Dougherty, Executive Director
  Initial approach: brief letter or proposal
  Deadlines: applications accepted throughout the year

The Boston Foundation
Sixty State Street
Boston, Massachusetts 02108
(617) 723-7415

Areas of interest: Grants to institutions or for programs that benefit the health, welfare, recreational, educational, cultural, planning, and housing needs of the metropolitan Boston-area community.

Restrictions: Grants for new or experimental programs of both new and established institutions, as well as for capital needs. Organizations must have federal tax-exempt status. No grants are made to individuals.

Focus of giving: Giving limited to the Boston Standard Metropolitan Statistical Area only.

$ Given: $8,799,100 in grants; amount given varies; average $20,000–$25,000.

Publications: Information leaflet.

   Deadlines: none

   Board meeting dates: 4 times a year

Boston Globe Foundation
The Boston Globe Building
Boston, Massachusetts 02107
(617) 929-2895

Areas of interest: Community development.

Restrictions: Grants for building funds.

Contact: George M. Collins, Executive Director

Cabot Corporation Foundation, Inc.
c/o Cabot Corporation
125 High Street
Boston, Massachusetts 02110
(617) 890-0200

Areas of interest: Community development.

Restrictions: Grants for building funds.

Focus of giving: Grants given in areas of company operations.

Contact: Ruth C. Scheer, Executive Director

Emhart Corporation
426 Colt Highway
Farmington, Connecticut 06032
(203) 678-3204

Areas of interest: Arts and humanities (museums/galleries, zoos, operas, arts centers, historic preservation/restoration), civic and public affairs (business/free enterprise, urban and community affairs), education, health, and social services.

Restrictions: Grants for general support, capital, endowment, and matching funds; grants to individuals.

Focus of giving: Giving primarily in areas where company has major facilities and a large number of employees: AL, CA (Anaheim, Los Angeles, Torrance), CT (Berlin, Farmington, Hartford, Shelton, Windsor), IL (Broadview), IN (Indianapolis), KY (Campbellsville), MA (Beverly, Fall River, Middleton, New Bedford, South Hadley, Whitman), MI (Mount Clemens), MO, NE (Lincoln), NH, NY (Elmira, Maspeth), OH (Cleveland), PA (Huntington Valley, Reading, Temple), TN, VT (Springfield).

$ Given: $738,865 for 200 grants: high $45,000; low $100; average $2,694.

Contact: John F. Budd, Jr., Chairman, Contributions and Grants Committee

> **Initial approach:** brief letter or proposal
>
> **Deadlines:** submit proposal before October
>
> **Final notification:** by December

Fidelity Foundation
82 Devonshire Street
Boston, Massachusetts 02109
(617) 570-6806

Areas of interest: Community development.

Restrictions: Grants for building funds.

Contact: Anne-Marie Soulliere, Foundation Director

George F. and Sybil H. Fuller Foundation
105 Madison Street
Worcester, Massachusetts 01610
(617) 756-5111

Areas of interest: Community development.

Restrictions: Grants for building funds.

Contact: Robert Hallock, Chairman

Godfrey M. Hyams Trust
One Boston Place, 33rd Floor
Boston, Massachusetts 02108
(617) 720-2238

Areas of interest: Youth agencies and neighborhood centers; support also for other social service and community development purposes.

Restrictions: Grants given for operating budgets, continuing support, annual campaigns, seed money, building funds, equipment, land acquisition, and matching funds.

Focus of giving: Giving limited to the Boston, Massachusetts, metropolitan area.

$ Given: $2,793,499, including $2,481,387 for 170 grants: high $87,000; low $2,500; average $5,000–$20,000.

Contact: Joan M. Diver, Executive Director

    Initial approach: full proposal

    Copies of proposal: 6

    Deadlines: submit proposal preferably in fall or winter; no set deadline

    Board meeting dates: 5 to 6 times a year regularly from October through June

    Final notification: 2 to 6 months

Morgan-Worcester, Inc.
15 Belmont Street
Worcester, Massachusetts 01605
(617) 755-6111

Areas of interest: Community development.

Restrictions: Grants for building funds.

Contact: Peter S. Morgan, President

Theodore Edson Parker Foundation
100 Franklin Street
Boston, Massachusetts 02110
(617) 357-1500

Areas of interest: Community development and historic preservation.

Restrictions: Grants for building funds.

Contact: Ala H. Reid, Administrator

The Mabel Louise Riley Foundation*
100 Franklin Street
Boston, Massachusetts 02110
(617) 357-1500

Name of Program: Dudley Street Neighborhood Initiative.

Areas of interest: Social services and education, especially for youth; community development including cultural, housing, urban environmental, and energy conservation programs.

Restrictions: Support for pilot projects and capital purposes. Grants with multiplier or community-wide effects are favored over projects limited in scope or to a smaller geographic area.

Focus of giving: Grants are usually limited to the Greater Boston area.

$ Given: $1,050,000 for grants: high $100,000; low $30,000; average $40,000.

Contact: Newell Flather, Administrator
Mary Philips-Hall, Administrative Assistant
(617) 357-1514

> **Application information:** application form required
>
> **Initial approach:** letter or telephone full proposal
>
> **Copies of proposal:** 1
>
> **Deadlines:** February 15 and August 15 for grant meetings in April and October

Shawmut Charitable Foundation
c/o Shawmut Bank, N.A., 10th Floor
One Federal Street
Boston, Massachusetts 02211
(617) 292-3748

Areas of interest: Community development.

---

* The Riley Foundation is in the process of reviewing its grant-making focus; applicants may contact the Foundation to make sure the above policies are still in effect.

Restrictions: Grants for building funds.

Contact: Ms. Win Barnard, Administrator, Contributions

The Nathaniel and Elizabeth P. Stevens Foundation
P. O. Box 111
North Andover, Massachusetts 01845
(508) 688-7211

Restrictions: Grants given for general purposes, seed money, building funds, emergency funds, equipment, special projects, matching funds, land acquisition, and program-related investments.

Focus of giving: Giving limited to Massachusetts.

$ Given: $343,620 for 47 grants: high $50,000; low $750; average $2,000–$5,000.

Assets: $5,527,448

Contact: Elizabeth A. Beland
    Initial approach: full proposal
    Copies of proposal: 1
    Deadlines: none
    Board meeting dates: monthly, except in July and August
    Final notification: 2 months

Stoddard Charitable Trust
370 Main Street, Suite 1250
Worcester, Massachusetts 01608
(617) 757-9243

Areas of interest: Community development.

Restrictions: Grants for building funds.

Contact: Paris Fletcher, Secretary

Edwin S. Webster Foundation
c/o Investors Bank & Trust Co.
24 Federal Street
Boston, Massachusetts 02110
(617) 357-1510

Areas of interest: Community development.

Restrictions: Grants for building funds.

Contact: Richard Harte, Jr., Secretary

MICHIGAN

Ann Arbor Area Foundation
121 West Washington, Suite 400
Ann Arbor, Michigan 48104
(313) 663-0401

Areas of interest: Innovative programs and projects in charitable, religious, scientific, civic, moral, literary, cultural, social, and economic areas.

Restrictions: Grants for seed money, building funds, emergency funds, equipment, special projects, matching funds, program-related investments, publications, conferences, and seminars.

Focus of giving: Giving limited to Ann Arbor, Michigan, area.

$ Given: $71,022 for 21 grants.

Assets: $1,993,994

Contact: Terry Foster, Executive Director
   Application information: application form required
   Initial approach: telephone
   Deadlines: middle of month prior to meetings
   Board meeting dates: January, March, May, September, and November
   Final notification: 30 to 60 days

Bemis Company Foundation
800 Northstar Center
Minneapolis, Minnesota 55402
(612) 340-6198

Areas of interest: Urban and community affairs, arts centers, cinema, performing arts (general), business/free enterprise, economic development, education, health, and social services.

Restrictions: Grants for general support, special projects, and matching funds, grants to individuals.

Focus of giving: Areas where company maintains facilities, with emphasis on Minneapolis, MN. AR (Crossett), CA (Los Angeles, Union City, Wilmington), CT (Plainfield, Stratford), FL (Panama City), IL (Murphysboro, Peoria, Schaumburg), IN (Indianapolis, Terre Haute), KS (Wichita), KY (Florence, Henderson, Louisville), MA (East Pepperell), MI (Grand Rapids, Zeeland), MN (Mankato, Minneapolis, Minnetonka), MO (Louisiana, Saint Louis, Springfield), MS (Verona), NC (Statesville), NE (Omaha), NH (Hudson, Nashua, North Walpole), NJ (Flemington), NY (Buffalo), OH (Stow), TN (Memphis), TX (Jacksonville), WA (Seattle, Vancouver), WI (Green Bay, New London, Oshkosh, Sheboygan).

$ Given: $700,000 for 826 grants; average $832.

Contact: Edward T. Dougherty, Executive Director

  Initial approach: brief letter or proposal

  Deadlines: applications accepted throughout the year

Chrysler Corporation Fund
12000 Chrysler Drive
Highland Park, Michigan 48203
(313) 956-5194

Areas of interest: Community development.

Restrictions: Grants for building funds.

Focus of giving: Grants given in areas of company operations.

Contact: Lynn A. Feldhouse, Administrator

The Richard and Helen DeVos Foundation
7154 Windy Hill Road, S. E.
Grand Rapids, Michigan 49506
(616) 676-6225

Areas of interest: Civic affairs (economic development, urban and community affairs, business/free enterprise, community centers).

Restrictions: Grants for capital, general support, and special projects; grants to individuals.

Focus of giving: National distribution with priority given to religious programs and associations in Grand Rapids area.

$ Given: $783,078 for 65 grants: high $102,000 low $24; average $1,000–$25,000.

Assets: $6,883,417

Contact: Richard M. DeVos, President
   Initial approach: letter

Herbert H. and Grace A. Dow Foundation
P. O. Box 2184
Midland, Michigan 48641
(517) 636-2482

Areas of interest: Community development.

Restrictions: Grants for building funds.

Contact: Herbert H. Dow, President

Emhart Corporation
426 Colt Highway
Farmington, Connecticut 06032
(203) 678-3204

Areas of interest: Arts and humanities (museums/galleries, zoos, operas, arts centers, historic preservation/restoration), civic and public affairs (business/free enterprise, and urban and community affairs), education, health, and social services.

Restrictions: Grants for general support, capital, endowment, matching funds; grants to individuals.

Focus of giving: Giving primarily in areas where company has major facilities and a large number of employees: AL, CA (Anaheim, Los Angeles, Torrance), CT (Berlin, Farmington, Hartford, Shelton, Windsor), IL (Broadview), IN (Indianapolis), KY (Campbellsville), MA (Beverly, Fall River, Middleton, New Bedford, South Hadley, Whitman), MI (Mount Clemens), MO, NE (Lincoln), NH, NY (Elmira, Maspeth), OH (Cleveland), PA (Huntington Valley, Reading, Temple), TN, VT (Springfield).

$ Given: $738,865 for 200 grants: high $45,000; low $100; average $2,694.

Contact: John F. Budd, Jr., Chairman, Contributions and Grants Committee

    Initial approach: brief letter or proposal

    Deadlines: submit proposal before October

    Final notification: by December

Eleanor and Edsel Ford Fund
100 Renaissance Center, 34th Floor
Detroit, Michigan 48243

Areas of interest: Community development.

Restrictions: Grants for building funds.

Contact: Pierre V. Heftler, Secretary

Ford Motor Company Fund
The American Road
Dearborn, Michigan 48126
(313) 845-8711

Areas of interest: Economic development.

Restrictions: Grants for building funds.

Focus of giving: Grants given in areas of company operations.

Contact: Leo J. Brennan, Jr., Executive Director

General Motors Foundation, Inc.
13-145 General Motors Building
3044 W. Grand Boulevard
Detroit, Michigan 48202
(313) 556-4260

Areas of interest: Community and economic development, urban affairs.

Restrictions: Grants for building funds.

Focus of giving: Grants given in areas of company operations.

Contact: J. J. Nowicki, Manager

Rollin M. Gerstacker Foundation
P. O. Box 1945
Midland, Michigan 48641
(517) 631-6097

Areas of interest: Community development.

Restrictions: Grants for building funds.

Contact: E. N. Brandt, Secretary

Grand Rapids Foundation[*]
209-C Waters Building
161 Ottawa NW
Grand Rapids, Michigan 49503
(616) 454-1751

Restrictions: Grants for seed money, building funds, emergency funds, equipment, matching funds, and land acquisition.

Focus of giving: Giving limited to Kent County, Michigan.

$ Given: $1,122,617 for 55 grants: high $123,300; low $83; average $500–$100,000. Also $51,904 for grants to individuals and $80,500 for 37 loans.

Publications: Annual report, program policy statement, application guidelines, informational brochure, and newsletter.

Contact: Diana Sieger, Executive Director
   Application information: application form required
   Initial approach: letter or telephone
   Copies of proposal: 10
   Deadlines: 4 weeks preceding board meeting
   Board meeting dates: bimonthly, beginning in August
   Final notification: 1 month

---

[*] Community foundation established in 1922 in Michigan by resolution and declaration of trust.

Hudson-Webber Foundation
333 West Fort Street
Detroit, Michigan 48226
(313) 963-8991

Restrictions: Concentrates efforts and resources in support of physical revitalization of downtown Detroit, reduction of crime in Detroit, and economic development of southeastern Michigan, with emphasis on the creation of additional employment opportunities.

Focus of giving: Giving primarily in the Wayne, Oakland, and Macomb tricounty area of southeastern Michigan, particularly Detroit.

$ Given: $2,176,592 for 62 grants: high $213,000; low $2,400; average $10,000–30,000. Also $188,871 for 236 grants to individuals and $43,946 for 11 employee matching gifts.

Contact: Gilbert Hudson, President
   Deadlines: April 15, August 15, and December 15

Kalamazoo Foundation
151 S. Rose Street, Suite 332
Kalamazoo, Michigan 49007

Areas of interest: Community development.

Restrictions: Grants for building funds.

Contact: Howard D. Kalleward, Executive Director

Albert L. and Louise B. Miller Foundation, Inc.
155 West Van Buren Street
Battle Creek, Michigan 49016
(616) 964-7161

Restrictions: Local municipal improvement, grants for seed money, building funds, equipment, land acquisition, endowment funds, and loans.

Focus of giving: Giving primarily in the Battle Creek, Michigan, area.

$ Given: $100,600 for 32 grants: high $18,000; low $400; average $3,000.

Assets: $5,791,706

Contact: Robert B. Miller, Chairman

Application information: application form required

Initial approach: letter

Copies of proposal: 10

Deadlines: none

Board meeting dates: monthly

Final notification: 2 months

Muskegon County Community Foundation, Inc.[*]
Frauenthal Center, Suite 304
407 West Western Avenue
Muskegon, Michigan 49440
(616) 722-4538

Restrictions: Grants for seed money, building funds, equipment, special projects, matching funds, and land acquisition.

Focus of giving: Giving limited to Muskegon County, Michigan.

$ Given: $373,094 for 46 grants: high $58,600; low $200; average $1,000–$5,000. Also $163,259 for 192 grants to individuals and additional amounts as loans.

Publications: Annual report and application guidelines.

Contact: Patricia B. Johnson, Executive Director

Application information: application form required

Initial approach: letter or telephone

Copies of proposal: 12

Deadlines: January, April, July, or October

Board meeting dates: February, May, August, and November

Final notification: 2 to 3 weeks

Skillman Foundation
333 W. Fort Street, Suite 1350
Detroit, Michigan 48226
(313) 961-8850

[*]Community foundation incorporated in 1961 in Michigan.

Areas of interest: Community development.

Restrictions: Grants for building funds.

Contact: Kari Schlachtenhaufen, Program Officer

The Simpson Foundation*
c/o City Bank & Trust Company
One Jackson Square
Jackson, Michigan 49201
(517) 788-2711

Restrictions: Grants for seed money, building funds, emergency funds, equipment, special projects, and matching funds.

Focus of giving: Giving limited to Hillsdale County or to programs benefiting Hillsdale County, Michigan.

$ Given: $100,445 for grants: average $10,000.

Contact: Robert E. Carlson, Vice-President and Trust Officer
   Application information: application form required
   Initial approach: letter, full proposal, or telephone
   Deadlines: submit proposal preferably in August or September
   Board meeting dates: October
   Final notification: 30 to 60 days

Trust Corporation, Inc. Foundation
c/o Trust Corporation Bank, Ohio
Three Seagate
Toledo, Ohio 43603
(419) 259-8217

Restrictions: Charitable purposes: primarily local giving, with emphasis on community funds. Grants given for continuing support, building funds, emergency funds, equipment, and land acquisition.

Focus of giving: Giving primarily in tristate area of Indiana, Michigan, and Ohio.

*Established in 1980 in Michigan.

$ Given: $212,350 for 19 grants: high $148,000; low $100; average $1,000–$10,000.

Assets: $291,394

Contact: J. E. Lupe, Vice-President
    Initial approach: letter
    Deadlines: none
    Board meeting dates: monthly
    Final notification: 2 months

Whirlpool Foundation
North Shore Drive
Benton Harbor, Michigan 49022
(616) 926-3461

Areas of interest: Community development.

Restrictions: Grants for building funds.

Focus of giving: Grants given in areas of company operations.

Contact: Patricia O'Day, Secretary

Harvey Randall Wickes Foundation
Plaza North, Suite 472
4800 Fashion Square Boulevard
Saginaw, Michigan 48601
(517) 799-1850

Areas of interest: Community development.

Restrictions: Grants for building funds.

MINNESOTA

Bemis Company Foundation
800 Northstar Center
Minneapolis, Minnesota 55402
(612) 340-6198

Areas of interest: Urban and community affairs, arts centers, cinema, performing arts (general), business/free enterprise, economic development, education, health, and social services.

Restrictions: Grants for general support, special projects, and matching funds; grants to individuals.

Focus of giving: Areas where company maintains facilities, with emphasis on Minneapolis, MN. AR (Crossett), CA (Los Angeles, Union City, Wilmington), CT (Plainfield, Stratford), FL (Panama City), IL (Murphysboro, Peoria, Schaumburg), IN (Indianapolis, Terre Haute), KS (Wichita), KY (Florence, Henderson, Louisville), MA (East Pepperell), MI (Grand Rapids, Zeeland), MN (Mankato, Minneapolis, Minnetonka), MO (Louisiana, Saint Louis, Springfield), MS (Verona), NC (Statesville), NE (Omaha), NH (Hudson, Nashua, North Walpole), NJ (Flemington), NY (Buffalo), OH (Stow), TN (Memphis), TX (Jacksonville), WA (Seattle, Vancouver), WI (Green Bay, New London, Oshkosh, Sheboygan).

$ Given: $700,000 for 826 grants; average $832.

Contact: Edward T. Dougherty, Executive Director

　　Initial approach: brief letter or proposal

　　Deadlines: applications accepted throughout the year

F. R. Bigelow Foundation
c/o First Trust Company, Inc.
West 555 First National Bank Building
St. Paul, Minnesota 55101
(612) 224-5463

Areas of interest: Community development.

Restrictions: Grants for building funds.

Contact: Paul A. Verret, Secretary

Charles K. Blandin Foundation*
100 Pokegama Avenue North
Grand Rapids, Minnesota 55744
(218) 326-0523

---

*Incorporated in 1941 in Minnesota.

Restrictions: Local giving for community projects and economic development. Support for seed money, emergency funds, special projects, loans, program-related investments, consulting services, and technical assistance.

Focus of giving: Giving limited to Minnesota, with emphasis on rural Minnesota.

$ Given: $4,192,734 for 152 grants: high $450,000; low $500. Also $215,071 for 378 grants to individuals and $110,000 for two loans.

Assets: $17,651,437

Publications: Annual report, program policy statement, and application guidelines.

Contact: Paul M. Olson, Executive Director

> **Initial approach:** letter
>
> **Copies of proposal:** 1
>
> **Deadlines:** submit proposal preferably 2 months prior to board meetings: March 1, June 1, September 1, and December 1
>
> **Board meeting dates:** first week of February, May, August, and November
>
> **Final notification:** 2 months after board meeting

First Bank System Foundation
P. O. Box 522
Minneapolis, Minnesota 55480
(612) 370-4359

Areas of interest: Community development.

Restrictions: Grants for building funds.

Focus of giving: Grants given in areas of company operations.

Graco Foundation
P. O. Box 1441
Minneapolis, Minnesota 55440
(612) 623-6679

Areas of interest: Community development.

Restrictions: Grants for building funds.

Focus of giving: Grants given in areas of company operations.

Contact: David L. Schoeneck, Executive Director

Honeywell Foundation
Honeywell Plaza
Minneapolis, Minnesota 55408
(612) 870-6821

Areas of interest: Community development.

Restrictions: Grants for building funds.

Focus of giving: Grants given in areas of company operations.

Contact: M. Patricia Hoven, Director

Mary Andersen Hulings Foundation
c/o Baywood Corporation
287 Central Avenue
Bayport, Minnesota 55003
(612) 439-1557

Restrictions: Support for general purposes, operating budgets, building funds, program-related investments, research, and seed money.

Focus of giving: Giving primarily in Minnesota, with emphasis on Bayport.

$ Given: $191,665 for 62 grants: high $35,000; low $100.

Assets: $4,169,468

Contact: Peggy Scott, Grants Consultant
   Application information: application form required
   Initial approach: letter or proposal
   Copies of proposal: 2
   Deadlines: submit proposal preferably in March, June, September, or December; no set deadlines
   Board meeting dates: May, August, November, and February
   Final notification: 3 months

The McNeely Foundation
444 Pine Street
St. Paul, Minnesota 55101
(612) 228-4444

Restrictions: Grants for community funds including operating budgets, continuing support, annual campaigns for building funds, emergency funds, matching funds, program-related investments, endowment funds, and seed money.

Focus of giving: Giving primarily in the St. Paul-Minneapolis area.

$ Given: $120,000 for 20 grants: high $40,000; low $500; average $3,000–5,000.

Assets: $2,600,000

Contact: Malcolm W. McDonald

    Initial approach: letter

    Copies of proposal: 1

    Deadlines: submit proposal preferably in September or December

    Board meeting dates: March, June, September, and December

The McKnight Foundation
410 Peavey Building
Minneapolis, Minnesota 55402
(612) 333-4220

Areas of interest: Grants for human and social services in the seven-county Twin Cities metropolitan area and in Minnesota; for multiyear comprehensive programs in mental health and developmental disabilities. Also support for programs for the chronically mentally ill in four different communities.

Restrictions: Grants for operating budgets, seed money, continuing support, building funds, emergency funds, equipment, matching funds, and program-related investments.

$ Given: $11,945,119 for 200 grants: high $700,000; low $250; average $5,000–$500,000. Also $3,519,338 for 53 for grants to individuals.

Assets: $509,422,638

Contact: Russell V. Ewald, Executive Vice-President

Initial approach: letter

Copies of proposal: 7

Deadlines: March 1, June 1, September 1, and December 1

Board meeting dates: February, May, August, and November

Final notification: $2\frac{1}{2}$ months

Northwest Area Foundation
West 975 First National Bank Building
St. Paul, MN 55101-1373
(612) 224-9635

Areas of interest: Economic development and community revitalization.

Restrictions: Tax-exempt, nonprofit organizations with appropriate interests located in Minnesota, South and North Dakota, Iowa, Montana, Idaho, Oregon, and Washington are eligible to apply.

$ Given: Grants vary in amount, depending upon the needs and nature of the request. The foundation has a policy limiting a single grant to a maximum of $300,000. $25,000 average.

Contact: Karl Stauber, Vice-President, Programs

   Initial approach: written proposal

   Deadlines: applications are reviewed at bimonthly meetings of the board of directors; allow a minimum of 10 to 12 weeks for study and processing of an application in preparation for review at a board meeting

   Board meeting dates: bimonthly

Otto Bremer Foundation
55 East Fifth Street, Suite 700
St. Paul, Minnesota 55101
(612) 227-8036

Areas of interest: Community funds and building grants.

Restrictions: Nonprofit, tax-exempt organizations and programs having a direct impact on the service areas of the 26 Bremer banks in Minnesota, North Dakota, and Wisconsin, and within the city of St. Paul.

$ Given: Grants vary in amount, depending upon the needs and nature of the request.

Contact: John Kostishack, Executive Director

Initial approach: contact the foundation staff by telephone or letter for assistance in the development of a proposal

Deadlines: requests are reviewed continually.

Board meeting dates: once a month

The St. Paul Foundation
1120 Norwest Center
St. Paul, Minnesota 55101
(612) 224-5463

Areas of interest: Educational, charitable, cultural, or benevolent purposes of a public nature as well as promotion of the well-being of humankind and, preferably, the inhabitants of St. Paul and its vicinity.

Restrictions: Grants for seed money, building funds, emergency funds, equipment, special projects, matching funds, and program-related investments.

$ Given: $13,033,824 for 381 grants: high $9,967,964; low $60. Also $324,168 for seven loans.

Assets: $73,859,367

Contact: Paul A. Verret, President

Initial approach: telephone, letter, or full proposal

Copies of proposal: 1

Deadlines: 3 months before next board meeting

Board meeting dates: Generally in March, June, September, November, and December

Tozer Foundation, Inc.
c/o First Trust Company, Inc.
180 East 5th Street
P. O. Box 64367
St. Paul, Minnesota 55164
(612) 291-5134

Areas of interest: Community development.

Restrictions: Grants for building funds.

Contact: Grant T. Waldref, President

MISSISSIPPI

Bemis Company Foundation
800 Northstar Center
Minneapolis, Minnesota 55402
(612) 340-6198

Areas of interest: Urban and community affairs, arts centers, cinema, performing arts (general), business/free enterprise, economic development, education, health, and social services.

Restrictions: Grants for general support, special projects, and matching funds; grants to individuals.

Focus of giving: Areas where company maintains facilities, with emphasis on Minneapolis, MN. AR (Crossett), CA (Los Angeles, Union City, Wilmington), CT (Plainfield, Stratford), FL (Panama City), IL (Murphysboro, Peoria, Schaumburg), IN (Indianapolis, Terre Haute), KS (Wichita), KY (Florence, Henderson, Louisville), MA (East Pepperell), MI (Grand Rapids, Zeeland), MN (Mankato, Minneapolis, Minnetonka), MO (Louisiana, Saint Louis, Springfield), MS (Verona), NC (Statesville), NE (Omaha), NH (Hudson, Nashua, North Walpole), NJ (Flemington), NY (Buffalo), OH (Stow), TN (Memphis), TX (Jacksonville), WA (Seattle, Vancouver), WI (Green Bay, New London, Oshkosh, Sheboygan).

$ Given: $700,000 for 826 grants; average $832.

Contact: Edward T. Dougherty, Executive Director
    Initial approach: brief letter or proposal
    Deadlines: applications accepted throughout the year

Phil Hardin Foundation
P. O. Box 4329
Meridian, Mississippi 39301
(601) 483-4282

Restrictions: Grants for operating budgets, continuing support, seed money, building funds, equipment, special projects, program-related investments, research, publications, conferences, and seminars.

Focus of giving: Giving primarily in Mississippi, but also out-of-state organizations or programs of benefit to the people of Mississippi.

$ Given: $342,664 for 28 grants: high $150,000; low $500; average $12,000.

Assets: $12,912,048

Contact: C. Thompson Wacaster, Vice-President

   Initial approach: telephone, letter, or proposal

   Copies of proposal: 2

   Deadlines: none

   Board meeting dates: as required, usually at least every 2 months

---

MISSOURI

Anheuser-Busch Companies, Inc.
Anheuser-Busch Foundation
One Busch Place
St. Louis, Missouri 63118
(314) 557-7368

Areas of interest: Building funds (especially for hospitals), capital campaigns, community and urban affairs, and general support.

Restrictions: Organizations must be tax-exempt under 501 (c) 3. No grants to individuals.

Focus of giving: National (most grants in company-operating areas); CA (Fairfield, Los Angeles, Oakland), CO (Fort Collins), FL (Jacksonville, Tampa), MN (Moorhead), MO (St. Louis), NH (Merrimack, Durham, Nashua), NJ (Newark), NY (Baldwinsville), OH (Columbus), TX (Houston), VA (Williamsburg).

$ Given: $20,000,000 for grants: average $10,000–$50,000.

Assets: $32,559,020

Contact: Cindy Garonne, Contributions Administrator

Application information: application form required

Initial approach: full proposal

Copies of proposal: 1

Deadlines: applications accepted throughout the year

Board meeting dates: committee meets every 2 months

Final notification: 6 to 8 weeks

Bemis Company Foundation
800 Northstar Center
Minneapolis, Minnesota 55402
(612) 340-6198

Areas of interest: Urban and community affairs, arts centers, cinema, performing arts (general), business/free enterprise, economic development, education, health, and social services.

Restrictions: Grants for general support, special projects and matching funds; grants to individuals.

Focus of giving: Areas where company maintains facilities, with emphasis on Minneapolis, MN. AR (Crossett), CA (Los Angeles, Union City, Wilmington), CT (Plainfield, Stratford), FL (Panama City), IL (Murphysboro, Peoria, Schaumburg), IN (Indianapolis, Terre Haute), KS (Wichita), KY (Florence, Henderson, Louisville), MA (East Pepperell), MI (Grand Rapids, Zeeland), MN (Mankato, Minneapolis, Minnetonka), MO (Louisiana, Saint Louis, Springfield), MS (Verona), NC (Statesville), NE (Omaha), NH (Hudson, Nashua, North Walpole), NJ (Flemington), NY (Buffalo), OH (Stow), TN (Memphis), TX (Jacksonville), WA (Seattle, Vancouver), WI (Green Bay, New London, Oshkosh, Sheboygan).

$ Given: $700,000 for 826 grants; average $832.

Contact: Edward T. Dougherty, Executive Director

   Initial approach: brief letter or proposal

   Deadlines: applications accepted throughout the year

Brown Group, Inc. Charitable Trust
8400 Mayland Avenue
St. Louis, Missouri 63105
(314) 845-4120

Areas of interest: Community development.

Restrictions: Grants for building funds.

Contact: J. Carr Gamble, Jr., Secretary

Butler Manufacturing Company Foundation*
BMA Tower, P. O. Box 917
Penn Valley Park
Kansas City, Missouri 64141

Areas of interest: Minorities and the handicapped, preservation of urban neighborhoods, and development and improvement of agriculture and industry.

Restrictions: Support for seed money, building funds, emergency funds, equipment, matching funds, general purposes, and special projects.

$ Given: $281,472 for 102 grants. $74,166 for 38 grants to individuals and $4,550 for five loans.

Assets: $2,431,279

Publications: Annual report, program policy statement, application guidelines, and informational brochure.

Contact: Barbara Fay

  Initial approach: letter or telephone

  Copies of proposal: 1

  Deadlines: submit proposal preferably in month prior to board meetings

  Board meeting dates: March, June, September, and December

  Final notification: 6 months

Centerre Bank, N.A. Charitable Trust
One Centerre Plaza, MS 28-03
St. Louis, Missouri 63101
(314) 554-6541

*Incorporated in 1922 in Missouri.

Areas of interest: Community development.

Restrictions: Grants for building funds.

Emhart Corporation
426 Colt Highway
Farmington, Connecticut 06032
(203) 678-3204

Areas of interest: Arts and humanities (museums/galleries, zoos, operas, arts centers, historic preservation/restoration), civic and public affairs (business/free enterprise, urban and community affairs), education, health, and social services.

Restrictions: Grants for general support, capital, endowment, and matching funds; grants to individuals.

Focus of giving: Giving primarily in areas where company has major facilities and a large number of employees: AL, CA (Anaheim, Los Angeles, Torrance), CT (Berlin, Farmington, Hartford, Shelton, Windsor), IL (Broadview), IN (Indianapolis), KY (Campbellsville), MA (Beverly, Fall River, Middleton, New Bedford, South Hadley, Whitman), MI (Mount Clemens), MO, NE (Lincoln), NH, NY (Elmira, Maspeth), OH (Cleveland), PA (Huntington Valley, Reading, Temple), TN, VT (Springfield).

$ Given: $738,865 for 200 grants: high $45,000; low $100; average $2,694.

Contact: John F. Budd, Jr., Chairman, Contributions and Grants Committee

    Initial approach: brief letter or proposal

    Deadlines: submit proposal before October

    Final notification: by December

The H&R Block Foundation
4410 Main Street
Kansas City, Missouri 64111
(816) 932-8424

Restrictions: Support for general purposes, building funds, emergency funds, equipment, matching funds, land acquisition, program-related investments, operating budgets, seed money, and deficit financing.

Focus of giving: Giving limited to the 50-mile area around Kansas City.

$ Given: $233,955 for 131 grants: high $26,000; low $50; average $500–25,000. Also $60,000 for 30 grants to individuals and $5,100 for 22 employee matching gifts.

Assets: $3,739,311

Publications: Informational brochure, program policy statement, and application guidelines.

Donor: H&R Block, Inc.

Contact: Terrance R. Wood, President
   Initial approach: full proposal
   Copies of proposal: 1
   Deadlines: 45 days prior to meetings
   Board meeting dates: March, June, September, and December
   Final notification: 2 weeks after board meeting

Hall Family Foundations
Charitable & Crown Investment—323
P. O. Box 419580
Kansas City, Missouri 64141-6580
(816) 274-5615

Areas of interest: Broad purposes, within four main areas of interest: (1) youth, especially education and programs that promote social welfare, health, and character building of young people; (2) economic development; (3) the performing and visual arts; and (4) the elderly.

Focus of giving: Giving limited to the Kansas City, Missouri, area.

$ Given: $155,550 for 110 grants to individuals and $3,768,407 for 52 grants: high $1,966,921; low $1,000; average $35,000. Also $130,600 for 89 loans.

Assets: $117,877,180

Contact: Sarah V. Hutchison, Margaret H. Pence, or Wendy Hockaday, Program Officers
   Initial approach: letter
   Copies of proposal: 1

Deadlines: 4 weeks before board meetings

Board meeting dates: March, June, September, and December

Final notification: 4 to 6 weeks

Monsanto Fund
800 N. Lindbergh Boulevard
St. Louis, Missouri 63166
(314) 694-2742

Areas of interest: Community development.

Restrictions: Grants for building funds.

Focus of giving: Grants given in areas of company operations.

Contact: Sharon R. Bull, Secretary

Pulitzer Publishing Company Foundation
900 North Tucker Boulevard
St. Louis, Missouri 63101
(314) 622-7357

Areas of interest: Arts and culture (museums/galleries, historic preservation/restoration), civic and public affairs (business/free enterprise), education, health, and social services.

Restrictions: Grants for capital, endowment, general support, and special projects; grants to individuals.

Focus of giving: Giving primarily in St. Louis metropolitan area.

$ Given: $551,487 for 105 grants: high $100,000; low $100; average $1,000–$10,000.

Contact: Ronald H. Ridgeway, Treasurer and Director
    Initial approach: letter or proposal
    Deadlines: none

J. B. Reynolds Foundation
3520 Broadway
P. O. Box 139
Kansas City, Missouri 64111
(816) 753-7000

Areas of interest: Community development.

Restrictions: Grants for building funds.

Contact: Walter E. Bixby, Vice-President

Union Electric Company Charitable Trust
1901 Gratiot Street
P. O. Box 149
St. Louis, Missouri 63166
(314) 621-3222

Areas of interest: Community and urban development.

Restrictions: Grants for building funds.

Focus of giving: Grants given in areas of company operations.

MONTANA

Fred Meyer Charitable Trust
1515 Southwest Fifth Avenue, Suite 500
Portland, Oregon 97201
(503) 228-5512

Restrictions: Support for seed money, building funds, equipment, special projects, and matching funds.

Focus of giving: Support primarily in Oregon, with occasional grants at the initiative of the trust for programs in Washington, Idaho, Montana, and Alaska.

$ Given: $6,365,583 for 94 grants: high $555,000; low $964; average $20,000–$75,000.

Assets: $171,639,900

Contact: Charles S. Rooks, Executive Director
    Application information: application form required
    Initial approach: letter or full proposal
    Copies of proposal: 1
    Deadlines: none

Board meeting dates: monthly

Final notification: 4 to 6 months for proposals that pass first screening; 2 to 3 months for those that do not

**Northwest Area Foundation
West 975 First National Bank Building
St. Paul, Minnesota 55101
(612) 224-9635**

Restrictions: Grants generally for experimental and demonstration projects that promise significant impact on the community and the well-being of society but for which there is not now general support.

Focus of giving: Giving limited to an eight-state region that includes Idaho, Iowa, Minnesota, Montana, North Dakota, Oregon, South Dakota, and Washington.

$ Given: $6,967,105 for 196 grants: high $250,000; low $150; average $20,000–$60,000.

Contact: Terry Tinson, President

  Initial approach: letter, telephone, or proposal

  Copies of proposal: 2

  Deadlines: varies

  Board meeting dates: bimonthly, beginning in February

  Final notification: 60 to 90 days

NEBRASKA

**Bemis Company Foundation
800 Northstar Center
Minneapolis, Minnesota 55402
(612) 340-6198**

Areas of interest: Urban and community affairs, arts centers, cinema, performing arts (general), business/free enterprise, economic development, education, health, and social services.

Restrictions: Grants for general support, special projects, and matching funds; grants to individuals.

Focus of giving: Areas where company maintains facilities, with emphasis on Minneapolis, MN. AR (Crossett), CA (Los Angeles, Union City, Wilmington), CT (Plainfield, Stratford), FL (Panama City), IL (Murphysboro, Peoria, Schaumburg), IN (Indianapolis, Terre Haute), KS (Wichita), KY (Florence, Henderson, Louisville), MA (East Pepperell), MI (Grand Rapids, Zeeland), MN (Mankato, Minneapolis, Minnetonka), MO (Louisiana, Saint Louis, Springfield), MS (Verona), NC (Statesville), NE (Omaha), NH (Hudson, Nashua, North Walpole), NJ (Flemington), NY (Buffalo), OH (Stow), TN (Memphis), TX (Jacksonville), WA (Seattle, Vancouver), WI (Green Bay, New London, Oshkosh, Sheboygan).

$ Given: $700,000 for 826 grants; average $832.

Contact: Edward T. Dougherty, Executive Director

    Initial approach: brief letter or proposal

    Deadlines: applications accepted throughout the year

Emhart Corporation
426 Colt Highway
Farmington, Connecticut 06032
(203) 678-3204

Areas of interest: Arts and humanities (museums/galleries, zoos, operas, arts centers, historic preservation/restoration), civic and public affairs (business/free enterprise, urban and community affairs), education, health, and social services.

Restrictions: Grants for general support, capital, endowment, and matching funds; grants to individuals.

Focus of giving: Giving primarily in areas where company has major facilities and a large number of employees: AL, CA (Anaheim, Los Angeles, Torrance), CT (Berlin, Farmington, Hartford, Shelton, Windsor), IL (Broadview), IN (Indianapolis), KY (Campbellsville), MA (Beverly, Fall River, Middleton, New Bedford, South Hadley, Whitman), MI (Mount Clemens), MO, NE (Lincoln), NH, NY (Elmira, Maspeth), OH (Cleveland), PA (Huntington Valley, Reading, Temple), TN, VT (Springfield).

$ Given: $738,865 for 200 grants: high $45,000; low $100; average $2,694.

Contact: John F. Budd, Jr., Chairman, Contributions and Grants Committee

Initial approach: brief letter or proposal

Deadlines: submit proposal before October

Final notification: by December

Omaha World-Herald Foundation
c/o Omaha World-Herald Company
14th and Dodge Streets
Omaha, Nebraska 68102
(402) 444-1000

Areas of interest: Community development.

Restrictions: Grants for building funds.

Contact: John Gottschak, Vice-President

NEVADA

E. L. Wiegand Foundation
One E. First Street, Suite 800
Reno, Nevada 89501
(702) 322-2242

Areas of interest: Community development.

Restrictions: Grants for building funds.

Contact: Raymond C. Avansino, President

NEW HAMPSHIRE

Bemis Company Foundation
800 Northstar Center
Minneapolis, Minnesota 55402
(612) 340-6198

Areas of interest: Urban and community affairs, arts centers, cinema, performing arts (general), business/free enterprise, economic development, education, health, and social services.

Restrictions: Grants for general support, special projects, and matching funds; grants to individuals.

Focus of giving: Areas where company maintains facilities, with emphasis on Minneapolis, MN. AR (Crossett), CA (Los Angeles, Union City, Wilmington), CT (Plainfield, Stratford), FL (Panama City), IL (Murphysboro, Peoria, Schaumburg), IN (Indianapolis, Terre Haute), KS (Wichita), KY (Florence, Henderson, Louisville), MA (East Pepperell), MI (Grand Rapids, Zeeland), MN (Mankato, Minneapolis, Minnetonka), MO (Louisiana, Saint Louis, Springfield), MS (Verona), NC (Statesville), NE (Omaha), NH (Hudson, Nashua, North Walpole), NJ (Flemington), NY (Buffalo), OH (Stow), TN (Memphis), TX (Jacksonville), WA (Seattle, Vancouver), WI (Green Bay, New London, Oshkosh, Sheboygan).

$ Given: $700,000 for 826 grants; average $832.

Contact: Edward T. Dougherty, Executive Director

    Initial approach: brief letter or proposal

    Deadlines: applications accepted throughout the year

Emhart Corporation
426 Colt Highway
Farmington, Connecticut 06032
(203) 678-3204

Areas of interest: Arts and humanities (museums/galleries, zoos, operas, arts centers, historic preservation/restoration), civic and public affairs (business/free enterprise, urban and community affairs), education, health, and social services.

Restrictions: Grants for general support, capital, endowment, and matching funds; grants to individuals.

Focus of giving: Giving primarily in areas where company has major facilities and a large number of employees: AL, CA (Anaheim, Los Angeles, Torrance), CT (Berlin, Farmington, Hartford, Shelton, Windsor), IL (Broadview), IN (Indianapolis), KY (Campbellsville), MA (Beverly, Fall River, Middleton, New Bedford, South Hadley, Whitman), MI (Mount Clemens), MO, NE (Lincoln), NH, NY (Elmira, Maspeth), OH (Cleveland), PA (Huntington Valley, Reading, Temple), TN, VT (Springfield).

$ Given: $738,865 for 200 grants: high $45,000; low $100; average $2,694.

Contact: John F. Budd, Jr., Chairman, Contributions and Grants Committee

Initial approach: brief letter or proposal

Deadlines: submit proposal before October

Final notification: by December

The New Hampshire Charitable Fund[*]
One South Street
P. O. Box 1335
Concord, New Hampshire 03302-1335
(603) 255-6641

Restrictions: Grants for seed money, loans, general purposes, and special projects; grants to individuals.

Focus of giving: Giving limited to New Hampshire.

$ Given: $1,239,056 for 354 grants: high $207,966; low $78. Also $349,636 for 175 loans and $349,636 for 205 grants to individuals.

Publications: Annual report, program policy statement, application guidelines, and newsletter.

Contact: Deborah Cowan, Associate Director

    Initial approach: telephone

    Deadlines: February 1, May 1, August 1, and November 1

    Board meeting dates: March, June, September, and December

    Final notification: 4 to 6 weeks

Norwin S. and Elizabeth N. Bean Foundation[**]
c/o New Hampshire Charitable Fund
One South Street
P.O. Box 1335
Concord, New Hampshire 03302-1335
(603) 225-6641

Restrictions: Grants for general purposes, building funds, emergency funds, equipment, special projects, matching funds, land acquisition, program-related investments, and seed money.

---

[*]Community foundation incorporated in 1962 in New Hampshire.

[**]Trust established in 1957 in New Hampshire; later became an affiliated trust of the New Hampshire Charitable Fund.

Focus of giving: Giving limited to Amherst and Manchester, New Hampshire.

$ Given: $274,691 for 31 grants: high $75,000; low $350; average $500–$5,000. Also $12,000 for one loan.

Assets: $5,298,067

Publications: Program policy statement and application guidelines.

Contact: Norwin S. Bean or Elizabeth N. Bean

> **Initial approach:** letter or telephone
>
> **Copies of proposal:** 6
>
> **Deadlines:** February 15, May 15, August 15, and November 15
>
> **Board meeting dates:** March, June, September, and December

---

NEW JERSEY

Allied-Signal Foundation
Allied-Signal, Inc.
Box 2245R
Morristown, New Jersey 07960
(201) 455-5876 or 455-5877

Restrictions: Grants for building funds, general support, matching funds, special projects, and seed money. Organizations that do not qualify as tax-exempt under 501 (c) 3 may be considered for funding by the corporation; organizations must be tax-exempt under 501 (c) 3 to be funded by the foundation.

Focus of giving: National (emphasis on principal company-operating areas in 600 plant communities).

$ Given: Grants: high $200,000; low $1,000; average $2,500–$5,000.

Assets: $10,226,000,000 (Corporate); $159,996 (Foundation)

Contact: Alan S. Painter, Vice-President and Executive Director

> **Initial approach:** letter or telephone
>
> **Copies of proposal:** 1
>
> **Deadlines:** applications accepted throughout the year, but foundation prefers to receive applications between June and August
>
> **Final notification:** decisions generally made as budget is prepared in the fall

Bemis Company Foundation
800 Northstar Center
Minneapolis, Minnesota 55402
(612) 340-6198

Areas of interest: Urban and community affairs, arts centers, cinema, performing arts (general), business/free enterprise, economic development, education, health, and social services.

Restrictions: Grants for general support, special projects, and matching funds; grants to individuals.

Focus of giving: Areas where company maintains facilities, with emphasis on Minneapolis, MN. AR (Crossett), CA (Los Angeles, Union City, Wilmington), CT (Plainfield, Stratford), FL (Panama City), IL (Murphysboro, Peoria, Schaumburg), IN (Indianapolis, Terre Haute), KS (Wichita), KY (Florence, Henderson, Louisville), MA (East Pepperell), MI (Grand Rapids, Zeeland), MN (Mankato, Minneapolis, Minnetonka), MO (Louisiana, Saint Louis, Springfield), MS (Verona), NC (Statesville), NE (Omaha), NH (Hudson, Nashua, North Walpole), NJ (Flemington), NY (Buffalo), OH (Stow), TN (Memphis), TX (Jacksonville), WA (Seattle, Vancouver), WI (Green Bay, New London, Oshkosh, Sheboygan).

$ Given: $700,000 for 826 grants; average $832.

Contact: Edward T. Dougherty, Executive Director

   Initial approach: brief letter or proposal

   Deadlines: applications accepted throughout the year

Campbell Soup Fund
Campbell Place
Camden, New Jersey 08103
(609) 342-6431

Areas of interest: Community development.

Restrictions: Grants for building funds.

Focus of giving: Grants given in areas of company operations.

Contact: Frank G. Moore, Vice-President

Geraldine R. Dodge Foundation, Inc.
95 Madison Avenue
P.O. Box 1239
Morristown, New Jersey 07960-1239
(201) 540-8442

Restrictions: Grant-making emphasis in New Jersey for projects and programs in the public interest. Grants for seed money, matching funds, and special projects. No grants to individuals.

$ Given: $4,015,288 for 199 grants: high $285,500; average $5,000–$100,000.

Assets: $97,285,629

Contact: Scott McVay, Executive Director

    Initial approach: letter or full proposal

    Copies of proposal: 1

    Deadlines: submit proposal preferably in March, June, September, or December; deadlines January 1 for local projects, October 1 for critical issues/public interest

    Board meeting dates: March, June, September, and December

    Final notification: by the end of the month in which board meetings are held

Merck Company Foundation
P. O. Box 2000
Rahway, New Jersey 07065
(201) 574-4375

Areas of interest: Community development.

Restrictions: Grants for building funds.

Focus of giving: Grants given in areas of company operations.

Contact: Vernon B. Baker, Executive Vice-President

Nabisco Foundation
195 River Road
East Hanover, New Jersey 07936

Areas of interest: Community development.

Restrictions: Grants for building funds.

Focus of giving: Grants given in areas of company operations.

Contact: Henry A. Sandbach, Vice-President, Public Relations

Prudential Foundation
Prudential Plaza
Newark, New Jersey 07101
(201) 877-7354

Areas of interest: Community development.

Restrictions: Grants for building funds.

Contact: Donald N. Treloar, Secretary

Union Camp Charitable Trust
c/o Union Camp Corporation
1600 Valley Road
Wayne, New Jersey 07470
(201) 628-2232

Areas of interest: Community development.

Restrictions: Grants for building funds.

Contact: Harold Hoss, Treasurer

Victoria Foundation, Inc.
40 S. Fullerton Avenue
Montclair, New Jersey 07042
(201) 783-4450

Areas of interest: Community development.

Restrictions: Grants for building funds.

Contact: Howard E. Quirk, Executive Officer

Warner-Lambert Foundation
201 Tabor Road
Morris Plains, New Jersey 07950
(201) 540-2243

Areas of interest: Community development.

Restrictions: Grants for building funds.

Focus of giving: Grants given in areas of company operations.

Contact: Evelyn Self, Director of Community Affairs

NEW MEXICO

Carlsbad Foundation, Inc.*
116 South Canyon
Carlsbad, New Mexico 88220
(505) 887-1131

Restrictions: Support given in the form of loans, operating budgets, building funds, emergency funds, equipment, special projects, matching funds, program-related investments, and seed money.

Focus of giving: Giving limited to South Eddy County, New Mexico.

$ Given: $249,513, including $62,853 for grants, $92,781 for grants to individuals, and $400,000 for one loan.

Assets: $2,464,031

Publications: Annual report, program policy statement, and application guidelines.

Contact: John Mills, Executive Director

NEW YORK

The Vincent Astor Foundation
405 Park Avenue
New York, New York 10022
(212) 758-4110

Restrictions: No formal restrictions on the purposes for which grants may be made; however, grants are confined almost without exception to institutions and projects in New York such as neighborhood revitalization projects, parks and landmark preservation, and community-based projects, often involving children or the elderly. No grants to individuals.

---

*Incorporated in 1977 in New Mexico.

$ Given: $6,702,833 in grants.

  Initial approach: letter

  Copies of proposal: 1

  Deadlines: one

  Board meeting dates: April, October, and December

  Final notification: several months

AT&T Foundation
550 Madison Avenue
New York, New York 10022
(212) 605-6734

Areas of interest: Community development.

Restrictions: Grants for building funds.

Focus of giving: Grants given in areas of company operations.

Contact: Sheila A. Connolly, Secretary

The Buffalo Foundation
237 Main Street
Buffalo, New York 14203
(716) 852-2857

Restrictions: Grants for operating budgets, seed money, building funds, emergency funds, equipment, special projects, matching funds, and land acquisition.

Focus of giving: Programs and agencies must benefit and enhance the quality of life of residents living in Erie County, New York.

$ Given: $1,289,111 for 123 grants: high $109,050; low $78. Also $245,263 for grants to individuals.

Contact: W. L. Van Schoonhoven, Director

  Initial approach: letter or proposal

  Copies of proposal: 1

  Deadlines: applications must be received by the last day of March, June, September, or December

Board meeting dates: the Governing Committee meets on the first Wednesday of February, May, August, and November

Final notification: First meeting after submission of proposal

Bemis Company Foundation
800 Northstar Center
Minneapolis, Minnesota 55402
(612) 340-6198

Areas of interest: Urban and community affairs, arts centers, cinema, performing arts (general), business/free enterprise, economic development, education, health, and social services.

Restrictions: Grants for general support, special projects, and matching funds; grants to individuals.

Focus of giving: Areas where company maintains facilities, with emphasis on Minneapolis, MN. AR (Crossett), CA (Los Angeles, Union City, Wilmington), CT (Plainfield, Stratford), FL (Panama City), IL (Murphysboro, Peoria, Schaumburg), IN (Indianapolis, Terre Haute), KS (Wichita), KY (Florence, Henderson, Louisville), MA (East Pepperell), MI (Grand Rapids, Zeeland), MN (Mankato, Minneapolis, Minnetonka), MO (Louisiana, Saint Louis, Springfield), MS (Verona), NC (Statesville), NE (Omaha), NH (Hudson, Nashua, North Walpole), NJ (Flemington), NY (Buffalo), OH (Stow), TN (Memphis), TX (Jacksonville), WA (Seattle, Vancouver), WI (Green Bay, New London, Oshkosh, Sheboygan).

$ Given: $700,000 for 826 grants; average $832.

Contact: Edward T. Dougherty, Executive Director

Initial approach: brief letter or proposal

Deadlines: applications accepted throughout the year

Cecil Charitable Trust
111 Broadway, Suite 512
New York, New York 10006

Areas of interest: Historic preservation.

Restrictions: Support for general purposes, special projects, matching funds, program-related investments, and seed money.

Focus of giving: Giving primarily in New York and Vermont.

$ Given: $111,950 for 55 grants: high $10,000; low $100.

Assets: $1,196,880

Contact: George B. Cameron, Trustee

    Initial approach: letter

    Copies of proposal: 1

    Deadlines: April 1 and November 1

    Board meeting dates: May and December

The Clark Foundation
30 Wall Street
New York, New York 10005
(212) 269-1833

Restrictions: Grants for general purposes, urban and community affairs, and housing.

Focus of giving: Giving limited to northern New York and New York City.

$ Given: $5,166,843 for 783 grants: high $200,950; low $700; average $5,000–$25,000.

Assets: $160,554,423

Contact: Edward W. Stack, Secretary

    Initial approach: letter

    Copies of proposal: 1

    Board meeting dates: October, May, and other times during the year

Continental Corporation Foundation
180 Maiden Lane
New York, New York 10038
(212) 440-7729

Areas of interest: Community development.

Restrictions: Grants for building funds.

Focus of giving: Grants given in areas of company operations.

Corning Glass Works Foundation
Houghton House
22 West 3rd Street
Corning, New York 14830
(607) 974-8719

Areas of interest: Community development.

Restrictions: Grants for building funds.

Focus of giving: Grants given in areas of company operations.

Contact: Kristin A. Swain, Executive Director

Cowles Charitable Trust
630 Fifth Avenue, Suite 1612
New York, New York 10111
(212) 765-6262

Areas of interest: Community development.

Restrictions: Grants for building funds.

Contact: Martha Roby Stephens, Secretary

Dillon Fund, Inc.
1270 Avenue of the Americas, Room 2300
New York, New York 10020
(212) 315-8343

Areas of interest: Historic preservation.

Restrictions: Grants for building funds.

Contact: Crosby R. Smith, President

Fred L. Emerson Foundation, Inc.
P. O. Box 276
Auburn, New York 13021
(315) 253-9621

Areas of interest: Community development.

Restrictions: Grants for building funds.

Contact: Ronald D. West, Executive Director

Emhart Corporation
426 Colt Highway
Farmington, Connecticut 06032
(203) 678-3204

Areas of interest: Arts and humanities (museums/galleries, zoos, operas, arts centers, historic preservation/restoration), civic and public affairs (business/free enterprise, urban and community affairs), education, health, and social services.

Restrictions: Grants for general support, capital, endowment, and matching funds; grants to individuals.

Focus of giving: Giving primarily in areas where company has major facilities and a large number of employees: AL, CA (Anaheim, Los Angeles, Torrance), CT (Berlin, Farmington, Hartford, Shelton, Windsor), IL (Broadview), IN (Indianapolis), KY (Campbellsville), MA (Beverly, Fall River, Middleton, New Bedford, South Hadley, Whitman), MI (Mount Clemens), MO, NE (Lincoln), NH, NY (Elmira, Maspeth), OH (Cleveland), PA (Huntington Valley, Reading, Temple), TN, VT (Springfield).

$ Given: $738,865 for 200 grants: high $45,000; low $100; average $2,694.

Contact: John F. Budd, Jr., Chairman, Contributions and Grants Committee

    Initial approach: brief letter or proposal

    Deadlines: submit proposal before October

    Final notification: by December

The Equitable Life Assurance Society of the United States
Corporate Support Programs
Office of External Affairs
1285 Avenue of the Americas
New York, New York 10019
(212) 554-1057

Areas of interest: Miscellaneous, including support for projects involving business and economic research, community development, and preservation.

Restrictions: Grants are restricted to organizations and programs; support for individuals is generally not provided.

$ Given: $2,294,590 for 198 grants: high $60,000; low $450; average: $5,000.

Contact: Ellen McGoldrick, Director, Corporate Programs
  Initial approach: letter
  Deadlines: none
  Final notification: 3 to 4 weeks

Rosamond Gifford Charitable Corporation
731 James Street, Room 404
Syracuse, New York 13203
(315) 474-2489

Areas of interest: Community development.

Restrictions: Grants for building funds.

Contact: Dean A. Lesinski, Executive Director

The Glens Falls Foundation
55 Colvin Avenue
Albany, New York 12206
(518) 793-6302

Areas of interest: Broad purposes, including the promotion of the mental, moral, and physical improvement of the people of Glens Falls and environs.

Restrictions: Grants for seed money, building funds, emergency funds, equipment, special projects, and matching funds; grants to individuals.

Focus of giving: Giving limited to Warren, Washington, and Saratoga counties, New York; no loans.

$ Given: $73,369 for 29 grants: high $10,000; low $35. Also $7,500 for 27 grants to individuals.

Contact: Robert Gibeault, Administrator
  Initial approach: letter, telephone, or full proposal
  Copies of proposal: 8
  Deadlines: submit proposal preferably in December, March, June, or September; deadline first day of months in which board meets

Board meeting dates: second Wednesday in January, April, July, and October

Final notification: 2 days after quarterly meetings

Grace Foundation
Avenue of the Americas
New York, New York 10036
(212) 819-6316

Areas of interest: Community development.

Restrictions: Grants for building funds.

Contact: Richard I. Morris, President

Manufacturers Hanover Foundation
600 Fifth Avenue
New York, New York 10020
(212) 286-7124

Areas of interest: Community development.

Restrictions: Grants for building funds.

Merrill Lynch & Company Foundation, Inc.
One Liberty Plaza
165 Broadway
New York, New York 10080
(212) 637-8165

Areas of interest: Community development.

Restrictions: Grants for building funds.

Focus of giving: Grants given in areas of company operations.

Contact: Westina L. Mattews, Secretary

Morgan Guaranty Trust Company of New York Charitable Trust
23 Wall Street
New York, New York 10015
(212) 483-2058

Areas of interest: Housing, community development, and community rehabilitation.

Restrictions: Grants for general operating support, capital programs, building funds, and special projects. Only nonprofit 501 (c)(3) organizations are eligible for support.

$ Given: Grants vary in amount, depending upon the needs and nature of the request; range from $1,000 to $100,000.

Contact: Roberta Ruocco, Secretary, Contributions Committee
    Initial approach: application form and detailed request in writing
    Deadlines: committee meets on an ongoing basis

New York Life Foundation
51 Madison Avenue
New York, New York 10010
(212) 576-7341

Areas of interest: Community development.

Restrictions: Grants for building funds.

Contact: Carol J. Reuter, Executive Director

N. L. Industries Foundation, Inc.
1230 Avenue of the Americas
New York, New York 10020
(212) 698-2372

Areas of interest: Community development.

Restrictions: Grants for building funds.

Focus of giving: Grants given in areas of company operations.

Contact: Richmond W. Unwin, Jr., President

A. Lindsay and Olive B. O'Connor Foundation
P.O. Box D
Hobart, New York 13788
(607) 538-9248

Areas of interest: Broad purposes: local giving, with emphasis on "quality of life," including support for town, village, and environmental improvement.

Restrictions: Grants are awarded for general purposes, continuing support, building funds, emergency funds, equipment, special projects, matching funds, land acquisition, program-related investments, and seed money.

Focus of giving: Giving primarily in Delaware County, New York, and contiguous rural counties in upstate New York

$ Given: $1,262,964 for 45 grants: high $500,000; low $500; average $1,000–$20,000.

Contact: Donald F. Bishop, II, Executive Director

   Initial approach: letter

   Copies of proposal: 1

   Deadlines: April 1

   Board meeting dates: May or June and September or October; committee meets monthly to consider grants under $5,000

   Final notification: 1 week to 10 days after semi-annual meeting

Pfizer Foundation, Inc.
235 East 42nd Street
New York, New York 10017
(212) 573-3351

Areas of interest: Community development.

Restrictions: Grants for building funds.

Contact: Wyndham Anderson, Executive Vice-President

Helena Rubinstein Foundation, Inc.
405 Lexington Avenue
New York, New York 10174
(212) 986-0806

Areas of interest: Community development.

Restrictions: Grants for building funds.

Contact: Diane Moss, Executive Director

The John Ben Snow Foundation, Inc.
P.O. Box 376
Pulaski, New York 13142
(315) 298-6401

Restrictions: Community betterment projects.

Focus of giving: Giving limited to central New York.

$ Given: $257,600 for 13 grants: high $45,000; low $1,000; average $3,500.

Assets: $3,175,900

Contact: Vernon F. Snow, President

   Application information: application form required

   Initial approach: letter

   Copies of proposal: 1

   Deadlines: submit proposal between September and April; deadline is April 15

   Board meeting dates: June

Watertown Foundation, Inc.
c/o Chase Lincoln First National Bank
Chase Lincoln First Bank Building
216 Washington Street
Watertown, New York 13601
(315) 782-7110

Areas of interest: Community development.

Restrictions: Grants for building funds.

Contact: James E. McVean, Executive Director

NORTH CAROLINA

ABC Foundation
1201 Maple
Greensboro, North Carolina 27405
(919) 379-6717

Areas of interest: Arts and humanities, civic and public affairs, education, and health.

Restrictions: Grants for building funds; foundation will fund part of a capital project.

Focus of giving: Primarily in communities where Cone Mills Corporation maintains production facilities.

$ Given: $397,786

Assets: $4,343,589

Contact: William O. Leonard, Vice-President

    Initial approach: letter and brief proposal

    Copies of proposal: 1

    Deadlines: applications accepted throughout the year

    Board meeting dates: board meets annually and as necessary

Mary Reynolds Babcock Foundation, Inc.
102 Reynolds Village
Winston-Salem, North Carolina 27106-5123
(919) 748-9222

Areas of interest: Broad purposes, but primarily for social services, including community development and youth employment.

Restrictions: Grants for operating budgets, emergency funds, special projects, program-related investments, and seed money.

Focus of giving: Giving primarily in North Carolina and the southeastern United States.

$ Given: $3,127,491 for 156 grants: high $175,000; low $1,000; average $10,000–$50,000. Also $200,000 for two loans.

Assets: $40,601,750

Publications: Annual report, program policy statement, and application guidelines.

Contact: William L. Bondurant, Executive Director

    Application information: application form required

    Initial approach: letter, telephone, or full proposal

    Copies of proposal: 1

Deadlines: submit proposal between December and February or June and August; deadlines March 1 and September 1

Board meeting dates: May and November

Final notification: first week of the month following a board meeting

Bemis Company Foundation
800 Northstar Center
Minneapolis, Minnesota 55402
(612) 340-6198

Areas of interest: Urban and community affairs, arts centers, cinema, performing arts (general), business/free enterprise, economic development, education, health, and social services.

Restrictions: Grants for general support, special projects, and matching funds; grants to individuals.

Focus of giving: Areas where company maintains facilities, with emphasis on Minneapolis, MN. AR (Crossett), CA (Los Angeles, Union City, Wilmington), CT (Plainfield, Stratford), FL (Panama City), IL (Murphysboro, Peoria, Schaumburg), IN (Indianapolis, Terre Haute), KS (Wichita), KY (Florence, Henderson, Louisville), MA (East Pepperell), MI (Grand Rapids, Zeeland), MN (Mankato, Minneapolis, Minnetonka), MO (Louisiana, Saint Louis, Springfield), MS (Verona), NC (Statesville), NE (Omaha), NH (Hudson, Nashua, North Walpole), NJ (Flemington), NY (Buffalo), OH (Stow), TN (Memphis), TX (Jacksonville), WA (Seattle, Vancouver), WI (Green Bay, New London, Oshkosh, Sheboygan).

$ Given: $700,000 for 826 grants; average $832.

Contact: Edward T. Dougherty, Executive Director

   Initial approach: brief letter or proposal

   Deadlines: applications accepted throughout the year

Burlington Industries Foundation
3330 W. Friendly Avenue
Greensboro, North Carolina 27410
(919) 379-2515

Areas of interest: Community development.

Restrictions: Grants for building funds.

Focus of giving: Grants given in areas of company operations.

Cannon Foundation, Inc.
P. O. Box 548
Concord, North Carolina 28026-0548

Areas of interest: Community development.

Restrictions: Grants for building funds.

Focus of giving: Grants given in areas of company operations.

Contact: Dan L. Gray, Executive Director

Fieldcrest Foundation
326 E. Stadium Drive
Eden, North Carolina 27288

Areas of interest: Community development.

Restrictions: Grants for building funds.

Foundation for the Carolinas
301 South Brevard Street
Charlotte, North Carolina
(704) 376-9541

Restrictions: Grants for operating budgets, seed money, building funds, emergency funds, equipment, special projects, matching funds, and land acquisition.

Focus of giving: Giving primarily in North Carolina and South Carolina.

$ Given: $2,385,853 for 1,225 grants: high $209,800; low $100; average $500–$10,000. Also $12,398 for grants to individuals.

Publications: Annual report, application guidelines, informational brochure, and newsletter.

Contact: William Spencer, President

Application information: application form required

Initial approach: letter

Copies of proposal: 11

Deadlines: none

Board meeting dates: quarterly, with annual meeting in March; distribution committee meets monthly

Final notification: 1 to 2 months

Salisbury Community Foundation, Inc.
P. O. Box 1327
Salisbury, North Carolina 28144

Areas of interest: Community development.

Restrictions: Grants for building funds.

Contact: W. A. Sherrill, Secretary

Piedmont Aviation, Inc.
P. O. Box 2720
Winston-Salem, North Carolina 27156
(919) 767-5414

Areas of interest: Project grants and community development.

Restrictions: No grants to individuals.

$ Given: $50 to $50,000.

Contact: Thomas H. Davies, Chairman of the Executive Committee

   Initial approach: letter

   Deadlines: none

   Board meeting dates: quarterly

The Kathleen Price and Joseph M. Bryan Family Foundation, Inc.
P. O. Box 1349
Greensboro, North Carolina 27407
(919) 379-7512

Restrictions: Grants for community projects, building funds, program-related investments, and seed money.

Focus of giving: Giving primarily in North Carolina; will consider proposals from other states.

$ Given: $105,500 for 29 grants: high $10,000; low $1,000; average $1,000–$10,000.

Assets: $1,566,000

Contact: Richard L. Wharton, Executive Director

    Initial approach: letter

    Copies of proposal: 1

    Deadlines: March 15 and September 15

    Board meeting dates: usually in March, May, and November

    Final notification: 3 months after board meeting

Fund for Southern Communities
57 Forsyth Street, Suite 1603
P. O. Box 927
Atlanta, Georgia 30303
(404) 577-3178

Areas of interest: Housing and economic development. The fund supports organizations working against discrimination based on race, sex, age, religion, economic status, sexual preference, ethnic background, or physical or mental disabilities.

Restrictions: Seed grants to new projects; general support and project grants to small organizations.

Focus of giving: Requests must be submitted from projects or programs operating in North Carolina, South Carolina, or Georgia.

$ Given: $144,700 for grants: high $3,000; low $750; average $1,570.

Publications: Annual report, program policy statement, and application guidelines.

Contact: Alan McGregor, Executive Director

    Application information: application form required

    Initial approach: telephone or letter

    Copies of proposal: 1

    Deadlines: the fund accepts applications once a year, usually in the fall

Board meeting dates: once a year

Final notification: 4 months

Unocal Foundation
P. O. Box 7600
Los Angeles, California 90051
(213) 977-6171

Areas of interest: Arts and culture (museums/galleries, arts centers), civic and public affairs (business/free enterprise, economic development, urban and community affairs), education, health, and social services.

Restrictions: Grants for capital, general support, and special projects; grants to individuals.

Focus of giving: Nationally, with preference given to areas where Unocal maintains corporate facilities: AK (Kenai), CA (Brea, Los Angeles, Mountain Pass, San Francisco, Santa Maria), CO, IL (Chicago, Palatine), LA, NC (Charlotte), OR (Rivergate), TX (Beaumont).

$ Given: $4,571,472 for 397 grants: high $491,860; low $250; average $500–$5,000.

Contact: R. P. Van Zandt, Vice-President and Trustee

Initial approach: telephone

Deadlines: requests in by September 15

NORTH DAKOTA

Northwest Area Foundation
West 975 First National Bank Building
St. Paul, Minnesota 55101
(612) 224-9635

Restrictions: Grants generally for experimental and demonstration projects that promise significant impact on the community and the well-being of society but for which there is not now general support.

Focus of giving: Giving limited to an eight-state region that includes Idaho, Iowa, Minnesota, Montana, North Dakota, Oregon, South Dakota, and Washington.

$ Given: $6,967,105 for 196 grants: high $250,000; low $150; average $20,000–$60,000.

Contact: Terry Tinson, President

>   **Initial approach:**   letter, telephone, or proposal
>
>   **Copies of proposal:**   2
>
>   **Deadlines:**   varies
>
>   **Board meeting dates:**   bimonthly, beginning in February
>
>   **Final notification:**   60 to 90 days

Otto Bremer Foundation, Suite 700
55 East Fifth Street
St. Paul, Minnesota 55101
(612) 227-8036

Areas of interest: Community funds and building grants.

Restrictions: Nonprofit, tax-exempt organizations and to programs having a direct impact on the service areas of the 26 Bremer banks in Minnesota, North Dakota, and Wisconsin, and within the city of St. Paul.

$ Given: Grants vary in amount, depending upon the needs and nature of the request.

Contact: John Kostishack, Executive Director

>   **Initial approach:**   contact the foundation staff by telephone or letter for assistance in the development of a proposal
>
>   **Deadlines:**   requests are reviewed continually
>
>   **Board meeting dates:**   once a month

NORTHEASTERN STATES

Ellis L. Phillips Foundation
13 Dartmouth College Highway
Lyme, New York 03768
(603) 795-2790

Areas of interest: Historic preservation.

Restrictions: Grants for operating budgets, continuing support, emergency funds, and seed money.

Focus of giving: Giving primarily in the northeastern United States.

$ Given: $268,658 for 45 grants: high $30,158; low $1,000; average $1,000–$10,000.

Assets: $4,198,892

Contact: Ellis L. Phillips, President
   Initial approach: one- to three-page letter
   Copies of proposal: 1
   Board meeting dates: October, February, and May

OHIO

Anderson Foundation
P. O. Box 119
Maumee, Ohio 43537
(419) 891-6481

Areas of interest: Community development.

Restrictions: Grants for building funds.

Focus of giving: Grants given in areas of company operations.

Contact: Executive Director

Leon A. Beeghly Fund
808 Stambaugh Building
Youngstown, Ohio 44503
(216) 743-3151

Areas of interest: Community development.

Restrictions: Grants for building funds.

Contact: James L. Beeghly, Chairman

Bemis Company Foundation
800 Northstar Center
Minneapolis, Minnesota 55402
(612) 340-6198

Areas of interest: Urban and community affairs, arts centers, cinema, performing arts (general), business/free enterprise, economic development, education, health, and social services.

Restrictions: Grants for general support, special projects, and matching funds; grants to individuals.

Focus of giving: Areas where company maintains facilities, with emphasis on Minneapolis, MN. AR (Crossett), CA (Los Angeles, Union City, Wilmington), CT (Plainfield, Stratford), FL (Panama City), IL (Murphysboro, Peoria, Schaumburg), IN (Indianapolis, Terre Haute), KS (Wichita), KY (Florence, Henderson, Louisville), MA (East Pepperell), MI (Grand Rapids, Zeeland), MN (Mankato, Minneapolis, Minnetonka), MO (Louisiana, Saint Louis, Springfield), MS (Verona), NC (Statesville), NE (Omaha), NH (Hudson, Nashua, North Walpole), NJ (Flemington), NY (Buffalo), OH (Stow), TN (Memphis), TX (Jacksonville), WA (Seattle, Vancouver), WI (Green Bay, New London, Oshkosh, Sheboygan).

$ Given: $700,000 for 826 grants; average $832.

Contact: Edward T. Dougherty, Executive Director

> **Initial approach:** brief letter or proposal
>
> **Deadlines:** applications accepted throughout the year

The William Bingham Foundation[*]
1250 Leader Building
Cleveland, Ohio 44114
(216) 781-3275

Restrictions: Grants for general purposes, building funds, equipment, special projects, matching funds, program-related investments, and seed money.

Focus of giving: Giving primarily in the eastern United States, with some emphasis on the Cleveland, Ohio, area.

$ Given: $640,244 for 27 grants: high $115,294; low $2,000; average $5,000–$30,000. Also $100,000 for one loan.

Assets: $16,137,000

Publications: Annual report, program policy statement, and application guidelines.

Donor: Elizabeth B. Blossom

Contact: Laura C. Hitchcox, Executive Director

[*]Incorporated in 1955 in Ohio.

Initial approach: letter of 2 pages or less

Copies of proposal: 1

Deadlines: submit proposal preferably in February or July; deadline 2 months prior to board meeting dates

Board meeting dates: usually May or October

Final notification: 3 to 6 months

Cleveland Electric Illuminating Foundation
P. O. Box 5000
Cleveland, Ohio 44101
(216) 622-9800

Areas of interest: Community development.

Restrictions: Grants for building funds.

The Cleveland Foundation
1400 Hanna Building
Cleveland, Ohio 44115
(216) 861-3810

Restrictions: Grants are made to private, tax-exempt, and governmental agencies and programs serving the greater Cleveland area in the fields of civic and cultural affairs, education and economic development, and health and social services. Current priorities are in economic development, neighborhood development, downtown revitalization, and lakefront enhancement. Grants serve mainly as seed money for innovative projects or for developing institutions or services addressing unmet needs in the community. Very limited support for capital purposes for highly selective construction or equipment projects.

Focus of giving: Giving limited to the greater Cleveland area, with emphasis on Cleveland and on Cuyahoga and Lake Counties, Ohio, unless specified otherwise by donor.

$ Given: $17,100,149 for 675 grants: high $500,000; low $250; average $5,000–$50,000. Also money for loans.

Contact: Steve A. Minter, Director

Deadlines: March 31, June 15, August 31, and December 15

Dana Corporation Foundation
P. O. Box 1000
Toledo, Ohio 43697
(419) 535-4500

Areas of interest: Community development.

Restrictions: Grants for building funds.

Focus of giving: Grants given in areas of company operations.

Contact: Pauline Marzollini, Assistant Secretary

Eaton Charitable Fund
P. O. Box 6179
Cleveland, Ohio 44101
(216) 523-4822

Areas of interest: Community development.

Restrictions: Grants for building funds.

Contact: Frederick B. Unger

Emhart Corporation
426 Colt Highway
Farmington, Connecticut 06032
(203) 678-3204

Areas of interest: Arts and humanities (museums/galleries, zoos, operas, arts centers, historic preservation/restoration), civic and public affairs (business/free enterprise, urban and community affairs), education, health, and social services.

Restrictions: Grants for general support, capital, endowment, and matching funds; grants to individuals.

Focus of giving: Giving primarily in areas where company has major facilities and a large number of employees: AL, CA (Anaheim, Los Angeles, Torrance), CT (Berlin, Farmington, Hartford, Shelton, Windsor), IL (Broadview), IN (Indianapolis), KY (Campbellsville), MA (Beverly, Fall River, Middleton, New Bedford, South Hadley, Whitman), MI (Mount Clemens), MO, NE (Lincoln), NH, NY (Elmira, Maspeth), OH (Cleveland), PA (Huntington Valley, Reading, Temple), TN, VT (Springfield).

$ Given: $738,865 for 200 grants: high $45,000; low $100; average $2,694.

Contact: John F. Budd, Jr., Chairman, Contributions and Grants Committee

    Initial approach: brief letter or proposal

    Deadlines: submit proposal before October

    Final notification: by December

Federated Department Stores Foundation
Seven W. Seventh Street
Cincinnati, Ohio 45202

Areas of interest: Community development.

Restrictions: Grants for building funds.

Focus of giving: Grants given in areas of company operations.

Firestone Trust Fund
c/o AmeriTrust Company, N. A.
P. O. Box 5937
Cleveland, Ohio 44101

Areas of interest: Community development.

Restrictions: Grants for building funds.

Focus of giving: Grants given in areas of company operations.

Firman Fund
1010 Hanna Building
Cleveland, Ohio 44115
(216) 696-3913

Areas of interest: Community funds.

Restrictions: Tax-exempt organizations may apply. No grants are awarded to individuals.

$ Given: $100–$50,000.

Contact: Richard R. Kermode, Secretary-Treasurer

    Initial approach: letter

    Deadlines: none

Fort Howard Paper Foundation
P. O. Box 11325
Green Bay, Wisconsin 54307
(414) 435-8821

Areas of interest: Arts and humanities (museums/galleries, libraries, music, historic preservation/restoration), civic and public affairs (professional associations, urban and community affairs), education, health, and social services.

Restrictions: Grants for capital, general support, and special projects; grants to individuals.

Focus of giving: Giving primarily in Green Bay, Wisconsin, Muskogee, Oklahoma, and limited areas surrounding these communities.

$ Given: $622,396 for 31 grants: high $135,000; low $29; average $2,000–$12,000.

Assets: $11,303,956

Contact: Bruce W. Nagel, Assistant Secretary
    Initial approach: brief letter or proposal
    Deadlines: applications accepted throughout the year

The Lorain Foundation
457 Broadway
Lorain, Ohio 44502

Restrictions: Grants for general purposes.

$ Given: $33,223.

Assets: $721,201

Contact: Edward J. Gould, Chairman

Lubrizol Foundation
29400 Lakeland Boulevard
Wickliffe, Ohio 44092
(216) 943-4200

Areas of interest: Community development.

Restrictions: Grants for building funds.

Contact: Raymond W. Hussey, Secretary

Marathon Oil Foundation, Inc.
539 South Main Street
Findlay, Ohio 45840
(419) 422-2121, Ext. 3708

Restrictions: Support for seed money and building funds.

Focus of giving: Giving limited to areas of company operations.

$ Given: $1,789 ,407 for 368 grants: high $2,000,000; low $300. Also $197,778 for 50 grants to individuals.

Assets: $2,568,574

Contact: Carol Mittermaien, Assistant Secretary
   Initial approach: full proposal
   Copies of proposal: 1
   Deadlines: none
   Board meeting dates: as required
   Final notification: 6 to 8 weeks

Mead Corporation Foundation
Courthouse Plaza Northeast
Dayton, Ohio 45463
(513) 222-6323

Areas of interest: Community development.

Restrictions: Grants for building funds.

Focus of giving: Grants given in areas of company operations.

Contact: Ronald F. Budzik, Executive Director

John P. Murphy Foundation
100 Public Square, 10th Floor
Cleveland, Ohio 44113
(216) 579-3650

Areas of interest: Community development.

Restrictions: Grants for building funds.

Contact: Herbert E. Strawbridge, President

National Machinery Foundation, Inc.
Greenfield Street
P. O. Box 747
Tiffin, Ohio 44883
(419) 447-5211

Areas of interest: Arts and humanities (museums/galleries, arts centers, historic preservation/restoration), civic and public affairs (economics, business/free enterprise, urban and community affairs), education, health, and social services (homes).

Restrictions: Grants for capital, general support, endowment, and special projects; grants to individuals.

Focus of giving: Giving primarily in county where company operates.

$ Given: $366,782 for 126 grants: high $35,000; low $50; average $500–$5,500.

Assets: $7,265,000

Contact: D. B. Bero, Secretary-Treasurer

>   **Application information:** application form required

>   **Initial approach:** brief letter or proposal

>   **Deadlines:** applications accepted throughout the year

Nationwide Foundation
One Nationwide Plaza
Columbus, Ohio 43215

Areas of interest: Community development.

Restrictions: Grants for building funds.

Focus of giving: Grants given in areas of company operations.

Contact: J. Richard Bull, Vice-President

NCR Foundation
1700 S. Patterson Boulevard
Dayton, Ohio 45479
(513) 445-2577

Areas of interest: Community development.

Restrictions: Grants for building funds.

Focus of giving: Grants given in areas of company operations.

Contact: R. F. Beach, Vice-President

Proctor & Gamble Fund
One Proctor & Gamble Plaza
Cincinnati, Ohio 45202
(513) 983-2201

Areas of interest: Community development.

Restrictions: Grants for building funds.

Focus of giving: Grants given in areas of company operations.

Contact: B. J. Nolan, Vice-President

Richland County Foundation of Mansfield, Ohio
$34\frac{1}{2}$ S. Park Street, Room 202
Mansfield, Ohio 44902
(419) 525-3020

Areas of interest: Community development.

Restrictions: Grants for building funds.

Contact: Betty J. Crawford, Executive Director

Louise Taft Semple Foundation
1800 First National Bank Center
Cincinnati, Ohio 45202
(513) 381-2838

Areas of interest: Community development.

Restrictions: Grants for building funds.

Contact: Dudley S. Taft, President

Sherwin-Williams Foundation
101 Prospect Avenue, N.W., 12th Floor
Cleveland, Ohio 44115
(216) 566-2511

Areas of interest: Community development.

Restrictions: Grants for building funds.

Stark County Foundation
United Bank Building, Suite 1180
220 Market Avenue, South
Canton, Ohio 44702
(216) 454-3426

Areas of interest: Community development.

Restrictions: Grants for building funds.

Contact: William K. Wilson, Executive Secretary

Stranahan Foundation
c/o Champion Spark Plug Co.
245 N. Summit Street
Toledo, Ohio 43604

Areas of interest: Community development.

Restrictions: Grants for building funds.

Contact: R. A. Stranahan, Jr., Trustee

Trust Corporation, Inc. Foundation
c/o Trust Corporation Bank, Ohio
Three Seagate
Toledo, Ohio 43603
(419) 259-8217

Restrictions: Charitable purposes: primarily local giving, with emphasis on community funds. Grants given for continuing support, building funds, emergency funds, equipment, and land acquisition.

Focus of giving: Giving primarily in tristate area of Indiana, Michigan, and Ohio.

$ Given: $212,350 for 19 grants: high $148,000; low $100; average $1,000–$10,000.

Assets: $291,394

Contact: J. E. Lupe, Vice-President
   Initial approach: letter
   Deadlines: none
   Board meeting dates: monthly
   Final notification: 2 months

TRW Foundation
1900 Richmond Road
Cleveland, Ohio 44124
(216) 291-7164

Areas of interest: Community development.

Restrictions: Grants for building funds.

Focus of giving: Grants given in areas of company operations.

Contact: Donna L. Cummings, Manager

White Consolidated Industries, Inc. Foundation
c/o White Consolidated Industries, Inc.
11770 Berea Road
Cleveland, Ohio 44111
(216) 252-3700

Areas of interest: Community development.

Restrictions: Grants for building funds.

Focus of giving: Grants given in areas of company operations.

Contact: Ronald G. Fountain, Treasurer

Wolfe Associates, Inc.
34 S. Third Street
Columbus, Ohio 43215
(614) 461-5220

Areas of interest: Community development.

Restrictions: Grants for building funds.

Contact: A. Kenneth Pierce, Jr., Secretary

The Leo Yassenoff Foundation
37 North High Street, Suite 304
Columbus, Ohio 43215
(614) 221-4315

Restrictions: Grants awarded for seed money, building funds, emergency funds, equipment, special projects, matching funds, and land acquisition.

Focus of giving: Giving limited to the central Ohio area, with emphasis on Franklin County.

$ Given: $722,960 for 98 grants: high $200,000; low $200; average $1,000–$20,000.

Assets: $10,637,830

Contact: Cynthia Cecil Lazarus, Executive Director

Application information: application form required

Initial approach: telephone, letter, or full proposal

Copies of proposal: 1

Deadlines: first business day of every other month, beginning in January

Board meeting dates: every other month, beginning in January

Youngstown Foundation
c/o The Dollar Savings & Trust Co.
P. O. Box 450
Youngstown, Ohio 44501
(216) 744-9000

Areas of interest: Community development.

Restrictions: Grants for building funds.

Contact: Herbert H. Pridham, Secretary

OKLAHOMA

Broadhurst Foundation
320 S. Boston, Suite 1111
Tulsa, Oklahoma 74103
(918) 584-0661

Areas of interest: Community development.

Restrictions: Grants for building funds.

Contact: Ann Shannon Cassidy, Chairman

McCasland Foundation
P. O. Box 400
McCasland Building
Duncan, Oklahoma 73534
(405) 252-5580

Areas of interest: Community development.

Restrictions: Grants for building funds.

Contact: W. H. Phelps, Trustee

Oklahoma City Community Foundation, Inc.
115 Park Avenue
Oklahoma City, Oklahoma 7310
(405) 235-5603

Areas of interest: Community development.

Restrictions: Grants for building funds.

Contact: Nancy B. Anthony, Executive Director

Phillips Petroleum Foundation, Inc.
Phillips Building, 16th Floor
Bartlesville, Oklahoma 74004
(918) 661-6248

Restrictions: Grants given for operating budgets, seed money, building funds, emergency funds, equipment, matching funds, and land acquisition.

Focus of giving: Giving primarily in area of company operations.

$ Given: $3,595,030 for 712 grants: high $520,801; low $60.

Contact: John C. West, Executive Director
  Application information: application form required
  Initial approach: telephone, letter, or proposal
  Copies of proposal: 1
  Deadlines: none
  Board meeting dates: January and as required
  Final notification: 6 to 8 weeks

Williams Companies Foundation, Inc.
Bank of Oklahoma Building
P. O. Box 2400
Tulsa, Oklahoma 74101
(918) 588-2106

Areas of interest: Community development.

Restrictions: Grants for building funds.

Focus of giving: Grants given in areas of company operations.

Contact: Hannah D. Robson, Manager

W. P. Wood Charitable Trust
P. O. Box 127
Shawnee, Oklahoma 74802
(405) 273-2880

Areas of interest: Community development.

Restrictions: Grants for building funds.

Contact: Steve Garner, Manager

OREGON

The Collins Foundation
909 Terminal Sales Building
Portland, Oregon 97205
(503) 227-1219

Restrictions: Grants are awarded for building funds, emergency funds, equipment, special projects, matching funds, and land acquisition.

Focus of giving: Giving limited to Oregon, with emphasis on Portland.

$ Given: $2,689,176, including $1,811,717 for 131 grants: high $250,000; low $725; average $2,500–$15,000. Also money for loans.

Contact: William C. Pine, Executive Vice-President

> **Initial approach:** letter
>
> **Copies of proposal:** 1
>
> **Deadlines:** none
>
> **Board meeting dates:** approximately 6 times a year
>
> **Final notification:** 2 months

The Jackson Foundation
c/o U. S. National Bank of Oregon
P. O. Box 3168
Portland, Oregon 97208
(503) 225-4461; (800) 547-1031, Ext. 6558

Restrictions: Broad purposes: local giving.

Focus of giving: Giving limited to Oregon

$ Given: $791,646 for 132 grants: high $64,200; low $300; average $2,000–$10,000. Also $764,330 for 18 loans.

Contact: Stephen W. Miller, Trust Officer

> **Deadlines:** none

Fred Meyer Charitable Trust
1515 Southwest Fifth Avenue, Suite 500
Portland, Oregon 97201
(503) 228-5512

Restrictions: Support for seed money, building funds, equipment, special projects, and matching funds.

Focus of giving: Support primarily in Oregon, with occasional grants at the initiative of the trust for programs in Washington, Idaho, Montana, and Alaska.

$ Given: $6,365,583 for 94 grants: high $555,000; low $964; average $20,000–$75,000.

Assets: $171,639,900

Contact: Charles S. Rooks, Executive Director

  Application information: application form required

  Initial approach: letter or full proposal

  Copies of proposal: 1

  Deadlines: none

  Board meeting dates: monthly

  Final notification: 4 to 6 months for proposals that pass first screening; 2 to 3 months for those that do not

Northwest Area Foundation
West 975 First National Bank Building
St. Paul, Minnesota 55101
(612) 224-9635

Restrictions: Grants generally for experimental and demonstration projects that promise significant impact on the community and the well-being of society but for which there is not now general support.

Focus of giving: Giving limited to an eight-state region that includes Idaho, Iowa, Minnesota, Montana, North Dakota, Oregon, South Dakota, and Washington.

$ Given: $6,967,105 for 196 grants: high $250,000; low $150; average $20,000–$60,000.

Contact: Terry Tinson, President

  Initial approach: letter, telephone, or proposal

  Copies of proposal: 2

  Deadlines: varies

  Board meeting dates: bimonthly, beginning in February

  Final notification: 60 to 90 days

Unocal Foundation
P. O. Box 7600
Los Angeles, California 90051
(213) 977-6171

Areas of interest: Arts and culture (museums/galleries, arts centers), civic and public affairs (business/free enterprise, economic development, urban and community affairs), education, health, and social services.

Restrictions: Grants for capital, general support, and special projects; grants to individuals.

Focus of giving: Nationally, with preference given to areas where Unocal maintains corporate facilities: AK (Kenai), CA (Brea, Los Angeles, Mountain Pass, San Francisco, Santa Maria), CO, IL (Chicago, Palatine), LA, NC (Charlotte), OR (Rivergate), TX (Beaumont).

$ Given: $4,571,472 for 397 grants: high $491,860; low $250; average $500–$5,000.

Contact: R. P. Van Zandt, Vice-President and Trustee

   Initial approach: telephone

   Deadlines: requests in by September 15

PENNSYLVANIA

Aluminum Company of America (ALCOA)
Alcoa Foundation
1501 Alcoa Building
Pittsburgh, Pennsylvania 15219
(412) 553-4696 or 522-2000

Areas of interest: Building funds, capital campaigns, community development, urban economic affairs, historic preservation, and special projects.

Restrictions: Organizations must be tax-exempt under 501 (c) 3; publicly supported agencies are eligible. No grants to individuals.

Focus of giving: National (most grants in company-operating areas); many grants in Pittsburgh.

$ Given: $10,453,387 for grants: high $200,000; low $200; average $1,000–$5,000.

Assets: $214,000,000

Publications: Annual report and application guidelines.

Contact: Earl L. Gadbery, President

 Initial approach: proposal with cover letter

 Copies of proposal: 1

 Deadlines: applications accepted throughout the year

 Board meeting dates: monthly

 Final notification: 4 to 6 weeks after board meeting

Claude Worthington Benedum Foundation*
223 Fourth Avenue
Pittsburgh, Pennsylvania 15219
(412) 288-0360

Areas of interest: Serves a variety of charitable purposes in West Virginia and southwestern Pennsylvania. Funds are provided for projects that address regional problems and needs, that establish demonstration projects with strong potential for replication in West Virginia, or that make outstanding contributions to the area. Local initiatives and voluntary support are encouraged by the foundation.

Restrictions: Grants are awarded for operating budgets, continuing support, building funds, special projects, matching funds, program-related investments, and seed money.

$ Given: $5,646,092 for 73 grants: high $1,000,000; low $2,500; average $75,000.

Assets: $108,939,234

Publications: Annual report and application guidelines.

Contact: Paul R. Jenkins, Executive Vice-President

 Initial approach: letter

 Copies of proposal: 1

 Deadlines: none

 Board meeting dates: March, June, September, and December

 Final notification: 6

*Incorporated in 1944 in Pennsylvania.

Emhart Corporation
426 Colt Highway
Farmington, Connecticut 06032
(203) 678-3204

Areas of interest: Arts and humanities (museums/galleries, zoos, operas, arts centers, historic preservation/restoration), civic and public affairs (business/free enterprise, urban and community affairs), education, health, and social services.

Restrictions: Grants for general support, capital, endowment, and matching funds; grants to individuals.

Focus of giving: Giving primarily in areas where company has major facilities and a large number of employees: AL, CA (Anaheim, Los Angeles, Torrance), CT (Berlin, Farmington, Hartford, Shelton, Windsor), IL (Broadview), IN (Indianapolis), KY (Campbellsville), MA (Beverly, Fall River, Middleton, New Bedford, South Hadley, Whitman), MI (Mount Clemens), MO, NE (Lincoln), NH, NY (Elmira, Maspeth), OH (Cleveland), PA (Huntington Valley, Reading, Temple), TN, VT (Springfield).

$ Given: $738,865 for 200 grants: high $45,000; low $100; average $2,694.

Contact: John F. Budd, Jr., Chairman, Contributions and Grants Committee

   Initial approach: brief letter or proposal

   Deadlines: submit proposal before October

   Final notification: by December

Howard Heinz Endowment
CNG Tower, 30th Floor
625 Liberty Avenue
Pittsburgh, Pennsylvania 15222
(412) 391-5122

Restrictions: Local giving, usually with one-time, non-renewable grants for new programs, seed money, and capital projects.

Focus of giving: Giving limited to Pennsylvania, with emphasis on Pittsburgh and the Allegheny County area.

$ Given: $4,637,323 for 108 grants: high $500,000; low $500; average $5,000–$150,000.

Contact: Alfred W. Wishart, Jr., Executive Director

Application information: application form required

Initial approach: letter, full proposal, or telephone

Copies of proposal: 1

Deadlines: none

Board meeting dates: spring and fall

Final notification: 3 to 4 months

Kennametal Foundation
P. O. Box 231
Latrobe, Pennsylvania 15650
(412) 539-5203

Areas of interest: General purposes, including community funds.

Restrictions: Support for building funds, equipment, program-related investments, and matching funds.

$ Given: $129,283 for 100 grants: high $33,198; low $25.

Assets: $473,704

Contact: Richard Gibson, Secretary-Treasurer

  Initial approach: letter

  Copies of proposal: 1

  Deadlines: submit proposal preferably in January

  Board meeting dates: monthly

Williamsport Foundation
102 West Fourth Street
Williamsport, Pennsylvania 17701
(717) 326-2611

Areas of interest: Charitable purposes: distribution of funds to serve the needs of Williamsport and vicinity.

Restrictions: Grants given for building funds, emergency funds, equipment, special projects, matching funds, program-related investments, seed money, and loans.

$ Given: $899,945 for 84 grants: high $115,000; low $24; average $1,000–$30,000.

Assets: $16,821,254

Contact: Harold D. Hershberger, Jr., Secretary
  Initial approach: letter
  Copies of proposal: 5
  Deadlines: none
  Board meeting dates: at least 4 times a year
  Final notification: 2 months

RHODE ISLAND

Old Stone Bank Charitable Foundation
180 South Main Street
Providence, Rhode Island 02903
(401) 278-2213

Areas of interest: Broad purposes; focus on local giving.

Restrictions: Grants awarded for building funds, special projects, land acquisition, program-related investments, and seed money.

Focus of giving: Giving limited to Rhode Island.

$ Given: $238,798 for 24 grants: high $140,000; low $150.

Assets: $518,089

Publications: Annual report, program policy statement, and application guidelines.

Contact: Kay H. Low, Manager
  Initial approach: letter or telephone
  Copies of proposal: 1
  Deadlines: first day of months when board meets
  Board meeting dates: bimonthly, beginning in January
  Final notification: 4 to 6 weeks

SOUTH CAROLINA

Foundation for the Carolinas
301 South Brevard Street
Charlotte, North Carolina
(704) 376-9541

Restrictions: Grants for operating budgets, seed money, building funds, emergency funds, equipment, special projects, matching funds, and land acquisition.

Focus of giving: Giving primarily in North Carolina and South Carolina.

$ Given: $2,385,853 for 1,225 grants: high $209,800; low $100; average $500–$10,000. Also $12,398 for grants to individuals.

Publications: Annual report, application guidelines, informational brochure, and newsletter.

Contact: William Spencer, President

    Application information: application form required

    Initial approach: letter

    Copies of proposal: 11

    Deadlines: none

    Board meeting dates: quarterly, with annual meeting in March; distribution committee meets monthly

    Final notification: 1 to 2 months

Fund for Southern Communities
57 Forsyth Street, Suite 1603
P. O. Box 927
Atlanta, Georgia 30303
(404) 577-3178

Areas of interest: Housing and economic development. The fund supports organizations working against discrimination based on race, sex, age, religion, economic status, sexual preference, ethnic background, or physical or mental disabilities.

Restrictions: Seed grants to new projects; general support and project grants to small organizations.

Focus of giving: Requests must be submitted from projects or programs operating in North Carolina, South Carolina, or Georgia.

$ Given: $144,700 for grants: high $3,000; low $750; average $1,570.

Publications: Annual report, program policy statement, and application guidelines.

Contact: Alan McGregor, Executive Director

    Application information: application form required

    Initial approach: telephone or letter

    Copies of proposal: 1

    Deadlines: the fund accepts applications once a year, usually in the fall

    Board meeting dates: once a year

    Final notification: 4 months

Spartanburg County Foundation
805 Montgomery Building
Spartanburg, South Carolina 29301
(803) 582-0138

Areas of interest: Social welfare, recreation, and health projects.

Restrictions: Grants for building funds.

Contact: James S. Barrett, Executive Director

Springs Foundation Fund, Inc.
P. O. Drawer 460
Lancaster, South Carolina 29720
(803) 286-2196

Areas of interest: Community development.

Restrictions: Grants for building funds.

Contact: Charles A. Bundy, President

SOUTH DAKOTA

Northwest Area Foundation West
975 First National Bank Building
St. Paul, Minnesota 55101
(612) 224-9635

Restrictions: Grants generally for experimental and demonstration projects that promise significant impact on the community and the well-being of society but for which there is not now general support.

Focus of giving: Giving limited to an eight-state region that includes Idaho, Iowa, Minnesota, Montana, North Dakota, Oregon, South Dakota, and Washington.

$ Given: $6,967,105 for 196 grants: high $250,000; low $150; average $20,000–$60,000.

Contact: Terry Tinson, President

    Initial approach: letter, telephone, or proposal

    Copies of proposal: 2

    Deadlines: varies

    Board meeting dates: bimonthly, beginning in February

    Final notification: 60 to 90 days

SOUTHEASTERN STATES

Mary Reynolds Babcock Foundation, Inc.
102 Reynolds Village
Winston-Salem, North Carolina 27106-5123
(919) 748-9222

Areas of interest: Broad purposes. Grants primarily for social services, including community development and youth employment.

Restrictions: Grants for operating budgets, emergency funds, special projects, program-related investments, and seed money.

Focus of giving: Giving primarily in North Carolina and the southeastern United States.

$ Given: $3,127,491 for 156 grants: high $175,000; low $1,000; average $10,000–$50,000. Also $200,00 for two loans.

Assets: $40,601,750

Publications: Annual report, program policy statement, and application guidelines.

Contact: William L. Bondurant, Executive Director

    Application information: application form required

    Initial approach: letter, telephone, or full proposal

    Copies of proposal: 1

Deadlines: submit proposal between December and February or June and August; deadlines March 1 and September 1

Board meeting dates: May and November

Final notification: first week of the month following a board meeting

Fund for Southern Communities
57 Forsyth Street, Suite 1603
P. O. Box 927
Atlanta, Georgia 30303
(404) 577-3178

Areas of interest: Housing and economic development. The fund supports organizations working against discrimination based on race, sex, age, religion, economic status, sexual preference, ethnic background, or physical or mental disabilities.

Restrictions: Seed grants to new projects; general support and project grants to small organizations.

Focus of giving: Requests must be submitted from projects or programs operating in North Carolina, South Carolina, or Georgia.

$ Given: $144,700 for grants: high $3,000; low $750; average $1,570.

Publications: Annual report, program policy statement, and application guidelines.

Contact: Alan McGregor, Executive Director

    Application information: application form required

    Initial approach: telephone or letter

    Copies of proposal: 1

    Deadlines: the fund accepts applications once a year, usually in the fall

    Board meeting dates: once a year

    Final notification: 4 months

TENNESSEE

Bemis Company Foundation
800 Northstar Center
Minneapolis, Minnesota 55402
(612) 340-6198

Areas of interest: Urban and community affairs, arts centers, cinema, performing arts (general), business/free enterprise, economic development, education, health, and social services.

Restrictions: Grants for general support, special projects, and matching funds; grants to individuals.

Focus of giving: Areas where company maintains facilities, with emphasis on Minneapolis, MN. AR (Crossett), CA (Los Angeles, Union City, Wilmington), CT (Plainfield, Stratford), FL (Panama City), IL (Murphysboro, Peoria, Schaumburg), IN (Indianapolis, Terre Haute), KS (Wichita), KY (Florence, Henderson, Louisville), MA (East Pepperell), MI (Grand Rapids, Zeeland), MN (Mankato, Minneapolis, Minnetonka), MO (Louisiana, Saint Louis, Springfield), MS (Verona), NC (Statesville), NE (Omaha), NH (Hudson, Nashua, North Walpole), NJ (Flemington), NY (Buffalo), OH (Stow), TN (Memphis), TX (Jacksonville), WA (Seattle, Vancouver), WI (Green Bay, New London, Oshkosh, Sheboygan).

$ Given: $700,000 for 826 grants; average $832.

Contact: Edward T. Dougherty, Executive Director

    Initial approach: brief letter or proposal

    Deadlines: applications accepted throughout the year

Benwood Foundation
1600 American National Bank Building
Chattanooga, Tennessee 37402
(615) 267-4311

Areas of interest: Historic preservation.

Restrictions: Grants for building funds.

Contact: William A. Walter, Executive Director

Community Foundation of Greater Chattanooga, Inc.
1600 American National Bank Building
Chattanooga, Tennessee 37402
(615) 267-4311

Areas of interest: Community development.

Restrictions: Grants for building funds.

Contact: William A. Walter, Executive Director

Emhart Corporation
426 Colt Highway
Farmington, Connecticut 06032
(203) 678-3204

Areas of interest: Arts and humanities (museums/galleries, zoos, operas, arts centers, historic preservation/restoration), civic and public affairs (business/free enterprise, urban and community affairs), education, health, and social services.

Restrictions: Grants for general support, capital, endowment, and matching funds; grants to individuals.

Focus of giving: Giving primarily in areas where company has major facilities and a large number of employees: AL, CA (Anaheim, Los Angeles, Torrance), CT (Berlin, Farmington, Hartford, Shelton, Windsor), IL (Broadview), IN (Indianapolis), KY (Campbellsville), MA (Beverly, Fall River, Middleton, New Bedford, South Hadley, Whitman), MI (Mount Clemens), MO, NE (Lincoln), NH, NY (Elmira, Maspeth), OH (Cleveland), PA (Huntington Valley, Reading, Temple), TN, VT (Springfield).

$ Given: $738,865 for 200 grants: high $45,000; low $100; average $2,694.

Contact: John F. Budd, Jr., Chairman, Contributions and Grants Committee

> **Initial approach:** brief letter or proposal
>
> **Deadlines:** submit proposal before October
>
> **Final notification:** by December

Lyndhurst Foundation
701 Tallan Building
Chattanooga, Tennessee 37402
(615) 756-0767

Areas of interest: Emphasis on health.

Restrictions: Support for general purposes, seed money, special projects, and matching funds.

Focus of giving: Grants generally limited to Chattanooga.

$ Given: $2,827,077 for 50 grants: high $355,000; low $2,000; average $30,000–$150,000. Also $305,000 for 13 grants to individuals.

Assets: $91,695,737

Contact: Deaderick C. Montague, President

Application information: application form required for grants to individuals; awards made only at the initiative of the foundation

Initial approach: letter

Copies of proposal: 1

Deadlines: 4 weeks before board meetings

Board meeting dates: February, May, August, and November

Final notification: 3 months

Plough Foundation
6055 Primacy Parkway, Suite 250
Memphis, Tennessee 38119
(901) 761-9180

Areas of interest: Community development.

Restrictions: Grants for building funds.

Tonya Memorial Foundation
1033 Volunteer State Life Building
Chattanooga, Tennessee 37402

Areas of interest: Community development.

Restrictions: Grants for building funds.

TEXAS

American General Corporation
2929 Allen Parkway
P. O. Box 3247
Houston, Texas 77253
(713) 522-1288

Areas of interest: Capital campaigns (many grants in Houston), general support, community and urban affairs, and special projects.

Restrictions: Organizations must be tax-exempt under 501 (c) 3. No grants to individuals. Groups supported mainly through United Way.

Focus of giving: CA (most grants in locations of major offices and in Sacramento), FL (Jacksonville), HI (Honolulu), IN (Evansville), ME, MD (Baltimore), NY (Syracuse), TN (Nashville), TX (Houston, Waco).

$ Given: $3,500,000 for grants: high $1,000,000 (multiyear); low $500; average $1,500–$3,000.

Assets: $28,008,000,000

Contact: James F. Moore, Vice-President, Operations

  Initial approach: letter

  Deadlines: applications accepted throughout the year

Bemis Company Foundation
800 Northstar Center
Minneapolis, Minnesota 55402
(612) 340-6198

Areas of interest: Urban and community affairs, arts centers, cinema, performing arts (general), business/free enterprise, economic development, education, health, and social services.

Restrictions: Grants for general support, special projects, and matching funds; grants to individuals.

Focus of giving: Areas where company maintains facilities, with emphasis on Minneapolis, MN. AR (Crossett), CA (Los Angeles, Union City, Wilmington), CT (Plainfield, Stratford), FL (Panama City), IL (Murphysboro, Peoria, Schaumburg), IN (Indianapolis, Terre Haute), KS (Wichita), KY (Florence, Henderson, Louisville), MA (East Pepperell), MI (Grand Rapids, Zeeland), MN (Mankato, Minneapolis, Minnetonka), MO (Louisiana, Saint Louis, Springfield), MS (Verona), NC (Statesville), NE (Omaha), NH (Hudson, Nashua, North Walpole), NJ (Flemington), NY (Buffalo), OH (Stow), TN (Memphis), TX (Jacksonville), WA (Seattle, Vancouver), WI (Green Bay, New London, Oshkosh, Sheboygan).

$ Given: $700,000 for 826 grants; average $832.

Contact: Edward T. Dougherty, Executive Director

  Initial approach: brief letter or proposal

  Deadlines: applications accepted throughout the year

The Clayton Fund
c/o Anderson, Clayton and Company
P. O. Box 2538
Houston, Texas 77252
(713) 651-0641

Areas of interest: Housing, community centers, and historic preservation/restoration.

Restrictions: Grants for general support; grants to individuals.

Focus of giving: Giving primarily to Texas, with limited support elsewhere.

$ Given: $1,223,936 for 47 grants: high $200,000; low $100; average $5,000–$20,000.

Assets: $16,254,955

Contact: S. M. McAshan, Jr., Trustee

Communities Foundation of Texas, Inc.
4605 Live Oak Street
Dallas, Texas 75204
(214) 826-5231

Areas of interest: Broad purposes: to promote the well-being of the inhabitants of Texas, primarily in the Dallas area.

Restrictions: Support for operating budgets, building funds, emergency funds, equipment, special projects, matching funds, land acquisition, program-related investments, and seed money.

Focus of giving: Giving primarily in Dallas, Texas, area.

$ Given: $11,310,838 for 925 grants: high $1,050,923; low $15; average $10,000–$25,000.

Assets: $89,520,522

Contact: Edward M. Fjorbak, Executive Vice-President
   Initial approach: letter
   Copies of proposal: 1
   Deadlines: 30 days before distribution committee meetings
   Board meeting dates: distribution committee for unrestricted funds meets in March, August, and November
   Final notification: 1 week after distribution committee meeting

Walter Hightower Foundation
c/o El Paso National Bank
P. O. Drawer 140
El Paso, Texas 79980
(915) 546-6515

Areas of interest: Health care for crippled children under the age of 21.

Restrictions: Giving limited to west Texas and southern New Mexico. Grants for operating budgets, building funds, equipment, program-related investments, and seed money; grants to individuals.

$ Given: $233,574 for grants: high $40,000.

Assets: $5,150,058

Contact: Terry Crenshaw, Charitable Services Officer
    Application information: application form required
    Initial approach: letter
    Copies of proposal: 2
    Deadlines: July 1
    Board meeting dates: annually
    Final notification: 2 months

Meadows Foundation, Inc.
Wilson Historic Block
2922 Swiss Avenue
Dallas, Texas 75204
(214) 826-9431

Restrictions: Support for operating budgets, continuing support, building funds, equipment, special projects, matching funds, land acquisition, program-related investments, and seed money.

Focus of giving: Giving limited to Texas, with emphasis on Dallas.

$ Given: $7,500,859 for 164 grants: high $1,000,000; low $607; average $25,000–$50,000.

Assets: $324,123,001

Contact: Dr. Sally R. Lancaster, Executive Vice-President
    Initial approach: full proposal
    Copies of proposal: 1

Deadlines: none

Board meeting dates: April and November on major grants; grants review committee meets monthly

Final notification: 3 to 4 months

The Moody Foundation
704 Moody National Bank Building
Galveston, Texas 77550
(409) 763-5333

Areas of interest: Historic restoration projects, performing arts organizations, and cultural programs; health, science, and education; community and social services; and religion.

Restrictions: Support given for seed money, building funds, emergency funds, equipment, special projects, and matching funds.

Focus of giving: Giving limited to Texas.

$ Given: $9,452,399 for 142 grants: high $515,000; low $600. Also $350,495 for 518 grants to individuals.

Publications: Annual report and application guidelines.

Contact: Peter M. Moore, Grants Officer

   Initial approach: letter or telephone

   Copies of proposal: 1

   Deadlines: 4 weeks prior to board meetings

   Board meeting dates: quarterly

   Final notification: 2 weeks after board meeting

Crystelle Waggoner Charitable Trust
c/o NCNB Texas
P. O. Box 1317
Fort Worth, Texas 76101
(817) 390-6925

Restrictions: Support for building funds, emergency funds, equipment, special projects, matching funds, land acquisition, program-related investments, and seed money.

Focus of giving: Giving limited to Texas, especially Fort Worth and Decatur.

$ Given: $339,922 for 33 grants: high $50,000; low $2,000; average $10,000.

Assets: $2,635,245

Contact: Darlene Mann, Vice-President

   Application information: application form required

   Initial approach: letter

   Copies of proposal: 1

   Deadlines: end of each quarter

   Board meeting dates: January, April, July, and October

   Final notification: 6 months, only if request is granted

Unocal Foundation
P. O. Box 7600
Los Angeles, California 90051
(213) 977-6171

Areas of interest: Arts and culture (museums/galleries, arts centers), civic and public affairs (business/free enterprise, economic development, urban and community affairs), education, health, and social services.

Restrictions: Grants for capital, general support, and special projects; grants to individuals.

Focus of giving: Nationally, with preference given to areas where Unocal maintains corporate facilities: AK (Kenai), CA (Brea, Los Angeles, Mountain Pass, San Francisco, Santa Maria), CO, IL (Chicago, Palatine), LA, NC (Charlotte), OR (Rivergate), TX (Beaumont).

$ Given: $4,571,472 for 397 grants: high $491,860; low $250; average $500–$5,000.

Contact: R. P. Van Zandt, Vice-President and Trustee

   Initial approach: telephone

   Deadlines: requests in by September 15

UTAH

Marriner S. Eccles Foundation
c/o First Security Bank of Utah
P. O. Box 30007
Salt Lake City, Utah 84130

Areas of interest: Projects concerning colleges and universities, and low-income families.

Restrictions: Grants for building funds.

Contact: Irma A. Hawkins, Manager

VERMONT

Cecil Charitable Trust
111 Broadway, Suite 512
New York, New York 10006

Areas of interest: Historic preservation.

Restrictions: Support for general purposes, special projects, matching funds, program-related investments, and seed money.

Focus of giving: Giving primarily in New York and Vermont.

$ Given: $111,950 for 55 grants: high $10,000; low $100.

Assets: $1,196,880

Contact: George B. Cameron, Trustee
   Initial approach: letter
   Copies of proposal: 1
   Deadlines: April 1 and November 1
   Board meeting dates: May and December

Emhart Corporation
426 Colt Highway
Farmington, Connecticut 06032
(203) 678-3204

Areas of interest: Arts and humanities (museums/galleries, zoos, operas, arts centers, historic preservation/restoration), civic and public affairs (business/free enterprise, urban and community affairs), education, health, and social services.

Restrictions: Grants for general support, capital, endowment, and matching funds; grants to individuals.

Focus of giving: Giving primarily in areas where company has major facilities and a large number of employees: AL, CA (Anaheim, Los Angeles, Torrance), CT (Berlin, Farmington, Hartford, Shelton, Windsor), IL (Broadview), IN (Indianapolis), KY (Campbellsville), MA (Beverly, Fall River, Middleton, New Bedford, South Hadley, Whitman), MI (Mount Clemens), MO, NE (Lincoln), NH, NY (Elmira, Maspeth), OH (Cleveland), PA (Huntington Valley, Reading, Temple), TN, VT (Springfield).

$ Given: $738,865 for 200 grants: high $45,000; low $100; average $2,694.

Contact: John F. Budd, Jr., Chairman, Contributions and Grants Committee

> **Initial approach:** brief letter or proposal
>
> **Deadlines:** submit proposal before October
>
> **Final notification:** by December

The Windham Foundation, Inc.
P. O. Box 70
Grafton, Vermont 05146
(802) 843-2211

Restrictions: A private operating foundation in which 85 percent of adjusted net income is applied to operating programs of the foundation. The foundation's primary activity is the preservation of properties in rural areas of Vermont to maintain their charm and historic, native, or unusual features, with emphasis on restoration of houses in Grafton. The remaining 15 percent of the foundations income is used for general charitable giving.

Focus of giving: Giving limited to Vermont, with emphasis on Windham County.

$ Given: $230,641 for 57 grants: high $30,000; low $100. Also $116,590 for 357 grants to individuals.

Contact: Stephan A. Morse, Executive Director

> **Initial approach:** letter
>
> **Copies of proposal:** 1
>
> **Deadlines:** none
>
> **Board meeting dates:** February, May, July, and October
>
> **Final notification:** following the board meeting

VIRGINIA

Norfolk Foundation
1410 Sovran Center
Norfolk, Virginia 23510
(804) 622-7951

Areas of interest: Community development.

Restrictions: Grants for building funds.

Contact: Lee C. Kitchen, Executive Director

UVB Foundation
919 East Main Street
Richmond, Virginia 23219
(804) 782-5618

Areas of interest: Community development.

Restrictions: Grants for building funds.

Contact: Lewis B. Flinn, Jr., President

WASHINGTON

Bemis Company Foundation
800 Northstar Center
Minneapolis, Minnesota 55402
(612) 340-6198

Areas of interest: Urban and community affairs, arts centers, cinema, performing arts (general), business/free enterprise, economic development, education, health, and social services.

Restrictions: Grants for general support, special projects, and matching funds; grants to individuals.

Focus of giving: Areas where company maintains facilities, with emphasis on Minneapolis, MN. AR (Crossett), CA (Los Angeles, Union City, Wilmington), CT (Plainfield, Stratford), FL (Panama City), IL (Murphysboro, Peoria, Schaumburg), IN (Indianapolis, Terre Haute), KS (Wichita), KY (Florence, Henderson, Louisville), MA (East Pepperell), MI (Grand Rapids, Zeeland), MN (Mankato, Minneapolis, Minnetonka), MO (Louisiana, Saint Louis, Springfield), MS (Verona), NC (Statesville), NE

(Omaha), NH (Hudson, Nashua, North Walpole), NJ (Flemington), NY (Buffalo), OH (Stow), TN (Memphis), TX (Jacksonville), WA (Seattle, Vancouver), WI (Green Bay, New London, Oshkosh, Sheboygan).

$ Given: $700,000 for 826 grants; average $832.

Contact: Edward T. Dougherty, Executive Director

    Initial approach: brief letter or proposal

    Deadlines: applications accepted throughout the year

Fred Meyer Charitable Trust
1515 Southwest Fifth Avenue, Suite 500
Portland, Oregon 97201
(503) 228-5512

Restrictions: Support for seed money, building funds, equipment, special projects, and matching funds.

Focus of giving: Support primarily in Oregon, with occasional grants at the initiative of the trust for programs in Washington, Idaho, Montana, and Alaska.

$ Given: $6,365,583 for 94 grants: high $555,000; low $964; average $20,000–$75,000.

Assets: $171,639,900

Contact: Charles S. Rooks, Executive Director

    Application information: application form required

    Initial approach: letter or full proposal

    Copies of proposal: 1

    Deadlines: none

    Board meeting dates: monthly

    Final notification: 4 to 6 months for proposals that pass first screening; 2 to 3 months for those that do not

Inland Northwest Community Foundation
400 Paulsen Center
Spokane, Washington 99201
(509) 624-2606

Restrictions: Grants for operating budgets, continuing support, seed money, building funds, special projects, matching funds, and land acquisition.

Focus of giving: Giving primarily in the inland Northwest.

$ Given: $169,024 for 157 grants: high $3,500; low $242; average $1,000. Also $18,550 for 53 grants to individuals.

Publications: Annual report, program policy statement, application guidelines, and 990-PF.

Contact: Jeanne L. Ager, Executive Director

    Application information: application form required

    Initial approach: letter

    Copies of proposal: 11

    Deadlines: varies depending on area of grant

    Board meeting dates: September through June

    Final notification: 3 months

ITT Rayonier Foundation
1177 Summer Street
Stamford, Connecticut 06904
(203) 348-7000

Areas of interest: Arts and humanities (aquariums, performing arts, museums/galleries), civic and public affairs (business/free enterprise, economic development, urban and community affairs), education, health, and social services (homes).

Restrictions: Grants for capital, general support, matching funds, and special projects; grants to individuals.

Focus of giving: Giving primarily near operating locations in Connecticut (Stamford), Florida, Georgia, and Washington.

$ Given: $259,985 for 129 grants: high $18,500; low $25; average $1,000–$5,000.

Assets: $2,635,096

Contact: Jerome D. Gregoire, Vice-President

    Initial approach: letter

    Deadlines: November 30

    Board meeting dates: February

    Final notification: 1 month

Northwest Area Foundation
West 975 First National Bank Building
St. Paul, Minnesota 55101
(612) 224-9635

Restrictions: Grants generally for experimental and demonstration projects that promise significant impact on the community and the well-being of society but for which there is not now general support.

Focus of giving: Giving limited to an eight-state region that includes Idaho, Iowa, Minnesota, Montana, North Dakota, Oregon, South Dakota, and Washington.

$ Given: $6,967,105 for 196 grants: high $250,000; low $150; average $20,000–$60,000.

Contact: Terry Tinson, President

    Initial approach: letter, telephone, or proposal

    Copies of proposal: 2

    Deadlines: varies

    Board meeting dates: bimonthly, beginning in February

    Final notification: 60 to 90 days

Puget Sound Power & Light Company
P. O. Box 97034
Bellevue, Washington 98009
(206) 462-3799

Areas of interest: Arts and culture (museums/galleries), civic and public affairs (economics, business/free enterprise, urban and community affairs), education, health, and social services.

Restrictions: Grants for capital and general support; grants to individuals.

Focus of giving: Primarily in Washington State.

$ Given: $500,000 for grants: average $1,000–$10,000

Contact: Neil L. McReynolds, Senior Vice-President, Corporate Relations.

    Initial approach: letter or proposal

    Deadlines: submit proposal preferably late summer/early fall

WEST VIRGINIA

Claude Worthington Benedum Foundation*
223 Fourth Avenue
Pittsburgh, Pennsylvania 15219
(412) 288-0360

Areas of interest: Serves a broad variety of charitable purposes in West Virginia and southwestern Pennsylvania. Funds are provided for projects that address regional problems and needs, that establish demonstration projects with strong potential for replication in Pennsylvania, or that make outstanding contributions to the area. Local initiatives and voluntary support are encouraged by the foundation.

Restrictions: Grants are awarded for operating budgets, continuing support, building funds, special projects, matching funds, program-related investments, and seed money.

$ Given: $5,646,092 for 73 grants: high $1,000,000; low $2,500; average $75,000.

Assets: $108,939,234

Publications: Annual report and application guidelines.

Contact: Paul R. Jenkins, Executive Vice-President
    Initial approach: letter
    Copies of proposal: 1
    Deadlines: none
    Board meeting dates: March, June, September, and December
    Final notification: 6 weeks

The Greater Kanawha Valley Foundation**
P. O. Box 3041
Charleston, West Virginia
(304) 346-3620

Restrictions: Grants for operating budgets, continuing support, seed money building funds, emergency funds, equipment, special projects, matching funds, and land acquisition.

*Incorporated in 1944 in Pennsylvania.
**Community foundation established in 1962 in West Virginia.

Focus of giving: Giving limited to the Greater Kanawha Valley, West Virginia area.

$ Given: $406,559 for 91 grants: high $25,000; low $89; average $500–$5,000. Also $200,371 for 200 grants to individuals.

Publications: Annual report and application guidelines.

Contact: Stanley Loewenstein, Executive Director
> **Initial approach:** letter or telephone full proposal

WISCONSIN

Judd S. Alexander Foundation, Inc.[*]
500 Third Street, Suite 509
P. O. Box 2137
Wausau, Wisconsin 54402-2137
(715) 845-4556

Restrictions: Grants for building funds, emergency funds, equipment, matching funds, land acquisition, program-related investments, and seed money.

Focus of giving: Giving primarily in Wisconsin.

$ Given: $270,472 for 56 grants: high $29,000; low $175. Also $157,723 for 3 loans.

Assets: $8,937,425

Publications: Application guidelines.

Contact: Stanley F. Staples, Jr., President
> **Initial approach:** letter, full proposal, or telephone
> **Copies of proposal:** 1
> **Deadlines:** none
> **Board meeting dates:** monthly
> **Final notification:** 60 days

[*]Incorporated in 1973 in Wisconsin.

Alvin R. Amundson Charitable Remainder Trust
c/o Marshall and Ilsly Bank,
Madison Trust Office
P. O. Box 830
Madison, Wisconsin 53701

Restrictions: Local giving for community development.

Focus of giving: Giving limited to the village of Cambridge and surrounding municipalities.

$ Given: $68,225 for 12 grants: high $38,225; low $1,000.

Assets: $1,083,756

Contact: Marshall and Ilsley Bank, Madison Trust Office

Bemis Company Foundation
800 Northstar Center
Minneapolis, Minnesota 55402
(612) 340-6198

Areas of interest: Urban and community affairs, arts centers, cinema, performing arts (general), business/free enterprise, economic development, education, health, and social services.

Restrictions: Grants for general support, special projects, and matching funds; grants to individuals.

Focus of giving: Areas where company maintains facilities, with emphasis on Minneapolis, MN. AR (Crossett), CA (Los Angeles, Union City, Wilmington), CT (Plainfield, Stratford), FL (Panama City), IL (Murphysboro, Peoria, Schaumburg), IN (Indianapolis, Terre Haute), KS (Wichita), KY (Florence, Henderson, Louisville), MA (East Pepperell), MI (Grand Rapids, Zeeland), MN (Mankato, Minneapolis, Minnetonka), MO (Louisiana, Saint Louis, Springfield), MS (Verona), NC (Statesville), NE (Omaha), NH (Hudson, Nashua, North Walpole), NJ (Flemington), NY (Buffalo), OH (Stow), TN (Memphis), TX (Jacksonville), WA (Seattle, Vancouver), WI (Green Bay, New London, Oshkosh, Sheboygan).

$ Given: $700,000 for 826 grants; average $832.

Contact: Edward T. Dougherty, Executive Director
    Initial approach: brief letter or proposal
    Deadlines: applications accepted throughout the year

Fort Howard Paper Foundation
P. O. Box 11325
Green Bay, Wisconsin 54307
(414) 435-8821

Areas of interest: Arts and humanities (museums/galleries, libraries, music, historic preservation/restoration), civic and public affairs (professional associations, urban and community affairs), education, health, and social services.

Restrictions: Grants for capital, general support, and special projects; grants to individuals.

Focus of giving: Giving primarily in Green Bay, Wisconsin, Muskogee, Oklahoma; and limited areas surrounding these communities.

$ Given: $622,396 for 31 grants: high $135,000; low $29; average $2,000–$12,000.

Assets: $11,303,956

Contact: Bruce W. Nagel, Assistant Secretary
   Initial approach: brief letter or proposal
   Deadlines: applications accepted throughout the year

Otto Bremer Foundation
55 East Fifth Street, Suite 700
St. Paul, Minnesota 55101
(612) 227-8036

Areas of interest: Community funds and building grants.

Restrictions: Grants are restricted to nonprofit, tax-exempt organizations and to programs having a direct impact on the service areas of the 26 Bremer banks in Minnesota, North Dakota, and Wisconsin, and within the city of St. Paul.

$ Given: Grants vary in amount, depending upon the needs and nature of the request.

Contact: John Kostishack, Executive Director
   Initial approach: contact the foundation staff by telephone or letter for assistance in the development of a proposal
   Deadlines: requests are reviewed continually
   Board meeting dates: once a month

7

Federal Money

The grants in this chapter consist primarily of awards made by government agencies. Many of these awards are made directly to individuals, but some require a fiscal sponsor (see previous section introduction on fiscal sponsorship). There is an enormous amount of money available from the federal government. Last year there were some 975 programs dispersing over $300 billion in grants and direct payments.

In addition to these sources, check with a local bank or the Small Business Administration (SBA) office about the possibility of obtaining an SBA loan. Small commercial real estate loans are all but off limits to individuals by most troubled savings and loans institutions and by banks accustomed to dealing exclusively with big accounts. Individual buyers of business properties, for example, have few options when it comes to financing $500,000 to $2 million. The few loans that are available often have to be paid back in less than ten years and carry prohibitively high interest rates.

To meet the requirements of an SBA loan, the borrower must be able to collateralize the loan. Repayment note terms vary from 7 to 25 years; however, because the SBA wants to keep its default rate at a minimum, it will structure the loan and work with the borrower to try to guarantee repayment, and there are usually no balloon payments. The SBA prefers that the property being bought or developed be used as the buyer's place of business, and the borrower should demonstrate a healthy cash flow and bottom line. Often, these SBA loans are viewed as business loans rather than real estate loans.

U.S. DEPARTMENT OF AGRICULTURE

Farmers Home Administration
U.S. Department of Agriculture
Washington, D.C. 20250
(202) 382-1474

Name of program: Rural Housing Loans and Grants (Section 504)

Restrictions: Grants to assist very low-income owner-occupants in rural areas to repair or improve their dwellings to make such dwellings sanitary and to remove hazards.

Focus of giving: FmHA is the credit agency for agriculture and rural development in the USDA. FmHA has offices at the state, district, and county levels that serve every county or parish in the 50 states, plus the Pacific Trust Territory, Guam, Puerto Rico, and the Virgin Islands.

$ Given: Up to $5,000 per grant; total amount of support: $12.5 million available nationwide for fiscal year 1986. Matching fund requirements: none.

Eligibility: Applicants must own and occupy houses in rural areas that need repair to remove health or safety hazards. Grant recipients must be 62 years of age or older and unable to pay for the cost of repairs with a loan.

Contact: James A. Weibel, FmHA Housing Specialist

  Application information: apply at the local county FmHA office

  Deadlines: none; awards are approved by county supervisor

Farmers Home Administration
U.S. Department of Agriculture
Washington, D.C. 20250
(202) 382-1632

Name of program: Emergency Loans

Restrictions: To assist farmers, ranchers, and aquaculture operators with loans to cover losses resulting from a major and/or natural disaster. Loans may be used to repair, restore, or replace damaged or destroyed farm property.

$ Given: Guaranteed/insured loans ranging from $500 to $6 million.

Eligibility: Individuals.

Contact: Administrator

Farmers Home Administration
U.S. Department of Agriculture
Washington, D.C. 20250
(202) 447-7967

Name of program: Low-Income Housing Loans

Restrictions: To assist rural low-income families to obtain decent, safe, and sanitary dwellings and related facilities. Loans may be used for construction, repair, or purchase of housing.

$ Given: Guaranteed/insured loans ranging from $1,000 to $60,000.

Eligibility: Individuals.

Contact: Administrator

U.S. DEPARTMENT OF COMMERCE

ECONOMIC DEVELOPMENT—BUSINESS DEVELOPMENT ASSISTANCE

Economic Development Administration
U.S. Department of Commerce, Room H7844
Herbert Hoover Building
Washington, D.C. 20230
(202) 377-5067

Restrictions: To sustain industrial and commercial viability in designated areas by providing financial assistance to businesses that create or retain permanent jobs or expand or establish plants in redevelopment areas for projects where financial assistance is not available from other sources, on terms and conditions that would permit accomplishment of the project and further economic development in the area.

Eligibility: Individuals, private or public corporations, or Indian tribes.

$ Given: Guaranteed/insured loans ranging from $260,000 to $111 million.

Contact: Deputy Assistant Secretary for Finance, Finance Directorate

U.S. DEPARTMENT OF HEALTH AND HUMAN SERVICES

LAND AND BUILDINGS

Office of Real Property
Office of Facilities Engineering
U.S. Department of Health and Human Services
Washington, D.C. 20201
(202) 245-1926

Restrictions: Eligible organizations and institutions can obtain surplus real properties to carry out health programs, including research. Property is awarded to the applicants whose programs or use are determined to be in the highest public interest.

Contact: Chief, Division of Realty

U.S. DEPARTMENT OF HOUSING AND URBAN DEVELOPMENT

HOUSING

Single Family Development Division
Office of Single Family Housing
U.S. Department of Housing and Urban Development
451 7th Street, S.W.
Washington, D.C. 20410
(202) 755-6720

Name of program: Rehabilitation Mortgage Insurance

Restrictions: To help families repair or improve, purchase and improve, or refinance and improve existing residential structures.

Eligibility: Individuals.

$ Given: Guaranteed/insured loans.

Contact: Director

Insurance Division
Office of Multifamily Housing Development
U.S. Department of Housing and Urban Development
Washington, D.C. 20410
(202) 755-6223

Name of program: Mortgage Insurance—Construction or Substantial Rehabilitation of Condominium Projects

Restrictions: To enable sponsors to develop condominium projects in which individual units will be sold to home buyers.

Eligibility: Individuals.

$ Given: Guaranteed/insured loans up to $36,000.

Single Family Development Division
Office of Single Family Housing
U.S. Department of Housing and Urban Development
Washington, D.C. 20410
(202) 755-6223

Name of program: Mortgage Insurance—Homes

Restrictions: To help families undertake home ownership, and insure lenders against loss on mortgage loans. These loans may be used to finance the purchase of proposed, under-construction, or existing one- to four-family housing.

Eligibility: Individuals.

$ Given: Guaranteed/insured loans averaging $39,356.

Single Family Development Division
Office of Single Family Housing
U.S. Department of Housing and Urban Development
Washington, D.C. 20410
(202) 755-6720

Name of program: Mortgage Insurance—Homes in Outlying Areas

Restrictions: To help families purchase homes in outlying areas, and to insure lenders against loss on mortgage loans. These loans may be used to finance the purchase of proposed, under-construction, or existing one-family nonfarm, or new farm housing on five or more acres adjacent to a highway.

Eligibility: Individuals.

$ Given: Guaranteed/insured loans up to $42,000.

Single Family Development Division
Office of Single Family Housing
U.S. Department of Housing and Urban Development
Washington, D.C. 20410
(202) 755-6720

Name of program: Mortgage Insurance—Homes in Urban Renewal Areas

Restrictions: To help families purchase or rehabilitate homes in urban renewal areas, and to insure lenders against loss on mortgage loans. These loans may be used to finance acquisition or rehabilitation of one- to eleven-family housing in approved urban renewal or code enforcement areas.

Eligibility: Individuals.

$ Given: Guaranteed/insured loans.

LAND FOR BUILDERS

Office of Surplus Land and Housing
New Communities Development Corporation
U.S. Department of Housing and Urban Development
451 7th Street, S.W.
Washington, D.C. 20410
(202) 426-3500

Restrictions: The U.S. Department of Housing and Urban Development sells and donates surplus federal land and property to those who use it for low- or moderate- income housing and related commercial and industrial use.

Eligibility: American Indians.

$ Given: Grants up to $45,000.

COMMUNITY PLANNING AND DEVELOPMENT

U.S. Department of Housing and Urban Development
451 7th Street S.W., Room 7100
Washington, D.C. 20410
(202) 755-6270

Restrictions: To provide decent housing, a suitable living environment, and expanding economic opportunities for persons of low and moderate income. Makes direct grants to severely distressed cities and urban counties for local economic development projects designed to stimulate new and increased private investment. Assists state and local governments with common or related planning development programs. Ensures fair treatment of persons displaced by federally-assisted projects. Implement policies and procedures for the protection and enhancement of environmental quality. Provides loans for rehabilitation of property and assistance to the urban homesteading program.

$ Given: Grants and loans.

U.S. Department of Housing and Urban Development
451 7th Street S.W., Room 7100
Washington, D.C. 20410
(202) 755-5544

Name of program: Mortgage Insurance—Experimental Rental Housing

Restrictions: To provide mortgage insurance to help finance the development of multifamily housing that incorporates new or untried construction concepts designed to reduce housing costs, raise living standards, and improve neighborhood design.

Eligibility: Individuals.

$ Given: Guaranteed/insured loans averaging $2,314,814.

Contact: Secretary for Policy Development and Research

Single Family Development Division
Office of Single Family Housing
U.S. Department of Housing and Urban Development
451 7th Street, S.W.
Washington, D.C. 20410
(202) 426-3500

Name of program: Mortgage Insurance—Land Development and New Communities

Restrictions: To assist the development of large subdivisions or new communities on a sound economic basis, and to insure lenders against loss on mortgage loans. These loans may be used to assist in financing the purchase of land and the development of building sites for subdivisions or new communities including water and sewer systems, streets and lighting, and other installations needed for residential communities.

Eligibility: Individuals.

$ Given: Guaranteed/insured loans.

Contact: Director

Insurance Division
Office of Multifamily Housing Development
U.S. Department of Housing and Urban Development
Washington, D.C. 20410
(202) 755-6223

Name of program: Mortgage Insurance—Group Practice Facilities

Restrictions: To help develop group health practice facilities and to insure lenders against loss on mortgage loans. These loans may be used to finance the construction or rehabilitation of facilities, including major movable equipment, for the provision of preventive, diagnostic, and treatment services by medical, dental, optometric, osteopathic, or podiatric groups.

Eligibility: Individuals.

$ Given: Guaranteed/insured loans.

FAIR HOUSING ASSISTANCE PROGRAM

Assistant Secretary for Fair Housing and Equal Opportunity
Department of Housing and Urban Development
451 7th Street, S.W.
Washington, D.C. 20410
(202) 426-3500

Restrictions: Grants to state and local governments

$ Given: Grants up to $250,000.

COMMUNITY HOUSING RESOURCE BOARD PROGRAM

U.S. Department of Housing and Urban Development
Office of Fair Housing and Equal Opportunity
Office of Voluntary Compliance
Washington, D.C. 20410
(202) 755-5992

Restrictions: To fulfill HUD's contractual agreement to provide assistance to local real estate boards in achieving Voluntary Affirmative Marketing Agreement goals by supporting projects that improve Community Housing Resource Boards performance and increase their ability to assist in implementing the VAMA.

Eligibility: The applicant must be a Community Housing Resource Board consisting of HUD-appointed representatives of community organizations or agencies formed to fulfill HUD's obligation to provide technical assistance to local real estate boards in the implementation and monitoring of progress under the Voluntary Affirmative Marketing Agreement.

$ Given: $15,000 for Community Housing Resource Boards in communities of 50,000 or less; $25,000 for Community Housing Resource Boards in communities of over 50,000.

PROPERTY FOR SALE—MULTIFAMILY

Office of Multifamily Financing and Preservation
Office of Housing
U.S. Department of Housing and Urban Development
451 7th Street, S.W., Room 6151
Washington, D.C. 20410
(202) 755-7220

Restrictions: Department of Housing and Urban Development—held multifamily properties are sold by sealed-bid auction throughout the country.

Contact: Multifamily Sales Division

PROPERTY FOR SALE—SINGLE FAMILY

Office of Single Family Housing
Office of Housing
U.S. Department of Housing and Urban Development
451 7th Street, S.W., Room 9170
Washington, D.C. 20410
(202) 755-5832

Restrictions: Department of Housing and Urban Development–held single family properties are sold by sealed-bid auction throughout the country.

Contact: Sales Promotion Branch

COMMUNITY PLANNING AND DEVELOPMENT

Office of Program Policy Development
Community Development and Planning
U. S. Department of Housing and Urban Development
451 7th Street, S.W.
Washington, D.C. 20410
(202) 755-6069

Name of program: Indian Community Development Block Grant Program

Restrictions: Assistance to Indian tribes and Alaskan natives in the development of viable Indian communities and to provide community development assistance to American Samoa, Guam, the Northern Mariana Islands, and the U. S. Virgin Islands.

$ Given: Grants.

Community Planning and Development
Office of Urban Rehabilitation
U.S. Department of Housing and Urban Development
451 7th Street, S.W., Room 7132
Washington, D.C. 20410
(202) 755-6336

Name of Program: Section 312 Rehabilitation Loans

Restrictions: To promote the revitalization of neighborhoods by providing funds for rehabilitation of residential, commercial, and other non-residential properties.

Eligibility: Individuals.

$ Given: Direct loans up to $27,000 per dwelling unit.

U.S. DEPARTMENT OF THE INTERIOR

INDIAN HOUSING ASSISTANCE

Division of Housing Assistance
Office of Indian Services
Bureau of Indian Affairs
18th and C Streets, N.W.
Washington, D.C. 20245
(202) 343-4876

Restrictions: To eliminate substantially substandard Indian housing.

Eligibility: American Indians.

$ Given: Grants up to $45,000.

INDIAN LOANS—ECONOMIC DEVELOPMENT (INDIAN CREDIT PROGRAM)

Office of Indian Services
Bureau of Indian Affairs
18th and C Streets, N.W., Room 4600
Washington, D.C. 20245
(202) 343-3657

Restrictions: To provide assistance to Indians, Alaskan natives, tribes, and Indian organizations to obtain financing from private and governmental sources which serve other citizens. When otherwise unavailable, financial assistance through the Bureau of Indian Affairs is provided to eligible applicants for any purpose that will promote the economic development of a federal Indian reservation.

Eligibility: Native Americans.

$ Given: Direct loans and guaranteed/insured loans ranging from $100 to $1 million.

GENERAL SERVICES ADMINISTRATION

DISPOSAL OF FEDERAL SURPLUS REAL PROPERTY

Office of Real Property
Federal Property Resource Service
General Services Administration
Washington, D.C. 20405
(202) 535-7084

Restrictions: Surplus property is offered for sale or use as public parks, recreation areas, public health centers, or educational centers. The property is generally offered for sale to the public on a competitive bid basis.

Eligibility: Individuals, state and local government agencies, tax-exempt agencies, and schools are eligible to apply for this property.

$ Given: Sale, exchange, or donation of property and goods.

Contact: Assistant Commissioner

SALE OF FEDERAL SURPLUS PERSONAL PROPERTY

Office of Federal Supply and Services
General Services Administration
Washington, D.C. 20405
(703) 557-0814

Restrictions: To sell in an economical and efficient manner property no longer needed by the government and obtain the maximum net return from sales. General Services Administration conducts the sale of personal property for most of the civil agencies; the Department of Defense handles the sale of its own surplus property.

Eligibility: Individuals, nonprofit organizations, and state and local governments.

$ Given: Sale, exchange, or donation of property and goods.

Contact: Director, Sales Division, Office of Property Management

SMALL BUSINESS ADMINISTRATION

PHYSICAL DISASTER LOANS

Disaster Assistance Division
Small Business Administration
1441 L Street, N.W.
Washington, D.C. 20416
(202) 653-6879

Restrictions: To provide loans to restore, as nearly as possible, the living conditions of victims of physical disasters.

Eligibility: Individuals.

$ Given: Direct loans and guaranteed/insured loans up to $500,000.

SMALL BUSINESS INVESTMENT COMPANIES

Office of Investment
Small Business Administration
1441 L Street, N.W.
Washington, D.C. 20416
(202) 653-6584

Restrictions: To make equity and venture capital available to the small business community with maximum use of private sector participation and a minimum of government interference in the free market.

Eligibility: Individuals.

$ Given: Direct loans and guaranteed/insured loans ranging from $50,000 to $35 million.

Contact: Director

LOANS FOR SMALL BUSINESSES

Small Business Administration
1441 L Street, N.W.
Washington, D.C. 20416
(202) 653-6881

Restrictions: To aid small businesses unable to obtain financing in the private credit marketplace, including agricultural enterprises. Funds may be used to construct, expand, or convert facilities; to purchase building equipment or materials; or for working capital.

Eligibility: Individuals.

$ Given: Direct loans and guaranteed/insured loans ranging from $1,000 to $500,000.

Contact: Associate Administrator for Management Assistance

CERTIFIED DEVELOPMENT COMPANY LOANS

Office of Economic Development
Small Business Administration, Room 720
1441 L Street, N.W.
Washington, D.C. 20416

Restrictions: To assist small businesses by providing long-term financing through the sale of debentures of the Federal Financing Bank. Loans are for the acquisition of land and buildings, construction, expansion, renovation and modernization, and machinery and equipment.

Eligibility: Incorporated companies.

$ Given: Guaranteed/insured loans up to $500,000.

Contact: Director

SMALL BUSINESS ENERGY LOANS

Small Business Administration
1441 L Street, N.W.
Washington, D.C. 20416
(202) 653-6570

Restrictions: To assist small businesses to finance plant construction, expansion, conversion, or start-up, and in the acquisition of equipment facilities, machinery, supplies, or materials to enable such businesses to manufacture, design, market, install, or service specific energy measures.

Eligibility: Individuals.

$ Given: Direct loans and guaranteed/insured loans.

Contact: Business Loans

BOND GUARANTEES FOR SURETY COMPANIES

Surety Bond Guarantee Branch
Small Business Administration
4040 North Fairfax Drive
Arlington, Virginia 22203
(703) 235-2907

Restrictions: To encourage the commercial surety market to make surety bonds more available to small contractors unable to obtain a bond without a guarantee.

Eligibility: Individuals.

$ Given: Guaranteed/insured loans ranging from $2,000 to $1 million.

Contact: Chief

TENNESSEE VALLEY AUTHORITY

NATIONAL FERTILIZER DEVELOPMENT

Tennessee Valley Authority
400 West Summit Hill Drive
Knoxville, Tennessee 37902
(615) 632-2101

Restrictions: To develop improved, cheaper fertilizer products and processes and to improve U.S. agriculture.

Eligibility: Land-grant colleges, fertilizer industry firms, and farmers.

$ Given: Sale, exchange, or donation of property and goods; use of property, facilities, and equipment.

Contact: General Manager

VETERANS ADMINISTRATION

VETERANS HOUSING

Veterans Administration
Central Office
810 Vermont Avenue, N.W.
Washington, D.C. 20420
(202) 389-2356

Name of program: Guaranteed and Insured Loans

Restrictions: To assist veterans, service persons, and certain unremarried widows or widowers of veterans in obtaining credit for the purchase of homes on more liberal terms than are available to nonveterans.

Eligibility: Individuals.

$ Given: Guaranteed/insured loans ranging from $39,000 to $78,600.

Veterans Administration
Central Office
810 Vermont Avenue, N.W.
Washington, D.C. 20420
(202) 389-2356

Name of program: Direct Loans for Disabled Veterans

Restrictions: To provide certain severely disabled veterans with direct housing credit and to supplement grants authorized to assist such veterans in acquiring suitable housing with special features or movable facilities made necessary by their disabilities.

Eligibility: Individuals.

$ Given: Direct loans up to $33,000.

Veterans Administration
Central Office
810 Vermont Avenue, N.W.
Washington, D.C. 20420
(202) 389-2356

Name of program: Manufactured Home Loans

Restrictions: To assist veterans, service persons, and certain unremarried widows or widowers of veterans in obtaining credit for the purchase of a mobile home on more liberal terms than are available to nonveterans.

Eligibility: Individuals.

$ Given: Guaranteed/insured loans ranging from $16,490 to $27,450.

FEDERAL EMERGENCY MANAGEMENT AGENCY

DISASTER ASSISTANCE

Office of Disaster Assistance Programs
Federal Emergency Management Agency
Washington, D.C. 20472
(202) 646-3618

Restrictions: To provide assistance to states, local governments, selected private nonprofit facilities, and individuals in alleviating suffering and hardship resulting from emergencies or major disasters declared by the President.

Eligibility: Individuals and state and local governments.

$ Given: Grants ranging from $21 to $39,202,722.

U.S. DEPARTMENT OF EDUCATION

FEDERAL REAL PROPERTY ASSISTANCE PROGRAM

Federal Real Property Assistance Program
Office of Management
U.S. Department of Education
400 Maryland Avenue, S.W.
Washington, D.C. 20202
(202) 245-0306

Restrictions: Sale, exchange, or donation of surplus federal real property for educational purposes.

Eligibility: Organizations providing educational programs.

8

State Government Sources

ALABAMA

Alabama Development Office
Industrial Finance Division
State Capitol
Montgomery, Alabama 36130
(205) 263-0048

Name of program: Industrial Development Bond Issues

Restrictions: Used for purchase of land and buildings for new industry and for new additions to existing industry.

$ Given: Can finance up to 100 percent of the project costs. Projects financed by IDB are 100 percent exempt from all property taxes for the entire bond amortization period, which is normally 20 years. Interest rate is 70–85 percent of prime, and the term is normally 10–20 years.

Alabama Development Office
Industrial Finance Division
State Capitol
Montgomery, Alabama 36130
(205) 263-0048

Name of program: Urban Development Action Grant

Restrictions: Subordinated loan for gap financing, which can be used for the purchase of land and buildings and for new expansions. Interest rates, which are generally below market rates, are set by the federal government. Term is 10–20 years.

Eligibility: Grant is available only in eligible communities and cannot exceed one-quarter of the project cost. There is no limit on the total amount of the project.

Alabama Development Office
Industrial Finance Division
State Capitol
Montgomery, Alabama 36130
(205) 263-0048

Name of program: State Economic Development Loan Program

Restrictions: Can be used for the purchase of land, buildings, and for new expansion.

$ Given: There is a $250,000 limit per project; the interest rate is normally two points below prime; terms are generally 5–15 years; and the program can finance up to 40 percent of the project costs.

Alabama Development Office
Industrial Finance Division
State Capitol
Montgomery, Alabama 36130
(205) 263-0048

Name of program: Small Business Administration (SBA) 503 Loan

Restrictions: Can be used for the purchase of land and buildings and for new expansion. With this type of loan package, small businesses get better financial programs than are otherwise available on the market.

$ Given: The bank loans 50 percent of the project cost; the SBA loans 40 percent of the project cost at below market rates (usually this is equivalent to the 20-year treasury note rate). The SBA portion will have a maturity of 15, 20, or 25 years, depending on the project.

Alabama Development Office
Industrial Finance Division
State Capitol
Montgomery, Alabama 36130
(205) 263-0048

Name of program: State Industrial Site Preparation Grants

Restrictions: To help new and expanding manufacturing industries pay for industrial site preparation. May be used for conducting land and labor surveys and for grading, draining, and providing access to specific sites.

$ Given: Amount of the grant depends upon the amount of expenses for construction and equipment.

Alabama Development Office
Industrial Finance Division
State Capitol
Montgomery, Alabama 36130
(205) 263-0048

Name of program: Speculative Building Revolving Loan Fund

Restrictions: Industrial development boards may borrow up to 25 percent of the cost of constructing a speculative building for industrial development purposes with no interest on the money borrowed from the fund.

ALASKA

Alaska Industrial Development Authority
1577 C Street, Suite 304
Anchorage, Alaska 99501-5177
(907) 274-1651

Name of program: AIDA Revenue Bond Financing Program

Restrictions: Eligible projects include most types of commercial and industrial activity involving construction or acquisition of new plants and equipment.

$ Given: Borrower must locate purchaser or purchasers to buy 100 percent of the revenue bonds issued by AIDA for this project. The interest rate on the loan and any other charges are determined jointly by the borrower and the lender. Current AIDA charges include a $100 preliminary application fee and a financing fee of one percent for the first $1 million of bonds, declining to .5 percent for the next $4 million; to .25 percent for the next $10 million of bonds; and to .10 percent for bonds above $10 million.

Alaska Industrial Development Authority
1577 C Street, Suite 304
Anchorage, Alaska 99501-5177
(907) 274-1651

Name of program: AIDA Federally Guaranteed Loan Program

Restrictions: Loan program to finance accounts receivable, inventory, working capital, equipment, and for some refinancing of existing debt.

$ Given: AIDA will provide up to $500,000 per borrower by purchasing from the lender a participation in a loan guaranteed by the United States or an agency or instrumentality of the United States. AIDA assesses no fees on these loans. The composite rate of interest to the borrower on a guaranteed loan purchased by AIDA may not exceed the rate charged by AIDA by more than 1.5 percent for loans of $100,000. Presently AIDA's rate is equal to the Moody's Aa Corporate Bond Index and is fixed for the entire term of the loan.

Currently there is a $100 preliminary application fee and a one percent commitment fee to AIDA. The bond sale costs vary but are usually about three percent of the loan amount. Interest rates are determined by the marketplace and may vary. Generally, the AIDA portion of a long-term loan will carry an interest rate approximately equal to the Weekly Bond Buyer's Revenue Bond Index plus .5 to one percent.

Eligibility: The borrower must locate a qualified financial institution to be the lender/originator.

ARIZONA

Arizona Enterprise Development Corporation
Arizona Department of Commerce
Development Finance Unit
1700 West Washington
Phoenix, Arizona 85007
(602) 255-5705

Name of program: Development Finance Program

Restrictions: Provides loans to small expanding businesses through the U.S. Small Business Administration 503 Program. Can be used for the purchase of land and buildings and for construction and renovation.

Eligibility: For-profit businesses generating an average net profit of less than $2 million for the preceding two years with a net worth of less than $6 million, and located in Arizona (but outside Phoenix and Tucson, which have similar programs).

Arizona Department of Commerce
Development Finance Unit
1700 West Washington
Phoenix, Arizona 85007
(602) 255-5705

Name of program: Revolving Loan Programs

Restrictions: Provides loans for economic development projects. Can be used for site/facility acquisition and for improvements, construction, and building rehabilitation.

Eligibility: Small for-profit businesses located throughout Arizona (except Maricopa and Pima counties).

Arizona Department of Commerce
Development Finance Unit
1700 West Washington
Phoenix, Arizona 85007
(602) 255-5705

Name of program: Urban Development Action Grants

Restrictions: Used by eligible cities and towns and all Indian reservations to provide subordinated loans to new and expanding businesses, usually at 10–25 percent of a project. Eligible uses include site improvements for, and/or construction of, commercial, industrial, and mixed-use developments, and for industrial and commercial rehabilitation. Working capital, debt refinancing, and consolidation are not eligible uses.

$ Given: Favorable rates and terms are negotiated to ensure that good projects will proceed.

ARKANSAS

Arkansas Industrial Development Commission
1 State Capitol Mall
Little Rock, Arkansas 72201
(501) 371-7786

Restrictions: Provides financial assistance for start-up and existing businesses.

$ Given: Offers a maximum of $500,000 fixed-asset financing to businesses with at least a three-year operating history.

Minority Business Development Department
1 Capitol Mall, Room 4C-300
Little Rock, Arkansas 72201
(501) 371-1060

Restrictions: Offers access to financial resources, including a $1 million Minority Economic Development Fund.

CALIFORNIA

California Self-Help Housing Program (CSHHP)
Department of Housing and Community Development
921 10th Street, 5L
Sacramento, California 95814-2774
(916) 445-0110

Areas of interest: The program's primary emphasis is on the expansion and improvement of the housing stock available to low-income persons (80 percent of median income and below).

Restrictions: Nonprofit corporations and public agencies capable of providing technical assistance and comprehensive information to self-helpers and owner-builders.

$ Given: Grants to $100,000.

Assets: Grants and loans in 1988-89 of $1 million.

Deadlines: applications are accepted on an over-the-counter basis

Office of Business and Industrial Development
California Department of Economic and Business Development
1121 L Street, Suite 600
Sacramento, California 95814
(916) 322-5665

Name of program: Industrial Development Bonds

Restrictions: Provides low-interest financing to businesses wanting to locate or expand their operations through the use of tax-exempt industrial development bonds. Can be used to finance land acquisition and building construction.

Office of Local Development
California Department of Commerce
1121 L Street, Suite 600
Sacramento, California 95814
(916) 322-1398

Areas of interest: The California Department of Commerce administers a variety of state and federal loan and grant programs through this office, including funding sources for renovation of abandoned industrial businesses and central business district revitalization.

State Coastal Conservancy
1300 Broadway, Suite 1100
Oakland, California 94612
(415) 464-1015

Name of program: Urban Waterfronts Restoration Program

Areas of interest: To assist local governments in planning and providing new public investment in waterfront and near-shore areas; to encourage the development of land uses designed as high-priority under the coastal act (commercial recreation, public recreation, shoreline access, coastal dependent industry); and to develop feasible means of preserving such facilities when they are in need of rehabilitation.

Restrictions: Any local government, special district, or nonprofit organization may apply. Also any public or private party may apply for revenue bond funding. Projects must be in coastal areas or in and around the San Francisco Bay area.

$ Given: Grants or loans; depends upon individual project. Amounts, terms, and conditions of funding are negotiable.

Contact: Marc Beyeler, Urban Waterfronts Program Manager
    Initial approach: telephone or letter
    Deadlines: continuous application process

Department of Housing and Community Development
921 10th Street, Room 402
Sacramento, California 95814
(916) 322-1561

Restrictions: Cities with 50,000 or less in population and counties with 200,000 or less in the unincorporated area.

$ Given: Grants to communities and loans to businesses; $6 million annually. Grants range from $100,000 to $600,000.

Contact: Rochelle Braly

    Deadlines: March 1, June 1, September 1, and December 1

COLORADO

Farmers Home Administration
2490 West 26th Avenue
Denver, Colorado 80211
(303) 964-0151

Restrictions: Guarantees business and industrial loans in non-metropolitan areas of Colorado. Guarantees up to 90 percent of a loan from a bank or other lender to any kind of business that benefits a rural community.

CONNECTICUT

Connecticut Development Authority
217 Washington Street
Hartford, Connecticut 06106
(203) 522-3730

Name of program: Industrial Revenue Bonds

Restrictions: Provides long-term industrial bond financing to cover the purchase and development of land or the construction, purchase, or remodeling of buildings. Eligible project types include manufacturing, processing, assembling, research facilities, offices, warehousing, and certain recreation facilities.

Connecticut Development Credit Corporation
P. O. Box 714
Meriden, Connecticut 06450
(203) 235-3327

Restrictions: Makes long-term loans to small- and medium-sized businesses. Funding is usually applied toward capital and to plant construction and renovation.

Eligibility: CDCC loans are made only in those cases where financing is not available from banks or other normal credit sources.

DELAWARE

Delaware Development Office
99 Kings Highway, P. O. Box 1401
Dover, Delaware 19903
(302) 736-4271

Name of program: Industrial Revenue Bonds

Restrictions: Used to finance fixed assets within the following categories: industrial, commercial, and agricultural. Long-term, low-interest-rate financing may be obtained.

DISTRICT OF COLUMBIA

National Development Council
1025 Connecticut Avenue, N.W.
Washington, D.C. 20036
(202) 466-3906

Name of program: Small Business Revitalization Program

Restrictions: The National Development Council coordinates and implements the Small Business Revitalization Program, a federally-sponsored plan for mobilizing private sector capital for growing smaller business and industry.

District of Columbia Office of Business and Economic Development
1350 Pennsylvania Avenue, N.W., Room 208
Washington, D.C. 20004
(202) 727-6600

Name of program: Revolving Loan Fund

Restrictions: Directs loans for short-term gap-financing (30 days to two years) to be used in conjunction with private funds.

FLORIDA

Florida First Capital Finance Corporation, Inc.
P. O. Box 5826
Tallahassee, Florida 32301
(904) 487-0466

Restrictions: Financing is available for land acquisition, building construction, purchase of buildings, renovation, and modernization.

GEORGIA

Georgia Department of Community Affairs
Community and Economic Development Division
40 Marietta Street, N.W., Suite 800
Atlanta, Georgia 30303
(404) 656-3839

Name of program: Community Development Block Grants

Restrictions: Individual communities apply for available funding. Selected businesses receive funding for development from the community. Also provides referrals to other sources of funding for businesses.

HAWAII

Small Business Information Service
Hawaii Department of Planning and Economic Development
250 South King Street, Room 724
Honolulu, Hawaii 96813
(808) 548-7645 or 548-7887

Name of program: Hawaii Capital Loan Program

Restrictions: Provides loans for small businesses for the financing of plant construction, conversion, or expansion; for land acquisition or expansion; or for working capital.

$ Given: Maximum loan amount is $250,000.

Eligibility: Applicants must be unable to obtain financing from private lending institutions.

IDAHO

U.S. Small Business Administration
1020 Main Street, Suite 290
Boise, Idaho 83702
(208) 334-1780

Name of program: Certified Development Company Loans

Restrictions: Provides long-term, fixed-rate second mortgage financing for the expansion of small- and medium-size businesses. There are eight Certified Development Companies operating in the district that promote, package, and service these loans. The objective of the program is economic development and increased employment.

ILLINOIS

Illinois Department of Commerce and Community Affairs
620 East Adams Street
Springfield, Illinois 62701
(217) 782-1460

Name of program: Illinois Venture Fund

Restrictions: Provides equity capital for start-up and early stage companies located in Illinois. Money can be used for research and development expenses, working capital needs, and fixed assets.

$ Given: Amount of investment ranges from less than $300,000 to $1 million or more.

Contact: Marketing Staff

Illinois Department of Commerce and Community Affairs
620 East Adams Street
Springfield, Illinois 62701
(217) 782-1460

Name of program: Illinois Development Finance Authority Direct Loan Fund

Restrictions: Provides subordinated, fixed-interest loans for 20 to 30 percent of the cost of fixed asset projects. Money can be used for purchase of land or buildings and for building construction and renovation.

Eligibility: Assists creditworthy small- or medium-sized industrial or manufacturing firms that cannot meet all their financial requirements from conventional sources, and is intended to create jobs in areas of high unemployment.

$ Given: The average amount of an IDFA loan is $150,000.

Contact: Marketing Staff

Illinois Department of Commerce and Community Affairs
620 East Adams Street
Springfield, Illinois 62701
(217) 782-1460

Name of program: Build Illinois Small Business Development Program

Restrictions: Provides direct financing to small businesses for expansion and subsequent job creation or retention. Money can be used for land or buildings, working capital, or building construction and renovation. Provides loans which will not exceed 25 percent of the total cost of a project. The maximum amount which may be invested in any one project is $750,000. Loans are long-term, fixed-rate, and low-interest.

Contact: Marketing Staff

INDIANA

Indiana Institute for New Business Ventures, Inc.
One North Capitol, Suite 501
Indianapolis, Indiana 46204
(317) 232-3061

Areas of interest: Builds financial resource networks to provide the professional expertise required to start and operate a small business. The institute has implemented a number of programs which provide one-on-one services to individuals in the emerging business sector, including the Indiana Seed Capital Network and Capital Matching Grants.

IOWA

Iowa Development Commission
600 East Court Avenue, Suite A
Des Moines, Iowa 50309
(515) 281-3925

Restrictions: Venture capital is available in certain situations to provide capital infusion to companies that a conventional lender may view as high-risk. Venture capital is not viewed as a loan; instead the investor may take an equity position in the company.

Iowa Finance Authority
550 Liberty Building
418 Sixth Avenue
Des Moines, Iowa 50309
(515) 281-4058

Name of program: Iowa Small Business Loan Program

Restrictions: Assists the development and expansion of new or existing small businesses in Iowa through the sale of bonds and notes exempt from federal tax. The loan may be used for purchasing land or for construction, building improvements, or equipment.

Eligibility: Small businesses having 20 or fewer employees or less than $3 million in sales.

$ Given: Maximum loan is $10 million.

KANSAS

Kansas Development Credit Corporation, Inc.
First National Bank Towers, Suite 1030
Topeka, Kansas 66603
(913) 235-3437

Name of program: Kansas Venture Capital, Inc.

Restrictions: Provides debt/equity capital to small businesses. Funds can be used for working capital, debt restructuring, business expansion, and acquisition of shareholder or partner interest.

$ Given: May loan up to $200,000 to any company that meets Small Business Administration requirements.

Kansas Development Credit Corporation, Inc.
First National Bank Towers, Suite 1030
Topeka, Kansas 66603
(913) 235-3437

Restrictions: KDCC operates by borrowing money from more than 400 member Kansas banks. Loans can be made to companies that could not secure financial assistance from conventional lenders.

$ Given: Loans range up to $250,000.

KENTUCKY

Kentucky Development Finance Authority
24th Floor
Capitol Plaza Tower
Frankfort, Kentucky 40601
(502) 564-4554

Name of program: SBA 503 Loan Program

Restrictions: Provides funds for up to 40 percent of the total cost of an expansion project for a term of up to 25 years at a fixed rate of interest. This program is generally for healthy, established small businesses. Project size is generally $100,000 to $5 million, but projects under $100,000 will be considered.

$ Given: Maximum of $500,000 participation per project.

Kentucky Development Finance Authority
24th Floor
Capitol Plaza Tower
Frankfort, Kentucky 40601
(502) 564-4554

Name of program: KDFA Direct Loan Program

Restrictions: Offers a mortgage loan program to supplement private financing. The program is designed to allow businesses to obtain the long-term financing needed to encourage growth. Projects must create new jobs or have a significant impact on the economic growth of a community.

Eligibility: Projects financed must be agribusiness, tourism, or industrial ventures.

$ Given: $5,000 per job, with a maximum loan amount of $250,000; minimum loan amount is $25,000.

Kentucky Development Finance Authority
24th Floor
Capitol Plaza Tower
Frankfort, Kentucky 40601
(502) 564-4554

Name of program: Industrial Revenue Bond Issue Program

Restrictions: This program allows companies with sufficient financial strength to take advantage of tax-exempt rates of interest. Bonds may be issued for any eligible project that does not require the approval of the Industrial Revenue Bond Oversight Committee.

LOUISIANA

Louisiana Department of Commerce
P. O. Box 94185
Baton Rouge, Louisiana 70804
(504) 342-5361

Name of program: Industrial Revenue Bonds

Restrictions: Allows local authorities, development boards, and public trusts to issue up to $10 million in tax-exempt revenue bonds to finance the construction and equipping of new industrial facilities and/or expansions. The facilities and equipment are then leased to the participating company at a rent sufficient to retire the bonds. At the end of the lease period the company has the option to purchase the facility at a nominal figure or to continue to lease at a low rate.

Louisiana Minority Business Development Authority
P. O. Box 44185
Baton Rouge, Louisiana 70804
(504) 342-5359

Restrictions: Promotes business opportunities by granting loans to minority businesses.

MAINE

Maine Development Foundation
One Memorial Circle
Augusta, Maine 04330
(207) 622-6345

Restrictions: Legislatively-established, nonprofit corporation through which business, government, and education leaders pool resources to stimulate business development in Maine. The foundation provides high-level, professional assistance in such areas as industrial and commercial real estate development; location and financing of industrial and commercial facilities; business financing; and joint public/private development projects.

Finance Authority of Maine
State House
Augusta, Maine 04333
(207) 289-3095

Restrictions: Loans available for individuals and small businesses with plans for establishing new or for expanding existing industrial, manufacturing, agricultural, fishing, or recreational ventures within Maine.

$ Given: Maximum amount of loan is $1 million.

MARYLAND

Development Credit Fund, Inc.
1925 Eutaw Place
Baltimore, Maryland 21217
(301) 523-6400

Restrictions: Provides below-market financing to minority-owned companies doing business in Maryland.

Department of Economic and Community Development
Maryland Business Assistance Center
45 Calvert Street
Annapolis, Maryland 21401
(301) 269-2945

Restrictions: Provides businesses with a comprehensive array of financing alternatives including insurance for working capital loans and long-term financing of fixed assets.

$ Given: Loans and guarantees vary from $35,000 to $10 million.

MASSACHUSETTS

SITE Program
Massachusetts Department of Commerce
100 Cambridge Street
Boston, Massachusetts 02202
(617) 727-3215

Name of program: Site Inventory Tracking Exchange (SITE)

Purpose: Maintains a computerized listing of available industrial and building space throughout Massachusetts with a comprehensive printout of site attributes.

Eligibility: In-state and out-of-state firms seeking to start up, locate, or expand in Massachusetts may request this free service at any time.

Massachusetts Industrial Finance Agency
125 Pearl Street
Boston, Massachusetts 02110
(617) 451-2477

Restrictions: Promotes employment growth through industrial revenue bonds, loan guarantees, and pollution control bonds. MIFA financing is available for commercial real estate if these projects are located in locally-identified Commercial Area Revitalization Districts (CARD), primarily in older downtown areas.

Massachusetts Technology Development Corporation
84 State Street, Suite 500
Boston, Massachusetts 02109
(617) 723-4920

Restrictions: Provides capital to new and expanding high technology companies which have the capacity to generate significant employment growth in Massachusetts as well as other public benefits.

Community Development Finance Corporation
131 State Street, Suite 600
Boston, Massachusetts 02109
(617) 742-0366

Restrictions: Provides flexible financing for working capital needs and real estate development projects when there is some clear public benefit. Offers three investment programs for economic development projects: Venture Capital Investment Program, Community Development Investment Program, and Small Loan Guarantee Program.

Massachusetts Business Development Corporation
One Boston Place
Boston, Massachusetts 02108
(617) 723-7515

Restrictions: Provides loans for businesses which cannot obtain all their financing requirements from conventional sources. Provides working capital loans, government guaranteed loans, Small Business Administration 503 loans, and long-term loans.

$ Given: MBDC can provide up to 100 percent financing.

Massachusetts Capital Resource Company
545 Boylston Street
Boston, Massachusetts 02116
(617) 536-3900

Restrictions: Invests in both traditional and technology-based industries, high-risk start-up companies, expanding businesses, and turnaround situations.

$ Given: MCRC will invest from $100,000 to $5 million.

Massachusetts Government Land Bank
6 Beacon Street, Suite 900
Boston, Massachusetts 02108
(617) 727-8257

Restrictions: Offers below-market mortgage financing to qualifying public-purpose development projects lacking sufficient public/private investment.

$ Given: Project investments generally range from $200,000 to $3 million.

MICHIGAN

Michigan Department of Commerce
Office of Development Finance
P. O. Box 30004
Lansing, Michigan 48909
(517) 373-7550

Name of program: Michigan Strategic Fund

Restrictions: Consolidates and streamlines state economic development efforts that provide financing to businesses. It also increases cooperation between public and private investors. Provides a range of financial services that meet carefully-defined criteria. Services include working capital loans, tax-exempt revenue bonds, loan guarantees, small business loans, and tax-exempt bond issues.

MINNESOTA

Minnesota Department of Energy and Economic Development
900 American Center
150 East Kellogg Boulevard
St. Paul, Minnesota 55101
(612) 296-6424

Name of program: The Minnesota Fund

Restrictions: Provides direct loans, at fixed interest, on fixed assets for new and existing businesses.

$ Given: Maximum loan amount is $250,000 and cannot exceed 20 percent of the total project cost.

Minnesota Department of Energy and Economic Development
900 American Center
150 East Kellogg Boulevard
St. Paul, Minnesota 55101
(612) 296-5021

Purpose: Assists businesses with financial packages utilizing a variety of resources.

Contact: Office of Program Management

Minnesota Department of Energy and Economic Development
900 American Center
150 East Kellogg Boulevard
St. Paul, Minnesota 55101
(612) 296-6424

Name of program: Minnesota Small Business Development Loans

Restrictions: Assists small businesses in start-up or expansion in Minnesota.

$ Given: Loans range between $250,000 and $1 million.

MISSISSIPPI

Mississippi Department of Economic Development
P. O. Box 849
Jackson, Mississippi 39205
(601) 359-3437

Restrictions: Offers loan guarantees to a maximum of $200,000; industrial revenue bonds up to $10 million; and Small Business Administration 503 loans with a maximum participation of $500,000 per project.

MISSOURI

Office of the State Treasurer
P. O. Box 210
Jefferson City, Missouri 65105
(314) 751-2372

Name of program: Missouri Time Deposits for Industrial Development

Restrictions: The State Treasurer of Missouri makes available $10 million to $15 million annually to be placed on deposit with banks that make loans to manufacturers locating new operations or expanding existing facilities in the state. Loans may be used for working capital, interim construction, financing, or site development.

MONTANA

Montana Economic Development Board
1424 Ninth Avenue
Helena, Montana 59620
(406) 444-2090

Name of program: Development Finance Programs

Restrictions: Offers a series of programs designed to help small businesses obtain attractive capital financing. The focus of these programs is to increase the availability of long-term, fixed-rate financing to Montana small businesses. All programs operate through existing commercial lending institutions.

NEBRASKA

Business Development Corporation of Nebraska
1044 Stuart Building
Lincoln, Nebraska 68508
(402) 474-3855

Name of program: Small Business Administration 503 Loan

Restrictions: Lenders provide small business customers with long-term, low-interest, fixed-asset financing.

$ Given: The SBA 503 loan package consists of three sources—the private lending institution, the Small Business Administration, and a small business. The private lending institution provides up to 50 percent of the total project cost at conventional interest rates. SBA provides up to 40 percent of the project cost not to exceed $500,000 at an interest rate approximately .75 percent above long-term U.S. treasury bond rates. The remaining project cost is the equity injection provided by the small business.

Nebraska Investment Authority
Gold's Galleria, Suite 304
1033 O Street
Lincoln, Nebraska 68508
(402) 477-4406

Restrictions: Provides lower-cost financing for industrial, agricultural, commercial, health care, and residential development.

Division of Community Affairs
Nebraska Department of Economic Development
P. O. Box 94666
301 Centennial Mall South
Lincoln, Nebraska 68509
(402) 471-3111

Name of program: Community Development Block Grant

Restrictions: Funds are intended to supplement other financial resources to address local economic development issues. Funded projects must address job-creation activities for low- and moderate-income residents.

Nebraska Department of Economic Development
P. O. Box 94666
301 Centennial Mall South
Lincoln, Nebraska 68509
(402) 471-3111

Name of program: Industrial Development Revenue Bonds

Restrictions: Lower-cost financing for eligible projects through tax-exempt bond issues authorized by counties and municipalities.

Eligibility: Eligible projects must be of an industrial nature.

NEVADA

Nevada Small Business Revitalization Program
Community Services Office
1100 East Williams, Suite 117
Carson City, Nevada 89710
(702) 885-4420

Restrictions: Provides financial assistance to small businesses and economic development planning through Small Business Administration loans and Housing and Urban Development block grant.

Nevada Department of Commerce
201 South Fall Street
Carson City, Nevada 89710
(702) 885-4340

Name of program: Industrial Development Revenue Bonds

Restrictions: Provides up to 100 percent financing for land, building, improvements, and capital equipment for firms that incur from $1 million to $10 million in development costs and that meet applicable state statutes and federal tax codes.

Nevada Small Business Revitalization Program
1100 East Williams Street, Suite 117
Carson City, Nevada 89710
(702) 885-4420

Name of program: Nevada Revolving Loan Program

Restrictions: Designed for small business expansion that creates jobs for low- to moderate-income persons.

$ Given: Can lend up to 40 percent, or $100,000, whichever is the lesser of the total project cost.

Nevada Commission on Economic Development
Capitol Complex
Carson City, Nevada 89710
(702) 885-4325

Purpose: Provides information on availability of financing and on economic development districts, industrial parks, and land availability.

NEW HAMPSHIRE

New Hampshire Small Business Program
110 McConnell Hall
Durham, New Hampshire 03824
(603) 862-3556

Name of program: Venture Capital Network

Purpose: A formal "market" where entrepreneurs and other growing businesses needing financing can be linked with individuals with means and other sources of venture capital.

Northern Community Investment Corporation
P. O. Box 188
Littleton, New Hampshire 03561
(603) 298-5546

Restrictions: Provides direct loans, loan guarantees, and technical and financial development for industrial, commercial, and residential property. Financing is available for working capital, lease-hold improvements, or major expansion.

Eligibility: Market area is limited to the New Hampshire counties of Carroll, Coos, and Grafton.

New Hampshire Business Development Corporation
10 Fort Eddy Road
Concord, New Hampshire 03301
(603) 224-1432

Restrictions: Provides additional financing to all types of promising new and existing businesses by establishing a medium of credit not otherwise available to them.

$ Given: $25,000 to $150,000 net investment.

Granite State Capital, Inc.
10 Fort Eddy Road
Concord, New Hampshire 03301
(603) 228-9090

Restrictions: Provides equity capital and constructive counsel to assist talented and capable entrepreneurs to build substantial businesses.

NEW JERSEY

New Jersey Economic Development Authority
Capitol Place One, CN 990
Trenton, New Jersey 08625
(609) 292-1800

Restrictions: Arranges low-interest, long-term financing and other forms of assistance for businesses locating or expanding in New Jersey. Programs include Tax-Exempt Industrial Development Bond Financing, Loan Guarantees and Direct Loans; Small Business Administration 503 Loan Program; and Local Development Financing Fund Loans.

Corporation for Business Assistance in New Jersey
200 South Warren Street, Suite 600
Trenton, New Jersey 08608
(609) 633-7737

Restrictions: Provides small businesses with fixed-asset financing up to 25 years for the acquisition of land and buildings and for construction, renovation, and restoration.

$ Given: $500,000 maximum per project.

NEW MEXICO

New Mexico Economic Development and Tourism Department
Bataan Memorial Building, Room 201 EDB
Santa Fe, New Mexico 87503
(505) 827-6200

Purpose: Provides information and assistance in obtaining loans. Available sources of financing include Economic Incentive Loan Program, Industrial and Agricultural Finance Authority, Small Business Administration 503 Guaranteed Loans, Business Development Corporation, Community Development Block Grants, Community Development Assistance Fund; and Industrial Revenue Bonds. Low-interest and long-term loans are available.

NEW YORK

New York Business Development Corporation
41 State Street
Albany, New York 12207
(518) 463-2268

Restrictions: Makes loans to small, undercapitalized firms when funding is not available from usual lending sources.

New York Job Development Authority
One Commerce Plaza
Albany, New York 12210
(518) 474-7580

Restrictions: Functions as a bank, making business and industrial loans for real estate, machinery, and equipment.

Urban Development Corporation
1515 Broadway
New York, New York 10036
(212) 930-9000

Restrictions: Provides financing for minority- and women-owned small businesses through a variety of programs.

NORTH CAROLINA

Business Assistance Division
North Carolina Department of Commerce
430 North Salisbury Street
Raleigh, North Carolina 27611
(919) 733-7980

Restrictions: Although the state of North Carolina has no loans available for small businesses, this office will assist small business owners and direct them to Small Business Administration programs. Provides information and guidance in economic development within the state and encourages small business growth.

NORTH DAKOTA

North Dakota Economic Development Commission
Liberty Memorial Building
Bismarck, North Dakota 58501
(701) 224-2810

Restrictions: Works closely with new or expanding businesses in advising or arranging the financial aspects of their venture. Staff members work with all major funding sources and will serve as liaisons between the business and the financier when appropriate. The EDC also administers the North Dakota Industrial Revenue Bond Guarantee Program.

OHIO

Women's Business Resource Program
Small and Developing Business Division
Ohio Department of Development
P. O. Box 1001
Columbus, Ohio 43266-0101
(614) 466-4945

Purpose: Helps companies locate financing methods and loan packaging and purchasing and procurement opportunities with government agencies and private industry. Additional services include a business reference library, statistics for women's business enterprises, listings of women's business and professional organizations, and a calendar of seminars and workshops of special interest to women entrepreneurs.

Economic Development Financing Division
Ohio Department of Development
P. O. Box 1001
Columbus, Ohio 43266-0101
(614) 466-5420

Restrictions: Offers direct loans, loan guarantees, and industrial and hospital revenue bonds.

OKLAHOMA

Venture Capital Exchange
Enterprise Development Center
The University of Tulsa
600 South College Avenue
Tulsa, Oklahoma 74104
(918) 592-6000, Ext. 3152 or 2684

Purpose: Introduces entrepreneurs to active, informal investors commonly referred to as venture capitalists or "angels."

Oklahoma Industrial Finance Authority
4024 Lincoln Boulevard
Oklahoma City, Oklahoma 73105
(405) 521-2182

Restrictions: Provides supplemental funding in loan packages involving manufacturing industries. May loan up to 25 percent of the project's total cost of the land, buildings, and stationary manufacturing equipment.

OREGON

Economic Development Department
595 Cottage Street, N.E.
Salem, Oregon 97310
(503) 373-1200

Purpose: Offers assistance in obtaining a variety of federal and state loans and grants through Industrial Development Revenue Bonds, Umbrella Revenue Bonds, Oregon Business Development Fund, Port Revolving Loan Fund, Oregon Resource and Technology Development

Corporation, Small Business Administration 503 Loan Program, Small Business Administration Loan Guarantee Program, and Urban Development Action Grants.

PENNSYLVANIA

Pennsylvania Department of Commerce
Bureau of Economic Assistance
Pennsylvania Industrial Development Authority
405 Forum Building
Harrisburg, Pennsylvania 17120
(717) 787-6245

Name of program: Pennsylvania Industrial Development Authority (PIDA)

Restrictions: Administers long-term, low-interest business loans to stimulate economic activity in areas of high unemployment. Funds may be used for land and building acquisitions, new construction and/or expansion of existing buildings.

$ Given: PIDA can provide up to 70 percent of the financing for eligible projects. Loans range from $500,000 to $1 million.

Pennsylvania Department of Commerce
Bureau of Economic Assistance
405 Forum Building
Harrisburg, Pennsylvania 17120
(717) 783-1768

Restrictions: Makes low-interest loans to businesses for capital development projects that will result in long-term new employment opportunities. Loans may be used for the purchase of buildings, for building renovation, and for working capital.

$ Given: Loans up to $50,000 or 20 percent of the total project cost.

Revenue Bond and Mortgage Program
Pennsylvania Department of Commerce
Bureau of Economic Assistance
405 Forum Building
Harrisburg, Pennsylvania 17120
(717) 783-1108

Restrictions: Provides tax-exempt financing for land, buildings, and equipment to businesses engaged in industrial and commercial activities.

Eligibility: Commercial businesses must have a minimum project cost of $200,000 and create 20 jobs, while a manufacturing project should have a minimum cost of $100,000 and create or preserve five jobs.

Pennsylvania Minority Business Development Authority
Headquarters/Central Region
406 South Office Building
Harrisburg, Pennsylvania 17120
(717) 783-1127

Restrictions: Provides long-term, low-interest loans and guarantees for the establishment and expansion of minority businesses. Economically disadvantaged businesses unable to obtain financing from traditional sources are eligible to obtain financing in medium amounts.

RHODE ISLAND

Rhode Island Department of Economic Development
7 Jackson Walkway
Providence, Rhode Island 02903
(401) 277-2601

Purpose: Provides information on the many financial assistance programs available to help new and expanding businesses. Such programs include industrial revenue bonds, insured mortgage financing, revolving loan funds, and business investment funds.

SOUTH CAROLINA

South Carolina State Development Board
P. O. Box 927
Columbia, South Carolina 29202
(803) 758-3046

Restrictions: Makes industrial revenue bonds available to enterprises engaged in agriculture, mining or industry, manufacturing or growing, processing or assembling, storing or warehousing, and distributing or selling.

Jobs-Economic Development Authority
Number One Main Building
1203 Gervais Street
Columbia, South Carolina 29201
(803) 758-2094

Name of program: Pooled Investment Program

Restrictions: Obtains low-cost variable and/or fixed-rate funds for small businesses through the sale of tax-exempt industrial revenue bonds.

$ Given: Loans available to a single enterprise range from $100,000 to $10 million.

Jobs-Economic Development Authority
Number One Main Building
1203 Gervais Street
Columbia, South Carolina 29201
(803) 758-2094

Restrictions: Direct state loans are available to assist private for-profit enterprises and are confined to manufacturing, industrial, or service businesses. Funds may be used for land, facility construction, acquisition, or renovation and, in some locations, working capital.

Business Development Corporation of South Carolina
Enoree Building, Suite 225
111 Executive Center Drive
Columbia, South Carolina 29210
(803) 798-4064

Restrictions: Provides financing to businesses unable to secure loans from conventional lending sources. Direct loans to businesses for new or expanding operations. Loans can be used for most business purposes, including working capital, as long as the expenditure is related to creating or maintaining jobs.

SOUTH DAKOTA

South Dakota Department of State Development
Capitol Link Plaza
Box 6000
Pierre, South Dakota 57501
1-800-843-8000 (in South Dakota, 800-952-3625)

Restrictions: Although the state does not have any loan or grant money available, this office will help new and expanding businesses prepare packages to obtain private financing, industrial revenue bonds, Small Business Administration loans, and block grants.

TENNESSEE

Tennessee Department of Economic and Community Development
Program Management Section
James K. Polk Building
Nashville, Tennessee 37219
(615) 741-6201

Purpose: Provides information on obtaining a wide variety of loans and grants for use as start-up financing, working capital, or funds for expansion.

TEXAS

Texas Economic Development Commission
410 East 5th Street, P. O. Box 12728
Capitol Station
Austin, Texas 78711
(512) 472-5059

Restrictions: The finance department administers several financial assistance programs including industrial revenue bonds, small business revitalization, rural loan fund, and the Texas Small Business Industrial Development Corporation.

UTAH

Utah Division of Economic and Industrial Development
6150 State Office Building
Salt Lake City, Utah 84114
(801) 533-5325

Restrictions: Provides small businesses with long-term financing for land/building acquisition and building construction, expansion, renovation, and modernization.

$ Given: Maximum loan is 40 percent, or up to $500,000.

Davis County Economic Development Department
P. O. Box 305
Farmington, Utah 84025
(801) 451-3264

Restrictions: Loans can be used for land and building acquisition, building construction and renovation, and working capital. Interest rates are negotiable.

VERMONT

Vermont Industrial Development Authority
58 East Street
Montpelier, Vermont 05602
(802) 223-7226

Restrictions: Makes low-interest loans to businesses for the purchase or construction of land or buildings.

Vermont Agency of Development and Community Affairs
109 State Street
Montpelier, Vermont 05602
(802) 828-3221

Name of program: Small Business Revitalization Program

Restrictions: Provides long-term debt financing at reasonable rates through the utilization of a combination of federal, state, and private sources of capital. Staff is available to examine the borrower's needs and sort through the variety of public programs to recommend the best combination of financial packages to meet those needs.

VIRGINIA

Division of Industrial Development
Community Development Division
1010 State Office Building
Richmond, Virginia 23219
(804) 786-4486

Name of program: Industrial Revenue Bonds

Restrictions: Financing covers the cost of land, buildings, machinery, and equipment.

$ Given: Bonds provide up to 100 percent financing.

Small Business Financing Authority
1000 Washington Building
Richmond, Virginia 23219
(804) 786-3791

Name of program: The Umbrella Industrial Development Bond Program

Restrictions: Provides long-term financing of fixed assets through a mechanism generally available only to larger businesses.

Virginia Department of Economic Development
Office of Small Business and Financial Services
1000 Washington Building
Richmond, Virginia 23219
(804) 786-3791

Name of program: Local Development Corporations

Restrictions: Some LDCs make direct loans to small businesses in their localities. Other services may include site selection and assistance in applying for industrial revenue bonds and Small Business Administration loans.

Virginia Department of Economic Development
Office of Small Business and Financial Services
1000 Washington Building
Richmond, Virginia 23219
(804) 786-3791

Name of program: Small Business Investment Companies

Restrictions: Provides equity capital and long-term loans to small firms.

$ Given: An SBIC may invest up to 20 percent of its capital in a single small business.

WASHINGTON

Industrial Development Division
Washington State Department of Commerce and Economic Development
101 General Administration Building, AX-13
Olympia, Washington 98504
(206) 753-3065

Name of program: Industrial Revenue Bonds

Eligibility: Limited to those industrial facilities intended for one of the
following purposes: manufacturing, processing, production, assembly,
warehousing, transportation, pollution control, solid waste disposal, or
energy production.

$ Given: Bonds provide up to 100 percent financing.

Washington Community Development Corporation
400 108th Street, N.E., Suite 300
Bellevue, Washington 98004
(206) 454-4188

Restrictions: Certified firms under the Small Business Administration
503 Program can lend up to 40 percent of a project's cost up to a maximum of $500,000 for a term of up to 25 years for less than market-rate
interest.

WEST VIRGINIA

Small Business Division
State Capitol Complex
Charleston, West Virginia 25305
(304) 348-2960

Name of program: West Virginia Development Authority Direct Loans

Restrictions: Offers direct loans to companies at low interest with flexible terms for up to 50 percent of the project.

$ Given: General ceiling on any loan has been $500,000.

Small Business Division
State Capitol Complex
Charleston, West Virginia 25305
(304) 348-2960

Name of program: West Virginia Certified Development Corporation

Restrictions: Provides long-term, fixed-rate loans for small- and medium-sized firms. Interest rates will be tied to rates on U.S. treasury bills at the time the loan is made.

$ Given: $500,000 maximum loan.

WISCONSIN

Wisconsin Department of Development
123 West Washington Avenue, P. O. Box 7990
Madison, Wisconsin 53707
(608) 266-1018

Purpose: Provides a booklet which contains a complete listing and brief description of the many federal, state, and local financing programs available to businesses for long-term capital, working capital, and other financing needs.

Wisconsin Housing and Economic Development Authority
James Wilson Plaza, Suite 300
131 West Wilson Street
Madison, Wisconsin 53701
(608) 266-7884

Name of program: Small Enterprise Economic Development (SEED) Program

Restrictions: Offers long-term, fixed-rate financing to small- and medium-sized businesses at less than prime rate. SEED money can be used for the purchase, expansion, and improvement of land, plants, and equipment, if such projects result in the creation and maintenance of jobs.

Eligibility: Businesses or individuals affiliated with a business that has current gross annual sales of $35 million or less, a satisfactory credit history, and an ability to support debt service.

Wisconsin Business Development Finance Corporation
P. O. Box 2712
Madison, Wisconsin 53701-2717
(608) 258-8830

Restrictions: Participates with financial institutions to provide small businesses with financing for up to 25 years for purchase of land and buildings and for construction and modernization of facilities.

$ Given: Financing varies from $100,000 to $500,000. Interest rates are always less than conventional financing.

WYOMING

Capital Corporation of Wyoming, Inc.
Box 612
Casper, Wyoming 82602
(307) 235-5438

Restrictions: Financing available for new facilities, plant expansion, shops and warehouses, professional offices, equipment inventory, or venture capital. Provides equity financing to new and expanding businesses.

Wyoming Department of Economic Planning and Development
Herschler Building
Cheyenne, Wyoming 82002
(307) 777-7285

Restrictions: Provides a comprehensive package of available financing. Programs include block grants, industrial revenue bonds, Small Business Administration 503 loans, and others.

Wyoming Department of Economic Planning and Development
Herschler Building
Cheyenne, Wyoming 82002
(307) 777-7285

Name of program: Local Development Companies

Restrictions: Provides list of 28 local development companies that offer financial assistance and information on sites, buildings, or other capital goods available for firms in their area. They work with private funds raised through the sale of stock, subscriptions or contributions, or by notes of indebtedness.